GLOBALIZING ROMAN CULTURE

Why is the concept of 'Romanization' flawed?

Was Rome the first global culture?

Romanization has been represented as a simple progression from barbarism to civilization. Roman forms in architecture, coinage, language and literature came to dominate the world from Britain to Syria. Hingley argues for a more complex and nuanced view in which Roman models provided the means for provincial elites to articulate their own concerns, while also enabling some less influential people to stress new identities.

Most work that has been done in this area has concentrated on specific areas or provinces. Hingley draws together the threads in a sophisticated theoretical framework that spans the whole Roman empire, and provokes intriguing comparisons with modern discussions of globalization and resistance to contemporary cultural domination.

Richard Hingley is Lecturer in Roman Archaeology at the University of Durham, and author of *Roman Officers and English Gentlemen* (Routledge, 2000).

GLOBALIZING ROMAN CULTURE

Unity, diversity and empire

Richard Hingley

LONDON AND NEW YORK

First published 2005
by Routledge
2 Park Square, Milton Park, Abingdon, Oxon OX14 4RN

Simultaneously published in the USA and Canada
by Routledge
270 Madison Ave, New York, NY 10016

Routledge is an imprint of the Taylor & Francis Group

Typeset in Garamond by The Running Head Limited, Cambridge
Printed and bound in Great Britain by The Cromwell Press,
Trowbridge, Wiltshire

British Library Cataloguing in Publication Data
A catalogue record for this book is available from the British Library

Library of Congress Cataloging in Publication Data
Hingley, Richard.
Globalizing Roman culture: unity, diversity and empire / Richard Hingley
p. cm.
Includes bibliographical references and index.
1. Rome—Civilization—Influence. 2. Acculturation—Rome. I. Title.
DG77.H54 2005
937—dc22 2004017692

ISBN 0–415–35175–8 (hbk)
ISBN 0–415–35176–6 (pbk)

To Christina, I could not have written this without you.

[T]he modern literature on Roman imperialism is . . . itself part of an imperialist discourse of remarkable longevity in a post-colonial age.

(Mattingly 1997a, 8)

CONTENTS

List of illustrations xi
Acknowledgements xiii

1 The past in the present **1**

The presence of the past 3
The role of archaeology 10
Criticism and creativity 12

2 Changing concepts of Roman identity and social change **14**

Classical inheritances 18
Interpreting Romanization in the context of Western culture 30
Reconstructing Roman culture in a global context 47

3 Roman imperialism and culture **49**

Defining Roman elite culture 50
Writing about Roman elite culture 59
Elite culture as imperial discourse 69

4 The material elements of elite culture **72**

Projecting Roman elite identity 74
Standard developments? 89

5 Fragmenting identities **91**

Spreading Roman culture? 91
'The empire writes back' 94

'Discrepant experiences' in the landscape 102
Consuming culture 105
The limits of connectivity 115

6 'Back to the future'? Empire and Rome **117**

Enabling and imposing 118

Notes 121
References 162
Index 195

ILLUSTRATIONS

1 Octavian and the globe. Drawing taken from a denarius dating to before 31 BC. Drawing by Christina Unwin. 2

2 The Roman empire during the early second century AD, showing places mentioned in the text. Drawing by Christina Unwin. 3

3 Agricola by J. Goldar from E. Barnard's *The New, Comprehensive, Impartial and Complete History of England* (1790), London, Alexander Hogg. 25

4 A schematic representation of Roman social structure under the Principate. Adapted from Alföldy 1985, Figure 1. Drawing by Christina Unwin. 59

5 Taracco (Tarragona, Spain). Adapted from Ruiz de Arbulo Bayona 1998, Figures 1, 2 and 3; Remola and Ruiz de Arbulo 2002, Figure 2 and Keay 2003, Figures 6 and 7. Drawing by Christina Unwin. 83

6 Verulamium (St Albans, England) in the late Iron Age/early Roman period. Adapted from Niblett 2001, Figure 19. Drawing by Christina Unwin. 86

7 The Roman-period settlement at Tiel-Passewaaij (the Netherlands), showing the findspots of seal boxes. Adapted from Derks and Roymans 2002, Figure 7.10. Drawing by Christina Unwin. 96

8 Nijmegen, in the early Roman period. Adapted from van Enckevort and Thijssen 2003, Figure 7.2. Drawing by Christina Unwin. 97

9 Citânia de Sanfins (Portugal). Adapted from Queiroga 2003, Figure 45. This extensive hilltop settlement was replanned during the early Roman period. Drawing by Christina Unwin. 103

10 The broch at Fairy Knowe (Stirling, Scotland). Adapted from Main 1998, illustration 9. Drawing by Christina Unwin. 112

ACKNOWLEDGEMENTS

I am very grateful to numerous friends and colleagues for advice and help with this work, particularly to Professor David Breeze of Historic Scotland, Professor David Mattingly of the University of Leicester and to Christina Unwin, whose advice and assistance has been invaluable. Others who have helped me to write the book include Dr John Chapman of the University of Durham; Dr Chris Gosden of the University of Oxford; Professor Edith Hall of the University of Durham; Dr Stephen Harrison of Corpus Christi College, University of Oxford; Professor Bruce Hitchner of Tufts University; Dr Simon James of the University of Leicester; Dr Paul Newson of the University of Durham; Professor Francisco Queiroga of Universidad Fernando Pessoa, Porto, Portugal; Professor Nicola Terrenato of the University of North Carolina at Chapel Hill and Professor Greg Woolf of St Andrews University. Discussions with my post-graduate students – particularly James Bruhn, Dimitris Grigoropoulos and Dr Chris Martins – have helped me to clarify a number of issues. A research leave grant from the Arts and Humanities Research Board helped me to finalize the text and I am grateful to the staff of the library at the University of Durham and to those at the Sackler Library, University of Oxford. Finally, I am very grateful to Dr Richard Stoneman for his help and support and to Annie Jackson of The Running Head for the careful editing of the text.

1

THE PAST IN THE PRESENT

> [The Senate] decreed . . . that [Julius Caesar's] statue in bronze should be mounted upon a likeness of the inhabited world, with an inscription to the effect that he was a demigod.
>
> (Dio 43. 14. 6)

In the late Republican era a powerful image arose of the world as a globe over which Rome had extended its dominion (Figure 1). This idea may have been introduced during the early first century BC as a result of imperial expansion and was adopted as a symbol of the authority of Caesar in 46 BC; it became one of the recurring representations of Augustan and later imperialism, used to project Rome's claim to a universal hegemony.[1] The city of Rome, with its immense and diverse population, was often linked to the idea of 'the world',[2] while the extension of the Roman empire was felt by some classical authors to project Roman identity across its territories, leading to the equation of *urbs* with *orbis* – the city with the world.[3] This book examines the extent to which a large part of the world was culturally incorporated into the Roman empire, but the term 'globalizing' in the title refers, specifically, to the relevance of the new forms of understanding of Roman society that derive from a growing awareness of our own global world. Jerry Toner has proposed that the Roman empire 'was the first "global" empire (despite what the Victorians said), stretching across time zones and cultures' and this provides one reason for the contemporary significance of Roman studies.[4] I shall examine how ideas of our current world are interacting with and, in turn, transforming understanding of the character of Roman society. The context for the exploration of these issues is the manner in which studies of the past interrelate with the interests and concerns of the present.

Globalization is a concept that has become increasingly popular in the social sciences and the media since the early 1990s,[5] being used by writers from various academic disciplines (including economics, sociology, politics and social anthropology) to discuss the current condition of the world in which we live.[6] Different authors hold widely varying views about the nature of the

Figure 1 Octavian and the globe. Drawing taken from a denarius dating to before 31 BC. Drawing by Christina Unwin.

concept and its significance in the world today.[7] 'Globalization', in this book, is used to study the relevance to the Roman empire of some of these approaches.[8] Much recent scholarship in Roman studies places an emphasis upon two interrelated aspects – a global perspective and regional cultural diversity – while a comparable frame of reference informs influential academic approaches to the contemporary global situation.[9] The relationship between unity and diversity in the world of Rome is a recurring issue of discussion in this book.

My ambitious aim is to provide an up-to-date review of useful approaches that have been developed to explain the ways that material culture related to 'Roman' identity. Past studies have developed the idea of 'Romanization' to explore the spread of Roman cultural identity at this time, but I aim to progress beyond the constraints imposed by this concept, as I feel that the inherited perspectives are holding the discipline back. Put plainly, it is time that we abandoned this term and the intellectual baggage that it carries with it. For this reason, 'Romanization' is avoided, except when addressing approaches that have used it.[10]

The main temporal focus of this book is upon the late first century BC and the first century AD, the time of Augustus (who came to power in 31 BC and died in AD 14) and the century or so after his death.[11] This was when the empire reached its fullest extent (Figure 2). Although much of the empire was conquered prior to Augustus, the effective cultural incorporation of its people was assisted through reforms carried out during the reign of the first emperor. This was a time at which 'Roman' culture is often argued to have spread to a considerable area of what we today call Europe, in addition to parts of what is now North Africa and the Near East. This book adopts an explicitly theoretical approach but draws upon past accounts, written by Roman archaeologists and ancient historians. The character of social change

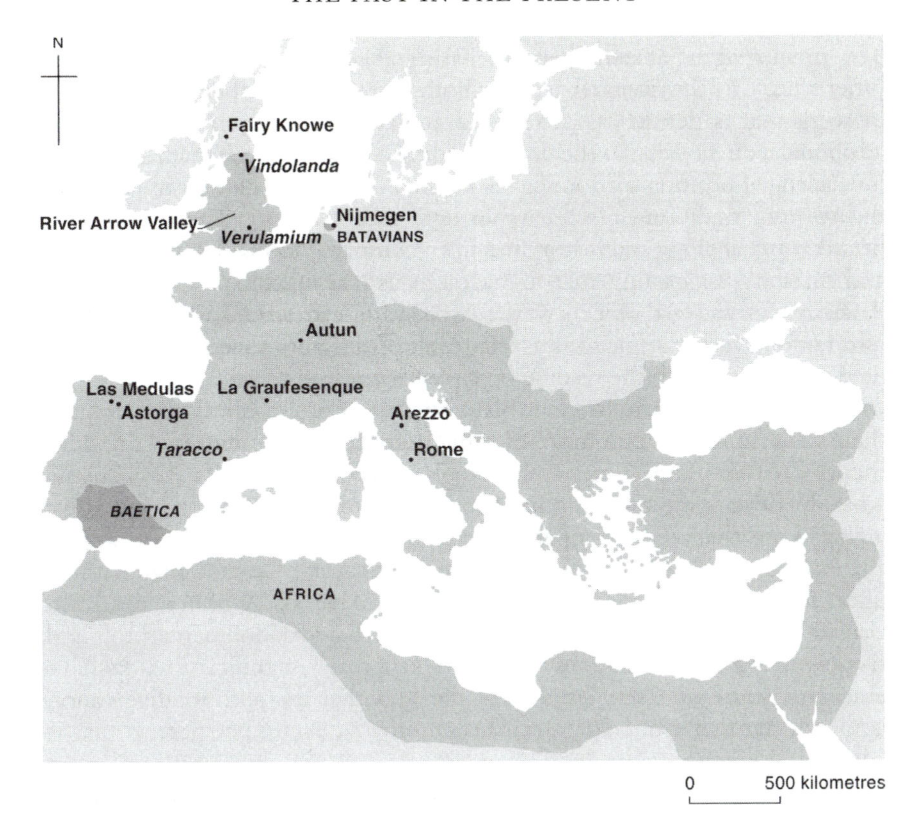

Figure 2 The Roman empire during the early second century AD, showing places mentioned in the text. Drawing by Christina Unwin.

within the Western empire is examined through selected case studies that draw upon archaeological information, while some reference is made to Italy, North Africa and the Near East.[12]

The presence of the past

In the past, ancient historians and archaeologists often used their source materials to attempt to construct grand historical narratives as definitive accounts of past society, based on the canonical status of classical knowledge and the supposed 'objectivity' of the scholarly pursuit.[13] The classical texts were often considered as a source with a privileged status and used unquestioningly in the interpretation of archaeological material. An uncritical connection had often been made between classical text and archaeological material in order to attempt to recognize historical events in the archaeological record. Within classical archaeology, this historical approach has long been characteristic of the subject, emerging with the origins of the discipline.

The 'privileging' of ancient literature has also been a characteristic of various other types of historical archaeology both in Europe and the USA,[14] leading to work that is defined as 'text-aided archaeology'.[15] Ancient literature is attributed a direct value to the understanding of the past, one that reflects the unchallenged position of dominance in which such texts have been placed in the Western tradition of scholarship until recent times.[16] The relationship between archaeology and history has been compared to that between servant and master,[17] suggesting that archaeology is 'the handmaid of history'.[18] Ancient sites and 'art' objects were searched for, excavated and transformed into famous visitor attractions as the result of a significance that was attributed to them through the reading of classical writings.[19]

Since the 1980s many ancient historians and classicists,[20] have redefined their subjects in new and more dynamic terms, drawing upon postmodern theory.[21] At the same time, archaeologists have responded to a changing world by developing various schools of 'post-processual' and 'interpretative archaeology' that adopt comparable approaches.[22] These works have gradually eroded the idea of the single privileged reading of each individual text upon which such 'historical' interpretations were based.[23] Within mainstream classics there is now a strong realization that each generation reinterprets and recontextualizes its important texts, and, as a result, significant works have emerged. Some of these emphasize the idea that the authoritative canon is merely another name for social hegemony,[24] a useful perspective that is adopted below.

An idealist position has sometimes been maintained by ancient historians and archaeologists, that the study of the past can effectively be isolated from the context of our lives in the present.[25] It is suggested that 'facts' can somehow be interpreted according to rational procedures in order to present a progressively more accurate picture about the past 'as it really was'.[26] This approach proposes that, through an informed analysis of the written texts (or, sometimes, of material remains) in their contexts, we can strive, to some degree, to escape the influence of our own concerns and interests. Over the past twenty years, numerous writers have undermined this idealist position by demonstrating that historical study can never be independent of the context in which it is undertaken.[27] An examination of the contemporary context of thought must form part of our attempt to interpret Roman society, since our writings about the past cannot escape the context in which they are produced – the present.

The works of these writers have undermined the idealism inherent in the traditional approaches to the classics and resulted in new ways of thinking. Charles Martindale has suggested that telling 'stories' with the past 'integrates us into our culture, while also allowing us to interrogate it'.[28] Imperial Rome has some particularly relevant stories to tell. Jerry Toner proposes that making the empire more relevant to the present should form part of the project to revitalize Roman studies.[29] The Roman empire, according to Cindy Benton and Trevor Fear, provides a valuable model of cultural interaction over a wide area and the 'consolidation' over time of 'a sense of subjectivity and cultural integration'.[30] Its interactions with other cultures provide material for studies of 'imperialism', 'alterity' and 'subjectivity'.[31] Since the empire incorporated substantial areas that lie outside contemporary Europe, Roman study has considerable potential for the exploration of stimulating relationships between ancient cultures of the East and West, and the ways in which these have been reconstructed in the contemporary world – issues that have a particular immediacy today.[32]

These writers claim that the relationship between past and present makes the Roman empire particularly significant today, but other authors have contested that the Enlightenment and the advent of modernity marked a dramatic discontinuity with the past.[33] This observation has led some to dismiss any but the most general attempts to compare the ancient world with that of the late twentieth and early twenty-first centuries. It is sometimes argued that, although modern society developed out of pre-modern societies and includes various elements that derive from this inheritance, the two worlds are quite distinct.[34] There is a major difference in scale between the societies that made up the ancient world and those that form part of the contemporary global world system.[35] This stress upon modernity as a disjuncture with the past emphasizes the need to understand the contemporary world in its own terms rather than as part of long-term social evolution and, perhaps, casts doubt upon any attempt at comparative work that examines the relationship between ancient and modern.

Anthony Giddens argues that the once dominant explanatory framework that relies upon social evolution has been undermined successively since the nineteenth century.[36] The emphasis in some past works on the evolution of society from prehistory to the present creates specious connections.[37] The evolutionary perspective is teleological in that it emphasizes the continuity and improvement of aspects of the past that are seen as having contributed to the present state of the world. In the process, it looks for continuity while doing damage to the specifics of the past. Following this argument, the ancient world and the modern require to be assessed in their own, different, terms. John Tomlinson, an influential writer on globalization, builds upon Giddens's observations by arguing that impressive examples of spatially spread systems of domination in the pre-modern world had none of the features of today's global connectivity.[38] He suggests that these ancient empires differed from those of the modern world in that they did not have the capacity for political or cultural integration over distance, nor the surveillance capacity to establish, monitor and police territorial boundaries.[39]

At this point in Tomlinson's discussion, the Roman specialist is likely to become curious. Current accounts of the empire of Augustus argue the existence of powerful methods of cultural and social integration that casts doubt upon Tomlinson's comments.[40] The Roman empire evidently also had the capacity to establish and maintain territorial borders, even if there appears to have been no high degree of central planning behind frontier policy.[41] Using the evidence of shipwrecks and other information, it has been proposed that the quantity of trade across the Mediterranean from the second century BC to the first century AD, and the degree of connectivity that this entailed, were greater than at any other time before the nineteenth century.[42] Rome also portrayed itself as a global empire, an image that has been drawn upon in the contemporary world. In fact, as a number of writers on globalization and postmodernism have observed, in response to accounts such as those of Giddens and Tomlinson, aspects of the current world system go back far further in time than the past 200 years.[43] For example, cross-regional trade and imperial conquests that lead to the long-distance transfer of resources, technology and culture occur both in the ancient and the modern worlds.[44] In effect, by focusing upon modernity as a thorough disjunction with what came before, studies of the contemporary world have created ahistorical perspectives upon the present, accounts that have developed because the previous global systems have proved not to be self-sustaining.[45] They also serve to create a sense of the 'otherness' of classical culture, which makes the past impenetrable and unobtainable to us in the present.[46]

There has been no such dramatic historical break between the contemporary world and what went before; indeed, the classical past retains a highly significant relationship to the present. Classical sources have been used to provide models for conscious adaptation; for instance, in literature, politics, architecture and art. Classical culture has a variety of powerful resonances for modern issues;[47] as a result, it is drawn upon in many complex ways to provide both parallels and contrasts with the present.[48] At the same time, the present is also used to inform the past.[49]

A discourse of domination[50]

Karl Galinsky writes in his book, *Augustan Culture*,[51] of the contemporary significance of the development of a distinctive cultural identity in the Rome of Augustus.[52] He argues that the Augustan period forms one of the most 'paradigmatic' in Western civilization.[53] Augustan literature often deals with significant issues that 'transcend time and . . . are inherently rich enough to allow for ever new perspectives that keep their appeal vital'. Indeed, they require each new generation to evaluate them anew.[54] Literature, in Galinsky's terms, forms just one element in this paradigmatic Augustan culture. He argues that writing within the empire developed as an aspect of the domination that Rome exercised over the ancient world.

According to Galinsky, however, the fact that each generation interprets classical works differently should not cause modern scholars to project contemporary sensibilities back into antiquity.[55] He suggests that we may be able to avoid these contemporary issues by differentiating between our own personal response, which is conditioned by our own culture, and the determination of the literary work in the milieu in which it was written.[56] In other words, through a scholarly consideration of a classical text within the context of the society that produced it, we can work to limit the impact that our contemporary context has upon our understanding of the issues raised. The scholar's task is to recover, as much as possible, the social and historical context of the literary work, including the nature and cultural assumptions of the intended audiences.[57] This enables some conclusions to be defined about the meaning of the work to the audience at the time and saves us from ahistoricism.[58] The use of contextual historical analysis forms a powerful methodological tool for ancient historians.[59] It is not, however, the only relevant task; another significant field of study is provided by the consideration of the reception of such works in later ages.[60]

There is a problem with Galinsky's approach, one that relates to issues of idealism and the context of interpretation. As he acknowledges elsewhere in the same volume, our interpretations of the past are, inevitably, greatly coloured by our own contemporary experiences and audiences.[61] The example that Galinsky provides is Ronald Syme's influential work *The Roman Revolution* (1939), which was written in a critical spirit that reflects the rise, during the 1920s and 1930s, of the dictatorships of Mussolini, Franco, Hitler and Stalin.[62] Augustus was seen at the time to provide a relevant historical parallel to these twentieth-century dictators and, as a result, his rule was viewed in negative terms. By the time a further study of this period was published in 1972,[63] the author of this new work felt that 'nothing in contemporary politics' helps us to make the effort of 'historical imagination' necessary to understand the frontier policy of Augustus in Germany.[64] Galinsky felt very differently about the power of the legacy of Augustan Rome within the USA of the 1990s.[65]

He informs the reader that he wrote his more positive assessment of Augustan culture in a different social context from that experienced by Syme. Galinsky argues that contemporary peoples in the West have witnessed that Fascist ideology and propaganda are inadequate foundations for a lasting political system – we live in a complex and changing world that defies 'conceptual straitjackets and facile bipolarities'.[66] As a result, he suggests that we have also come to realize the need for 'true values, guiding ideas and a sense of direction'.[67] Later in the same section, Galinsky considers Augustus' claimed restoration of the Roman *res publica* and the establishment of stability and order throughout the empire.[68] The acts that created these results are seen in a positive light and considered in comparison to the adoption of the idea of the Republic within the constitution of the USA. The detailed contextual analysis of the ancient sources that Galinsky champions is a vital methodological tool; but such an approach cannot, as he himself both records and demonstrates, enable a scholar to avoid imposing his or her own sensibilities upon the information.

Indeed, the claim to a classical inheritance appears fundamental to the interpretation championed by Galinsky.[69] His writings follow a long and powerful tradition. The classics have held a canonical status in the West, performing a direct role in perpetuating a dominant ideology in an ever-changing world.[70] The period of the empire under Augustus is viewed as 'laudable' precisely because it is considered to have been fundamental to the establishment of 'civilization' and the formulation of its defences against the 'barbarians'.[71] It is therefore felt that the empire laid the foundations for the modern achievements of the West.[72] As Hans-Peter Stahl has written, in a review of the reception of Virgil's *Aeneid*, such an idea has particular power within a hierarchically structured society whose main tenets the interpreter shares.[73] The past is made to serve as a justification for the thoughts and actions of people and, therefore, has a direct political value and a distinct purpose in the present.[74]

The writings that were produced by educated elite males within the Roman empire define what David Potter has described as a 'discourse of domination', one which has provided a significant legacy for those who have inherited power and influence within the modern West.[75] Thomas Habinek has argued that certain ideas that have been inherited from classical Rome continue to absorb the interest of 'contemporary beneficiaries' of Rome's 'self proclaimed civilizing mission'.[76] The literary and material inheritance from imperial Rome has served to provide highly effective cognitive models for the exercise of power within later societies.[77] For example, the author Posidonius, writing in the early first century BC, expressed the need for the scope and limits of the new world to be set out and for the relationship between its peoples to be recorded. These ideas served to assist Western colonial adventurers, from the sixteenth century onwards, in understanding the exotic places that they explored.[78] Later, the writings of Augustan authors were used to define new systems of imperial domination,[79] and the Roman parallel provided a particularly powerful source of imperial inspiration for the British and the French.[80] From around 1840, French military men studied and drew inspiration from archaeological remains during their colonial occupation of Algeria, revitalizing the former military accomplishments of Rome.[81] During the late nineteenth and early twentieth centuries, many British politicians, novelists and academics argued that their country had taken on the imperial mantle of Rome, while Roman civil and military policy were felt to be particularly informative to the contemporary imperial generations.[82] In addition, classical Rome was made to perform a role in the formation of the national unity of several modern European states. Writing in the second century AD, Appian provided a significant picture of Roman unity across Italy. This proved a valuable model during the second half of the nineteenth century when the nations of Germany and Italy were created.[83]

Galinsky's comparison of Rome and the USA forms part of a broader trend in contemporary discussion. In the late twentieth and early twenty-first centuries, the relationship between the USA and classical Rome has been subject to much critical attention, drawing upon the idea that both nations form, or formed, the super-powers of their respective ages. Michael Hardt and Antonio Negri, in their book *Empire*, emphasize the ancient genealogies of postmodern globalization.[84] They argue that the Roman Republican system has been reinvented by the USA and, in turn, has come to form the core of the current global world system.[85] The writings of the classical author Polybius on the Roman empire, form a fundamental part of their understanding of today's world.[86] Others have drawn directly upon ancient Rome to enlighten the contemporary world situation.[87]

It is important to recognize that the contemporary context of what we think and write about is bound up with the ways that we create pattern in the information for the past – we impose form on the information that we study. Indeed, as Ernest Gellner has stated, 'We inevitably assume a pattern of human history. There is simply no choice concerning *whether* we use such a pattern'.[88] This suggests that:

> The only choice we do have is whether we make our vision as explicit, coherent and comparable with available facts as we can, or whether we employ it more or less unconsciously and incoherently. If we do the latter, we risk using ideas without examination and criticism, passed off tacitly as some kind of 'common sense'.[89]

Analysis that openly reveals its theoretical basis involves the explicit adoption of a set of principles of interpretation, while a 'non-theoretical' analysis in reality adopts a non-explicit version of the same approach.[90]

In these terms, Galinsky's honesty in proclaiming his inspiration is laudable, since he outlines his personal agenda in terms that enable us to explore the context of his work.[91] The discussion that he provides explains some of his own motivation and this, in turn, enables the reader to consider his thoughts about the world of Augustus in our contemporary context. Despite this, Galinsky's avowed aim, to avoid projecting contemporary sensibilities back into the past, appears unachievable. Augustan culture is 'paradigmatic' for him partly because he feels that it can help to provide true values, guiding ideas and a sense of direction in a contemporary world order that he defines from his own particular historical and geographical perspective.[92] The world is, in fact, full of different perspectives, and the type of approach to the Roman empire followed by Galinsky and others fits a dominant Western perspective, in which former Roman authority is seen as fundamental to the power-politics of the present.

There have, of course, been significant challenges, from Augustan times onwards, to such dominant ideas of a central discourse of imperial identity.[93] As Anthony Grafton has argued, 'the ancient texts provide not only the intellectual foundations of European hegemony, but also the sharpest challenges to it'.[94] These challenges enable the contemporary scholar to consider alternative ways of being – ideas that do not draw so directly upon the discourses of domination that emerge from the classical written texts and which are also fundamental to the rewriting of this discourse within modern scholarship. Critical perspectives, such as those of Potter and Habinek, project current concerns onto the evidence for the past, while providing stimulating alternative conceptions.

The role of archaeology

Mario Torelli, in his discussion of the Romanization of the area of Daunia in ancient Apulia in Italy, observes that:

> Romanization . . . has frequently been disarticulated by two diverse and separate fields of study. On the one hand, scholars of the indigenous world, for the most part archaeologists who pay careful attention to the development and structure of the local culture, have emphasized the destructuring nature of the Roman presence. On the other hand, scholars of the Roman world, usually historians, generally have emphasized the political and military procedures which were adapted from the formulae found at Rome, especially about the organization of the Roman commonwealth.[95]

This process of archaeological destructuring is seen to provide a useful counter to the tendencies of ancient authors to over-generalize.[96] Other classicists have made comparable observations. Writing about the subject of classics, Mary Beard and John Henderson suggest that:

> Most archaeologists are no longer concerned with the discovery and excavation of famous classical monuments, and the treasures of ancient art that they might contain . . . Their attention has shifted to the 'underside' of classical culture, to the life of the peasant farmers in the countryside, the general pattern of human settlement . . ., the crops . . ., the animals . . ., and the food.[97]

It is argued that archaeology gives more of a 'bottom-up' perspective, while ancient history focuses upon the 'top-down'.

Matthew Johnson's model for the relationship between history and archaeology sets out a number of oppositions (Table 1.1).[98] While these simplify a complex reality, they are useful for thinking about the way that Roman archaeology and ancient history have developed.[99] The supposedly egalitarian trend within archaeology, noted in Table 1.1, relates to the increasing democratization of the subject from the 1960s onward, which is reflected in the broader range of sites that are studied by archaeologists today.[100] Ideas about

Table 1.1 Dualities in historical archaeology

Archaeology	*History*
Artefact	Document
Physical	Symbolic
(Objective)	(Subjective)
Vernacular	Elite
Bottom-up	Top-down
Colonized	Colonizer
Destructuring	Structuring

Adapted from M. Johnson 1999b, Figure 2.1, with the final example added. Johnson provides notes to support this diagram and includes the idea that the objective/subjective dichotomy is on occasions turned around.

regional diversity in Italy and across the Mediterranean and western Europe have arisen as a result of the important field surveys and excavations undertaken over the last forty years, projects that have transformed our understanding of classical society.[101]

Roman archaeology is seen to have a distinct role within classical studies and this helps to justify the subject. In the process, however, a number of oppositions are set up as ways of conceiving the relationship between disciplines. Moving beyond these oppositions should help the subject of Roman studies to progress,[102] yet in the discipline as a whole there appears to be a resistance to approaches that combine objectives. One way forward, defined by Johnson, for exploring the link between history and historical archaeology, is to establish and explore areas of common interest.[103] He argues that, if material culture is text, text is also material culture. Texts have a materiality that can be studied through archaeological means. In fact archaeological excavations on sites of Roman date sometimes uncover written texts (including inscriptions, writing-tablets and writing on wood and papyrus) and these, while transforming our understanding, also create an area in which the work of classicists and archaeologists overlap.[104]

The discovery by archaeologists of written texts has contributed highly important new knowledge. For instance, inscriptions and writing-tablets are literary texts that provide new insights but also materials that have been excavated by archaeologists.[105] Collaborative work helps towards the integration of different interests within the broader subject of classical studies.[106] At the same time these discoveries enable discussion to move beyond the centralizing perspectives that are characteristic of much of the Graeco-Roman 'literature'.[107] In fact, archaeological research can perform such a task on a broader front. David Mattingly has suggested that archaeological research on the Western empire has provided material 'texts' that contain pattern and significance;[108] perhaps these might enable a different story to be told.[109]

Criticism and creativity

If we cannot avoid imposing the present upon the past, how should we proceed? One of the most useful insights that we can gain through our research and writing concerns the relationship of the past to ideas that we hold about the current world. A relevant example is provided by Henrik Mouritsen who, writing about Italian unification in the ancient and modern worlds, comments:

> This study has attempted to update the 'Italian question' in the hope of presenting a version which better reflects the values and experiences of the late twentieth century. This aim does not in itself exclude the possibility of gaining insights into the past: it is simply an acknowledgment of the old truth that 'each generation writes its own history'.[110]

Present concerns influence the pictures of the past that we derive from the evidence. At the same time, as Mouritsen explores in some detail, the past is constantly drawn upon to inform the present and this makes the interrelationship of past and present highly complex. Historiographical analysis can aim to tease apart the relationship of past scholarship to its contemporary context, with the aim of making us aware of our assumptions, but we still require ideas in order to interpret the evidence that remains from the past.

Katherine Clarke, in a scholarly study of geography and history in the works of Polybius, Posidonius and Strabo, argues that it appears logical to apply to these ancient texts some of the issues raised in modern debates about geography and history.[111] This is in part because the beginning of modern geographical understanding developed with knowledge of the thoughts of ancient authors,[112] but also because many of the issues that emerge from ancient texts coincide with some of the modern debates that have grown up against the backdrop of this tradition.[113] Clarke argues that studies that combine the ancient with the modern serve to enrich both areas of debate.[114] Pushing this point slightly further, we can develop approaches that directly investigate the relationship between modern and ancient. Being explicit about these relationships makes it possible to judge an author's motivation and intention, while to ignore the issue follows in a long academic tradition through which the individual scholar composes text in a manner that covers his or her ideological tracks.[115]

What I take from the works that I have reviewed is that critical thought has an important role if we are to avoid total anachronism, but at the same time there is a need to balance this with an emphasis upon the importance of imagination and creativity.[116] Postmodernism has liberated us from the burden of arguing for the ultimate objectivity of any one idealized past that is independent of context. As a result, we have been freed to explore any number of different accounts,[117] but with an eye upon the reliability of the interpretations that we draw.[118]

This intellectual position does *not* mean that information derived from study of the past is unimportant, or that the past was actually the same as the present. Anachronism is always a problem for those engaged in historical study. John Barrett has argued that it is too easy to make the lives of people in the past dance to rhythms that we find pleasing, rather than seeing them as moving to the music of their own times.[119] Rather than inferring inappropriate parallels, we need to attempt to ensure that our writings about the Roman empire are consistent with a critical appreciation of the information that we have available.[120] History, as a form of discourse about the past, should aim to distinguish itself from fiction, myth and propaganda by the emphasis that it places upon the critical examination of surviving traces.[121] At the same time, part of this critical awareness must involve the investigation of historical contingency if we are to achieve understanding, since this forms a vital part of any explicit and self-conscious analysis. Dominant academic discourses often push rhythms of life in the past into pre-determined patterns and contextual analysis may enable scholars to define the limits of understanding and, perhaps, to push interpretation in new directions that are both more original and more challenging. The most valuable examples of reinterpretation will always, however, involve a serious engagement with materials (written texts, objects, deposits, sites and landscapes) that derive from the past societies that we study.

2

CHANGING CONCEPTS OF ROMAN IDENTITY AND SOCIAL CHANGE

> The West makes sense only within an authentic history which is not wholly deterministic and does not seek to explain the past wholly through the present.
>
> (Latouche 1996, 6)

This book focuses upon the suggestion that 'Roman' identity and social change have a particular resonance at the present time. This observation must be addressed if we are to create relevant and appropriate accounts of the Roman past. We have a wealth of archaeological and historical information about the empire, which should make the topic of social change and identity relevant to archaeologists and historians in general, but the power of the issue in the contemporary world is limited by the inheritance of certain approaches and ideas. Some writers have recently taken a directly critical approach to the theory of Romanization,[1] deriving their critique from 'post-colonial' reviews of Western imperialism. In brief, Romanization theory is over-simplistic, focusing attention on the elite of the empire, and conceiving of identity and social change in terms that are both too crude and too concrete. Nevertheless, the term 'Romanization' is still adopted by many Roman specialists and the history of the way that it has been used helps us to think about the way that the subject is developing.[2]

This chapter turns in detail to the way in which the scholars who have studied ancient Rome have created a usable past and how this helps us to think about the subject today. In particular, it focuses upon why new understandings need to move on, by abandoning the use of the term 'Romanization' and the approaches that it subsumes. Past interpretations of social change (usually called Romanization) are explored, in order to show how the topic has moved forward to engage directly with changing intellectual and political circumstances. The complexity of the debate in the various countries in which it has been conducted means that I cannot account for the entire variability of the explanations within the broad school (or schools) of Romanization across the whole of Europe and the USA over the past 150 years; it is necessary to simplify a variety of complex accounts in order to provide a coherent narrative.

Attitudes have been in a constant state of change over the past 100 years and, at the same time, Roman specialists have constantly re-defined their understandings of the Roman past. Romanization has been reinvented in each age to reflect upon the contemporary situation. It is a cultural construct and not a self-evident entity.[3] Initially, Romanization was viewed as a centralizing and civilizing process, and it was felt to operate in fairly simple ways. Times, however, have changed. Many of the scholars who have contributed to the debate since the 1970s – both in the north-western periphery and, increasingly, in the Mediterranean core – have aimed to decentre our understanding of Roman identity and social change by challenging the coherence of many of the concepts that have been adopted. This development of theory forms part of broader critiques of modernity, in which concepts in general have been subject to critical analysis and sometimes pulled apart.

Archaeologists and ancient historians have, over the past 100 years, used various forms of the term Romanization to explore the spread of Roman culture.[4] Many of the accounts that adopt the Romanization perspective do not provide any detailed discussion of the concept, effectively assuming that it derives directly from classical society. Traditional approaches often appear to consider that the term provides an account of a spontaneous process that requires no explanation,[5] a description of 'what really happened', free of any conscious bias.[6] Romanization, however, is problematical. Classical authors did not use it: Romanization was invented in the relatively recent past to explore an issue that modern scholars have felt to be important.[7] Ronald Syme described it as a term that is 'ugly and vulgar, worse than that, anachronistic and misleading'.[8]

Romanization was invented to account for the process of social change that is argued to have occurred under Roman rule, first across Italy and then throughout the provinces of the Western empire and also across some areas of the East.[9] Many of the terms in which the Romanization debate has been defined (including 'Roman', 'Greek', 'Hellenic', 'Etruscan', 'Italic', 'Celtic', 'Germanic', 'native', 'barbarian' and 'civilization') are themselves derived from classical texts, as is some of the conceptual framework within which they operate.[10] This is significant, since it means that there is a hermeneutic aspect to the debate. Romanization is, at one and the same time, linked to more recent national and imperial ideologies,[11] while owing much to accounts of empire and civilization formulated during the late Republic and early empire in writing, art and rhetoric. At its core are imperial images that presented the idea of empire as divinely sanctioned, conceiving that Rome had a mission to civilize the barbarians.[12]

This reuse of the past is a significant issue, since the incorporation of ideas that are derived from the classical past into the contemporary analytical framework has often been used to provide powerful intellectual support for the authenticity of the concepts that have been developed. Ideas derived from classical sources were felt to have a particular authority, since these inherited traditions were often attributed with an unchallengeable status within Western academic tradition. In reality, the core concept – Romanization – was first formulated in the late nineteenth and early twentieth centuries. It was the intellectual product of a group of nineteenth- and early twentieth-century historians, perhaps the most significant of whom were Theodor Mommsen, Francis Haverfield and Camille Jullian.[13] It drew in various ways upon contemporary concepts of nationhood and empire.[14] Classical images formed a rich source of inspiration for the ruling classes of European nations during the imperial ventures of the late nineteenth and early twentieth centuries, because they spoke within these contexts in powerful and authoritative ways.[15] In more general terms, some of the ideas inherent from the past – for instance, 'civilization', 'barbarism' and the idea of the 'just war' – have remained popular, and are redefined again today in order to justify the international actions of Western nations.[16]

Many past accounts suggest that the spread of Roman culture (often termed 'civilization' in works that were written in the first half of the twentieth century) occurred through a process of Romanization. Material culture, the objects and material structures that are found across the empire, is then thought to have spread as part of this expansion of Roman culture. This historical process is argued to have encouraged the adoption of the culture by groups of varying status. The process of Romanization was seen as involving a form of social change from one way of being to another, a change that has sometimes been conceived to have, in effective terms, a moral quality.

Those who have followed this approach in the creation of several distinct schools of theory have twisted a concept that was developed in the late nineteenth and early twentieth centuries in various ways to meet the changing contemporary contexts of thought. This is not to suggest that the concepts of Romanization that have been articulated in all of the work over the past ten decades are identical in nature to the theory that was outlined by Mommsen and Haverfield, or even that contemporary interpretations are broadly similar to one another. Romanization has been used in a variety of ways by numerous modern authors and it forms a broad church characterized by different opinions.

Several regional schools have emerged which are defined by at least a degree of coherence. Scholars who work on one part of the empire sometimes appear relatively unaware of developments elsewhere, although a variety of recent publications have helped in the breaking down of national and regional boundaries by including international collections of papers.[17] For example, it is argued that distinct approaches to Romanization are followed by archaeologists and ancient historians who study Italy and the Mediterranean core of the empire on the one hand, and those who work within the north-western provinces on the other.[18] In works about the Italian core various 'Italic' people are often viewed as having been united and drawn into an essentially unified body of Roman citizens from the late third century BC to the time of Augustus, through the influence and power of Rome.[19] As a result, they are often argued to have lost their own distinctive local cultures and to have adopted that of Rome, although the degree to which this process of adoption resulted in the complete abandonment of native identity varies from account to account.[20] In the context of the Western empire, pre-Roman populations are often felt to have been in a 'barbaric' or 'native' state of existence prior to conquest and, as a result of their incorporation within the empire, they were able to draw upon imperial culture and thus become 'Roman'.[21]

A third tradition has been developed by those who study the Eastern empire,[22] where classical Greece is often seen to have provided a more complex context for cultural development and where the concept of Romanization has been found to be less useful.[23] Nevertheless, a comparable perspective to that adopted in the West has been used to suggest that the Roman conquest introduced the 'less civilized' or 'barbarian' (i.e. the non-Greek) peoples of this part of the empire, and those of North Africa, to the benefits of Roman civilization.[24] Often, for reasons that are partly tied up with the politics of our contemporary world, it has been thought that these Roman offerings were not fully accepted by the native populations.

Bill Hanson suggested in 1994 that Romanization is 'the single topic which effectively underpins and potentially unites all aspects of the study of the Roman period in Britain',[25] while the term is also applied to the societies of Italy, the Mediterranean, Iberia and northern Europe, and is used by numerous writers in Europe and the USA.[26] In the final twenty years of the twentieth century, a plethora of books was published that focus on Romanization, taking their detailed subject matter from Italy, Athens, Spain, Gaul, the Low Countries, Britain and the West.[27] In addition, a significant and highly impressive archaeological project, focused upon Romanization (*Romanisierung*), has been undertaken on an area to either side of the Rhine, with generous funding provided by the German Research Council.[28]

Since the mid-1990s, a more lively and critical debate on the value of Romanization has developed. A number of authors have called for the complete abandonment of the term itself and the approaches that it represents and for the development of more flexible interpretations that deal more adequately with the variability that occurs across the empire.[29] Susan Alcock has written about the way in which concepts which were held in high regard in previous generations, such as Romanization or the city, have been destabilized by a 'critical outburst, fuelled to a great extent by post-colonial readings and concerns [which] ripped through the concept of "R(r)omanization" in the years prior to 1998'.[30]

Despite the growing critiques of Romanization over the past ten years, the concept has not gone away. A number of authors have looked for a compromise that allows them to continue to use Romanization theory. They argue that the concept did not ultimately exist, but that it is still a useful tool for archaeologists and ancient historians, providing that it is subject to reflection and adopted in a flexible manner. For Leonard Curchin, it is necessary to deconstruct the concept and then to 'find a model of Romanization that will faithfully describe its operation'.[31] Kathryn Lomas, in a study of Romanization in southern Italy, defines the term to mean:

> The transition [to] a characteristically Roman set of cultural attributes and assumptions, assuming that the speed and mode of transmission and the nature of their reception vary according to the nature of the recipient and the social and economic level at which the transmission operates at any given moment.[32]

Others follow comparable approaches to Romanization.[33] Such approaches enable a greater degree of flexibility in analysis than many past works. These writers seek to establish an effectively global concept to help with the analysis of local variability.[34]

During the first five years of the new millennium the use of 'Romanization' in the title of books has become, if anything, even more frequent than it was before, with new books published that address Spain, Gaul, Germany, Palestine and the empire as a whole.[35] In addition, books that use the term in their titles are greatly outnumbered by other recent works that adopt some form of the theory in their narrative. These publications indicate that Mommsen, in particular, and Haverfield created a theory that remains of vital importance for many of those who currently study the empire.

Classical inheritances

Romanization developed within the context of the ideas of classical civilization that were current within Europe during the nineteenth and early twentieth centuries, concepts that were themselves derived from earlier origins. In western Europe, classical study originated during the Renaissance from a revival of the Roman interest in visiting monuments and collecting ancient works of art.[36] The observation of ruins and collection of exotic objects represented one of the ways in which scholars who studied classical Greece and Rome attempted to understand and interpret the ancient world.[37] Classical archaeology and classics share a fascination with the inheritance of Western 'civilization' from Greece and Rome.[38] Classics, as a discipline grew, in particular, out of the Grand Tour of the eighteenth and nineteenth centuries, but it performed a specific role in Britain during the nineteenth and twentieth centuries, to educate future colonial administrators.[39] Classical archaeology became a distinct discipline during the late nineteenth and twentieth centuries as a result of the growing specialization of various topics within the broader categories of classical and historical studies.[40]

Knowledge of the classical past was a significant element in the creation of what today constitutes 'Europe' and 'the West'. The past, in general terms, has been deployed by Europeans, and peoples of the Western world, to construct identities which have often been defined in opposition to others, to construct the West and the non-West and to create ideas about ancestry.[41] Serge Latouche has stated that the concept of 'the West' has a lengthy and deeply 'sedimented' history of ambiguous usage that draws upon ideas derived from the Roman empire.[42] The idea originates from the division between the eastern and western halves of the empire, but also incorporates religious aspects that defined the West as Christian, the East as Muslim, Hindu and Buddhist. This is ironic, since Christianity originated in what is today the Middle East, while the Eastern empire inherited this religion and survived the fall of the Western empire by almost a millennium. Also reflected is the post-war division between the capitalist West and the Communist East.[43] Ideas about the identity of Europe have a significant role with regard to the definition of the West, although some eastern European countries are often not included entirely within the area.[44] The West also incorporates 'neo-Europeans', descendants of the people who settled in the Americas, Australia and elsewhere.[45] The construction of the past of the West, and that of Europe, has never been a neutral or an unbiased activity.[46] The role that the classical past has been given in the definition of the identity of people in the 'Western world' is a vital topic. Although dominant ideas of the core significance of classical society to Western identity remain powerful, this issue has only recently become subject to informed discussion.[47]

The 'civilization' of classical Rome has been drawn upon directly since the fall of the Western empire in the fifth century. This inheritance is one of two broad – but dichotomous – myths of origin within western and northern European society.[48] Barbarity, the second myth, also originated with Greece and Rome. The idea of the inheritance of classical culture and the variety of images and concepts derived from the barbarian origins of Western nations have interacted in complex ways in the development of knowledge about the ancient past.

Civilization

In a study of the significance of classical knowledge to present-day society, Mary Beard and John Henderson have suggested that the academic subject of classics links us to the world of the Greeks and Romans.[49] This means that the aim of those who study classical society is not only to uncover the ancient world but also to define and interpret our relationship to that world.[50] The questions that classical study raises are the result of our distance from the world of Greece and Rome and, at the same time, our familiarity with it,[51] as classical culture remains central to our own. For Beard and Henderson, it is this centrality that binds Western society to its heritage.[52] They choose two particular examples – the Parthenon and Virgil's *Aeneid* – to underline this argument.

Beard and Henderson deliberately use single examples derived, respectively, from Greece and Rome. Classical Greece provides an alternative series of ideas to those derived from Rome, concepts that have often been felt to have a more pure historical significance,[53] an original and untainted source for many Western traditions. In fact, this idea draws directly upon a Roman attitude towards the cultural superiority of Greece.[54] A lively debate has developed about the social origins of past studies of ancient Greece, including the roles performed by ancient history and archaeology.[55] In these terms, 'Hellenism' involves the idealization of Greece as the birthplace of a European spirit.[56] That classics can be argued to have appropriated the Greek past for political purposes is felt by some recent writers to make the subject central to any attempt to study the place of archaeology in Western society.[57]

Classical Rome shares a special place with Greece in the definition of Western history and thought.[58] This is at least in part a result of the range of practices and beliefs that people of Western origin are often argued to share in common – core Western values. Part of the fundamental importance of this idea of a classical inheritance has been the significant role that Rome is perceived to have performed in passing on a broadly conceived Western civilization to the modern world. We shall see that the manner in which civilization is considered to have been passed through to us is not entirely straightforward, as, in addition to a considerable lapse of time, it has had to account for the writings of classical authors that address the 'barbarian' populations of what is today western Europe.

An inheritance from imperial Rome has, however, been drawn upon in Europe from the early medieval period. Roman civilization forms part of an inherited tradition that has been handed down from antiquity, through the Middle Ages, on to modern times. Despite the 'fall of the Western empire' in the fifth century, Rome retained a vital role in the definition of political leadership. Charlemagne's imperial coronation in AD 800 drew upon the idea of the re-establishment of the empire of Rome.[59] From the middle of the ninth century onward the Germanic empire, which included a large part of modern Italy, was regarded as the successor to Rome.[60] Communities in the Italian peninsular drew upon the Roman imperial past as a 'golden age' of prosperity and centrality from the early Middle Ages onward.[61] From the fifteenth and sixteenth centuries, classical texts became available within Europe as a result of their rediscovery in the Renaissance and were used in a variety of ways.[62] In Spain during the fifteenth century the image of classical Rome provided a useful political model for the new monarchy after the conquest of the territories under Islamic control.[63] The elite classes of various European nations between the sixteenth and the twentieth century exploited the image of classical Rome in the development of art, architecture, literature, education and politics.[64] Christian Europe inherited its religious traditions from classical Rome. In addition, classical authors spoke, through their surviving writings, to the educated elite classes of modern Europe in Latin, a language that they were schooled to interpret and one that helped to define their identity.[65] Many felt a direct association with classical Rome through the inheritance of common tradition, language, religion and civilization. Ideas derived from Republican and imperial Rome have also been significant in modern times within the USA and other areas that have been colonized and settled by Western peoples.[66]

Knowledge of classical Greece and Rome has been made to play a fundamental role in the ways that people in the West have imagined both their past and present. In particular, during the nineteenth and twentieth centuries, people in the West created a classical past that served their own nationalist and imperialist aims.[67] To introduce the reason for this, it is necessary to review in greater detail some simple and linear concepts of cultural origins that have formed a significant element of ideas of Western identity. An idea that has been explored in various 'post-colonial' readings of the writing of history in the West is that of 'Eurocentrism'. This concept turns critical attention to the types of discourse of dominance that were introduced above. It provides a rather simple and linear idea, which does not allow for the full complexity of the ways in which the classical past has been interpreted. It has a direct value, however, since it enables an assessment of the often unquestioned ways in which classical society has been used to formulate images of Western superiority.

Eurocentrism focuses upon the idea of a classical inheritance. From the middle of the nineteenth century, European powers controlled or influenced most parts of the world and from the early twentieth century the USA has taken over much, although not all, of the former economic and political power of European states. It has been suggested that during this lengthy period of Western dominance, a Eurocentric perspective focused attention upon the importance of Europe in world history.[68] In these terms, it provided, and is still taken to provide, part of the justification for Western superiority and the resultant acts of imperialism.[69] It embeds, takes for granted and 'normalizes' the hierarchical patterns that are established through imperial actions.[70] 'Civilization' and Western origins are, effectively, used as an excuse and justification for the imperial domination that Western powers exercise over others. The Eurocentric perspective suggests that civilization was successively displaced in time and space from the ancient Near East through 'Western' (and democratic) classical Greece and then to Rome.[71] Rome acted as the link to the Christian Middle Ages and then civilization passed through the western European Renaissance and to the modern European imperial powers, finally to form the inheritance of the countries of contemporary Europe and of the USA.[72] In these terms, Eurocentric discourse renders history as a sequence of empires: *Pax Romana*, *Pax Hispanica*, *Pax Britannica* and *Pax Americana*.[73] In all cases western Europeans, or their descendants, are seen to provide the 'motor', or impetus, for historical change.

During the nineteenth and early twentieth centuries, this image of the classical origin of an inherited Western civilization was drawn upon in Britain, France and elsewhere as a powerful support for imperialism.[74] Writers in the West appropriated ancient cultures for their own interests in terms of a form of teleology in which the significance of the past lay primarily in its relevance to the imperial present.[75] The study of ancient history and classical archaeology, in these terms, was of value in establishing the roots of contemporary Western society,[76] but this approach can also be argued to have established an over-simplistic view of the past, one that was deeply influenced by the historical context in which it developed. Although this inherited perspective has been subject to increasing criticism, as the result of recent research that reassesses information in a search for new understanding, the central idea of classical inheritance remains powerful today, while the Eurocentric perspective has not disappeared with the 'decline' of Western territorial empires.[77]

Barbarity

Classical Rome has been used to provide alternative contributions to the origins of people across Europe; identities that form the second half of the civilization–barbarism dichotomy defined above.[78] Romans inherited knowledge from ancient Greek society, communicated through the writings of previous authors about the 'barbarians' that they had experienced during earlier colonial actions. Roman generals and traders also encountered non-Roman peoples during imperial expansion across the Italian peninsular and when they ventured across the Mediterranean, the Near East and beyond, into northern and western Europe.[79] Classical authors described and classified native peoples by contrasting their own civilization to the actions and institutions of these 'others' on the periphery of contact and control.[80] By describing the appearance and actions of these others, classical writers came to provide ideas that had a lasting relevance.[81] This image of barbarity, however, was not simple, but was attributed widely differing and contrasting meanings at different times and places.[82]

Classical accounts became widely available to the educated elite in western Europe from the fifteenth and sixteenth centuries onwards. Contrasting traditions of study developed well before the twentieth century, drawing upon classical ideas of barbarian otherness to define contemporary national identity. The classical authors recorded the names of various ethnic groups in Italy, the Western empire and elsewhere, including Etruscans, Iberians, Gauls, Batavians, Germans, Britons and Dacians.[83] Although sometimes developed in very dismissive terms, at other times these accounts glorified indigenous peoples, arguing that they represented the pristine virtues that had been lost in Rome.[84] The classical texts also contained useful information that described the habits and natures of these ancient peoples and the valiant warriors who led them in opposition to the armies of imperial Rome. These positive renditions of barbarians came, from the sixteenth century to the twentieth, to serve particular roles, since they provided powerful images that were of direct value for the bringing into being of modern nations across western Europe. Native peoples became adopted into national consciousness in differing ways, but usually in the guise of ancestors.[85]

The classical texts sometimes included information that enabled the former homelands of these ancient groups to be established and, as a result, from the seventeenth century onwards, writers and artists in the countries bordering the North Sea explored national identities by drawing upon knowledge about prehistoric peoples derived from the classical texts.[86] With the rise of antiquarianism from the late sixteenth century, physical evidence (artefacts and structures) derived from the past could be employed to locate these peoples in the contemporary landscape of western Europe. This evidence came to be used to translate classical descriptions of pre-Roman peoples onto the map of Europe, using the developing techniques of survey and classification,[87] to provide a concrete and physical link.

Classical writings included accounts of the ways in which Rome came into conflict with these 'barbarians', and the tales of the resistance by various peoples of western Europe to Roman imperial expansion were sometimes developed in a strongly anti-Roman fashion. This often, in effect, gave a voice to certain individuals and peoples within the prehistoric West. Texts named and described native leaders who led these pre-Roman groups in armed resistance. The classical authors also put words into the mouths of native rebels, including Arminius/Herman in Germany, Vercingetorix in Gaul, Boadicea/Boudica in Britain, Civilis in the Netherlands, Viriatus in Iberia and Decabalus in Dacia.[88] These individuals were, in turn, called upon to play an important role in the definition of self-identity – staunch figureheads of national autonomy. Between the eighteenth and twentieth centuries, various nations adopted these ancient leaders in order to project territorial claims derived from classical writings on to the contemporary landscapes of Europe.

Within the disparate national traditions of archaeological research that exist in many of the countries that make up western Europe, the ethnic or tribal terms that were recorded by the classical authors have been used to identify the inhabitants of various countries in the period immediately prior to Roman annexation. With the further development of archaeological methodology by the late nineteenth to early twentieth centuries, archaeologists were using techniques to locate, date, describe and classify material remains in some detail. This work enabled the writing of stories about the origins of monuments, artefacts and specific named individuals that assisted in the articulation of national self-identity. As a result of this information, and the development of knowledge about the pre-Roman monuments, prehistoric archaeology in western Europe has developed according to an alternative logic to that adopted within Romano-centric classical studies.

Those with interests in prehistoric Europe often aimed to counter the classical myth of origin that emphasized the idea of the barbaric character of the peoples in the West prior to the Roman invasion, by emphasizing the 'civilization' of the pre-Roman cultures.[89] This prehistoric civilization was explored through study of the impressive monuments that these peoples left behind and also of their evocative material culture.[90] The identification and description of these pre-Roman peoples within Europe has often formed the basis for the exploration of national identity.[91] In these stories, the physical elements of prehistoric culture – the artefacts, barrows, henges, hillforts and houses – provided tangible connections with an imagined ethnic past.[92] Sense of place is vital in national self-definition, and the tying of ethnic identity to certain physical forms of archaeological evidence has provided a useful tool for regional and state nationalism in various countries.[93] The most extreme example of the nationalistic use of barbarians arose through the development of racist and exclusionist accounts of Germanic peoples within Germany during the early twentieth century,[94] but comparable visions of exclusive archaeological cultures were constructed in other European countries during the late nineteenth and early twentieth centuries.[95]

The idea of a clearly defined barbarian identity was adopted from the classical sources, but reconfigured in contemporary terms through the mapping of cultural groups as clearly bounded and unchanging territorial units. In creating such clear boundaries, these accounts usually followed the lead of the classical texts by setting up their interpretations of native and Roman in opposition to one other. Classical writings, however, enabled another significant story to be told, one that allowed for the accommodation of native and classical civilizations. Certain classical writers had explored the manner in which barbarians might become civilized through contact and involvement with Roman culture.[96] Some classical writings, therefore, provided the potential for an accommodation between the important but apparently conflicting images of classical and barbarian origin, an idea that was adopted in Britain, and elsewhere, from the sixteenth century onwards (Figure 3).[97]

This highly significant idea, which was particularly influential in Britain and France during the late nineteenth and early twentieth centuries, built upon the Roman concept of the civilizing mission by arguing that imperial incorporation provided the opportunity for barbarian valour to be combined with an imported classical civilization. In Britain this image was articulated through the creation of an idea of mixed racial origin that had a contemporary imperial relevance. It drew upon the writings of classical authors who presented the empire as divinely sanctioned and with a mission to civilize the barbarians of the West.[98] Rome is made to represent the means by which classical civilization was transferred through the conquest and incorporation of territories that came in due course to form parts of western Europe. The archaeological evidence that survives for Roman sites had a particular importance from this perspective, since it provided physical evidence for the introduction of civilization from the Mediterranean – roads, towns, villas, bath-houses, forts, frontier works and churches. These physical traces had a

Figure 3 Agricola by J. Goldar. This illustration is from E. Barnard's *The New, Comprehensive, Impartial and Complete History of England* (1790), London, Alexander Hogg. It shows an early conception of the idea of Romanization.

particular immediacy with regard to the tracing of cultural identity, as they focused attention upon particular locations that provided physical links between classical past and imperial present. For many, this material link had a far more direct relevance than the descriptions provided by the classical writers, which emphasized, alongside their valour, the barbarity (or 'otherness') of native peoples across western Europe. For some, it also had a more direct relevance than the remains left behind by prehistoric populations.

The inheritance from classical Rome had a directly political purpose. Classically educated English administrators and politicians derived guidance from the example of classical Rome with regard to the topics of decline and fall, contemporary frontier issues and matters of 'race relations' within the empire.[99] Late Victorian and Edwardian administrators and politicians used the Roman conception of a linear legacy of Mediterranean civilization to suggest that the British empire had inherited and improved upon the Roman example.[100] The study of archaeological monuments had a direct role in this claim, since, increasingly, it was used to support the argument that Roman civilization had been passed on to the native peoples of Roman Britain.[101] During the late nineteenth and early twentieth centuries, this idea of a classical inheritance was developed in academic circles, and also in some popular accounts, through the creation of the idea of Romanization. Romanization provided a simple account of how Western barbarians were able to adopt Roman civilization. The search for the homes of the Romanized natives, therefore, had a role in the development of a concept of the history of the nation, since they were felt to have become civilized through their exposure to Rome and were, in turn, the civilizers of those within their contemporary imperial domains.

The role of classical literature was highly significant in creating this idea of the continuity of the history of the West. Within the Roman context, the concept of *humanitas* had become an ideological justification for the Roman elite that supported conquest and domination.[102] Some classical authors considered that *humanitas* had originated in classical Greece and was spread to a wider world through Roman imperial expansion. By representing Greek culture as the first stage in a universal process, authors within the empire could assert the superiority of Rome in a manner that served to counter anxiety over their own identity and status.[103] The ideas of the Roman inheritance of *humanitas* from the Greeks and that of the Roman cultural superiority over the peoples of the West were adopted during the later nineteenth and early twentieth centuries in the context of Western imperialism. This was because the concepts, in turn, helped to justify the imperial domination of other peoples by Western nations.[104]

Rome was argued to have brought classical civilization to barbarian peoples and, in turn, modern peoples in the West have drawn upon these classical sources both in defining their own ideas of imperial purpose and in their dealings with others.[105] With regard to western Europe, knowledge derived from the classical past was used to help to define national ancestry, while the theory of Romanization mapped the course by which influential native peoples were able to adopt civilization under the influence of Rome.[106] It was felt that, as a result of the Roman conquest, these indigenous peoples had been able to learn the lessons provided by the imperial power. Romanization enabled a clear link to be reaffirmed between the civilization of the ancient Mediterranean and that of the contemporary West,[107] even though, in the West, this link had been broken by the barbarian invasions and the subsequent fall of the Western empire.

Politicians and intellectuals of Western nations could therefore argue that contemporary empire was passing on an inherited civilization that had itself been brought into their countries in the distant past by a previous race of imperialists.[108] The 'gift' of this (supposedly) inherited civilization helped to define acts of colonialism as 'civilizing missions', supposedly providing justification for the associated acts of violence and oppression.[109] As Martin Bernal has argued:

> Classics has incorporated social and cultural patterns in society as a whole and has reflected them back, to provide powerful support for the notion of Europe possessing a categorical superiority over all the other continents, which in turn justifies imperialism or neo-colonialism as *missions civilisatrices*.[110]

This type of perspective arises naturally from the adoption of the classical concept of *humanitas* and from the development of this perspective within the modern concept of progress.[111] Both *humanitas* and progress suggest that the adoption of civilization represents a form of transition from a barbarian state to one that is closer to the present day. As such, the topics that have been discussed helped to supplement each other. A teleological perspective on technology and innovation helped to articulate ideas of imperialism and progress that then fed back into images of imperial purpose and power.[112] Effectively, modern authors drew upon the Roman example to argue the historical continuity of a European identity that was passed from civilization to civilization, while being improved in the process. Rome presented the example of an extensive, powerful and well organized world-empire – a parallel that could be drawn upon in a variety of ways.

Classical accounts were also used, from the sixteenth century onwards, to provide a directly contrasting representation of otherness that was utilized during the exploration of the 'New World'.[113] Re-evaluation of the classical texts at this time led to the revitalization of geographical knowledge, as ancient writings were adopted and adapted in the context of the new information derived from voyages overseas.[114] Ancient texts provided intellectuals with facts about 'others'.[115] The classical idea of the barbarian was adapted in the contemporary context to play a role in European colonization, as the ancient sources were called upon in order to help people to understand the natives and territories in these new lands.[116] Concepts of savagery suggested that some of these contemporary people might be in a comparable condition to the barbarians described by classical authors and, in a complementary manner, native peoples of the New World were used as ethnographic analogies in order to inform writings about the prehistoric peoples of western Europe and also the engravings and drawings that were produced.[117]

In the context of the development during the nineteenth century of modern concepts of imperialism, the construction of an absolute racial difference often formed the essential grounding for the conception of a homogeneous national identity, while images and ideas of the character of the barbarian continued to play a part.[118] Wilfried Nippel has suggested that:

> The structure of the concept of the Barbarian as 'a concept of asymmetrical opposition' . . . justified and made possible its being reserved to define, every time afresh, now pagans, now Muslims, now 'primitives' . . . Even the conceptual pairing of Europe/Asia could be employed in differing situations: to repel Arabs, Mongols, Turks, . . . to justify European colonialism, as well as to understand Europe's role in the course of world history.[119]

Doubts were sometimes expressed about the ability of non-European 'races' to absorb the 'gift' of civilization offered by the West and permanent assistance was often felt to be necessary;[120] in the mind of the colonizers, this force did not invalidate the potential of the gift itself.[121]

In the writing of the Roman past, during the colonial era, a similar logic was developed in the direct contrast that was often defined between the areas of Europe that formed the core of the West and areas of North Africa and the Near East that formed the possessions of Western nations. During the late nineteenth and early twentieth centuries, the French drew upon the Roman concept of the civilizing mission in their colonial occupation of North Africa, while the Italians argued a comparable motivation in the first half of the twentieth century during their occupations of North Africa and Albania.[122] In North Africa, French colonial administrators and military men saw themselves as the direct descendants of the Romans.[123] They adopted concepts from classical historical sources and used knowledge derived from the study of Roman monuments in the creation of their colonial present. The expansion of Italian territory to include parts of Africa during the 1910s and 1940s, and the campaign to conquer Albania, were projected as attempts to regain lands that were formerly part of the Roman empire and were seen as properly belonging to Italy.[124] In this context, modern colonialism provided both the opportunity and motive for the colonial authorities to map and interpret Roman monuments.[125]

In recent accounts of what is today the Maghreb of North Africa, the indigenous people of the Roman period were often regarded as stereotypical barbarians, incapable of a peaceful existence, self-rule or advancement without assistance.[126] While these ideas have subsequently been challenged by many authors in their studies of the Roman period within the Maghreb,[127] it has been argued that a comparable Romano-centric image remains influential in contemporary accounts of the Roman Near East.[128] Warwick Ball has mentioned that, in the contemporary world, such a view is likely to appear both arrogant and confrontational to many of the inhabitants of this area.[129]

An anti-Oriental interpretation of history has formed one significant element of Eurocentric discourse and is particularly common in Western accounts of history.[130] Interpretations of North Africa and the Near East in the Roman period have often been marred by ethnic and cultural prejudice and it is significant that such modern attitudes often draw upon ancient sources – once again, the writings of classical authors have been made to serve modern agendas.[131] Although more extreme versions of these imperialist conceptions have declined within classical archaeology since the mid-1980s, general frameworks of thought remain difficult to critique.[132] In fact, a more challenging perspective in a post-colonial context is to make allowance for the two-way character of cultural influence across the whole of the empire.[133]

The relationships constructed between imperial Rome and the contemporary world have never been simple and the discussion above has relied upon the use of a theory of Eurocentrism that simplifies a very complex picture. The argument that I have been developing suggests that Rome was made to share a particularly vital role with classical Greece in the course of Western history. Attention has been focused upon the passing of classical Greek culture to the West through the medium of the Roman empire. From this perspective, the Romans are seen to have brought forward various vital innovations that form the core of Western cultural value systems, and Rome is seen to have a focal purpose in the history of the development of Western society.[134] Indeed, Roman imperialism has been made to form part of this idea of dominance which, in turn, was an essential element in Western identity and served a role in modern imperialism.[135]

These studies of ideas of inherited civilization and barbarism indicate some of the contrasting ways in which the Roman past has been used to articulate ideas derived from contemporary contexts with evidence from the past. The Western empire, which formed the territorial base for modern Europe, has been emphasized in Roman studies at the expense of the southern and eastern areas: interpretations of the latter have been coloured by ideas of the 'oriental' domains of Byzantine and Ottoman civilizations.[136] The past has been recast in the context of the present for particular reasons. In the remainder of this chapter, I shall examine the development of accounts of Romanization in greater detail to explore how they have changed through time.

Interpreting Romanization in the context of Western culture

The theory of Romanization, as it has been developed during the past century, has often been written around a dichotomy. On the one hand, accounts of social change in the empire have focused upon a metanarrative that describes the creation of imperial unity. In defining this unified picture of Roman imperial culture, scholars have adapted ideas derived from the surviving writings of classical authors by connecting these up in new ways to account for the known archaeological evidence. At the same time, these accounts have seldom totally lost sight of the diversity of individual responses that occurred as a result of the Roman conquest and the control of particular places. Even a superficial knowledge of the archaeological material indicates that the culture of the empire varied from location to location. Early accounts of Romanization (prior to about 1960) tended to play up the creation of cultural unity and, conversely, to play down any evidence for regional variation across the empire. This was partly a result of the limits of archaeological knowledge, deriving from the focus of attention at this time upon the remains that appeared particularly 'Roman' (the cities, villas, monumental architecture, forts and 'art' that occur widely across the empire). During the past forty years a refocusing of study has drawn upon the developing knowledge of the archaeology of Roman Italy and the provinces, resulting, in particular from landscape field surveys. The accumulation of archaeological evidence, and also the growth of understanding that this information has brought, gradually led to an enhanced appreciation of the variation of regional cultures, which has had an increasing impact upon accounts of Romanization.

There is, however, also a broader factor in changing intellectual traditions that relates to the attitudes of people in the West towards social evolution and progress in the contemporary world. Since the 1960s, Romanization has developed from a modernist concept, in which it was made to operate as a relatively simple and unquestioned process of progress from barbarian identity to Roman, to a situation, in which the local context of individual provincial societies, and their potentially hybrid identities, have taken on increasing significance. The stress upon hybrid identities has occurred as a result of the growing critique of previous Romano-centric interpretations.

The idea of a move from modernist to postmodern conceptions provides a very simple account of the development of the theory of Romanization, itself based upon the type of binary abstractions that postmodernism often claims to sets itself against.[137] It does, however, capture a general change in the views of those who have studied the empire, focusing upon the years between 1960 and the present day. In fairly broad terms, over time, Roman specialists have come to question the initial focus of Romanization theory upon the centrality, or coherence, of Roman identity. This questioning has occurred as a result of a situation in which many people in both western Europe and the USA have become less supportive of some of the ideas that were used to justify imperialism during the nineteenth and earlier twentieth centuries.[138]

Modernist Romanization

To explore the roles that classical society has been made to perform with regard to the identity of the West, it is useful to assess in greater detail the development of Romanization and its relationship to social thought. Modernity is usually identified as something that defines the recent past of Western society,[139] although serious debates continue over whether modernity has in fact ended.[140] For the purposes of this study, modernity can be defined (in simple terms) as a conceptual schema that was a vital part of the imperial history of Western powers – a body of thought through which the world was imagined and manipulated. Knowledge was constructed through modernist thought that mapped the world from the secure position of the centre, a place that was seen as the highest and most advanced in symbolic and material terms.[141]

In this context, certain factors are key to an understanding of the early history of the theory of Romanization, including:

1 a focus upon coherent and monolithic cultural units (or peoples);
2 the idea of teleology which was inherent in dominant concepts of progress; and
3 a focus upon the central importance of the West with regard to human history as a whole.[142]

The past had a fundamental relevance to the present, as Western society has drawn deeply upon the knowledge derived from classical cultures through the study of their literature and monuments. Romanization theory, in this context, developed in a way that reflected core ideas about the central place of Rome within the identity of the West.

In the first three volumes of his *Römische Geschichte* (1845–6), Theodor Mommsen drew upon work by A. Kiene, to define a 'unitary' model of republican Italy; an image that was deeply rooted in contemporary society and politics.[143] The unitary framework adopted by Mommsen was used to explain why the indigenous communities of Italy, from the third century BC onwards, chose to abandon their traditional autonomy in favour of integration into the developing empire of Rome. This centralizing image reflected Mommsen's own political desire for a united Germany. The admiration that he felt for the domination that Rome exercised over Italy embodied a patriotic idealization of Germany and Prussia at a time when a struggle for German national unification was taking place.[144]

Mommsen drew directly upon certain aspects of the writing of the classical author Appian in order to create this image of the centralizing influences of Roman imperial control.[145] Appian wrote his account of the unification of Italy in the mid-second century AD, in the process projecting an anachronistic picture of Roman coherence onto the early history of the empire.[146] Mommsen argued that, from the third century BC onwards, the independent peoples of the Italian peninsula became drawn into a Roman confederation and that, through the influence of Rome, they also came to adopt a unified Roman culture. This image of a linear 'Italian question', focusing upon the struggle of the allies for equality with the Roman state, appealed to Mommsen because of his wish for a united Germany. He argued that regional differences had disappeared in a trend towards growing uniformity that he felt was entirely complete long before the time of Augustus.[147]

Mommsen also explored relevant issues in the fifth volume of his *Römische Geschichte*, published in 1885,[148] which turned to the history of the Roman empire. He discussed 'the carrying out of the Latin–Greek civilizing process in the form of the perfection of the constitution of the urban community, and the gradual bringing of the barbarian or at any rate alien elements into this circle'.[149] These were actions that took centuries of steady activity, and Mommsen suggested that:

> It constitutes the very grandeur of these centuries that the work once planned and initiated found this very long period of time, and the prevalence of peace . . . to facilitate its progress . . . [T]he Roman empire fostered the peace and prosperity of the many nations under its sway longer and more completely than any other leading power has ever succeeded in doing.[150]

This statement contrasts with some of Mommsen's earlier critical comments about the value of the Roman imperial venture in areas outside Italy.[151] In this new work of 1885, Mommsen developed an approach – 'Romanising' – which explained cultural change across the empire.[152] Although this process was not discussed in any detail, it was significant for the narrative that Mommsen developed. For example, he wrote that 'Roman Britain sustained a relation to Romanising similar to that of northern and central Gaul'.[153] He proposed that this process was the action through which the urban community was perfected across the empire.

In his four volumes, Mommsen emphasized the homogeneity of the Roman empire and this had an impact upon later accounts. It has been suggested that, because of the approach that he took, Roman studies grew in a way that tended to place emphasis on the consistency of Roman culture across the empire and the centralization of power.[154] In the face of this, any local variation in the nature of classical society across Italy and the empire tended, essentially, to be played down. The idea of a centralized Roman Italy has remained influential, for some classical scholars in Italy and elsewhere in Europe, down to the present day.[155]

The position of Mommsen's work in the context of developing German and Italian nationhood was highly significant.[156] The general idea behind this approach to Roman identity and social change also came to have a role in the imperial actions of Italy from 1910 onwards, when archaeology was used for distinctly political purposes.[157] Romanizing, or Romanization, as Francis Haverfield defined it in 1905, performed a comparable but contrasting role in Britain. It came to define the material correlates of the progressive adoption of Roman culture by natives within the province of Britannia.

Political concerns in Britain during the late nineteenth and early twentieth centuries differed in significant ways from those of the Germans and Italians. Britain ruled an extensive empire and was more united at home. The idea of Romanization that developed in Britain derived from a popular image that stressed the way in which Roman civilization and native barbarity became blended together; at the same time, this supposed historical process was used to provide concrete support for the contemporary identity and imperial might of the British nation.[158] Scholars and other writers, drawing upon classical sources and archaeological information, found it useful to argue that the indigenous groups of ancient Britain that were incorporated into the empire were also deeply influenced by the 'civilization' of the Romans. The strength of the English character, in the minds of some writers, was the result of the mixing of inherent qualities of distinct peoples in the past. In particular, the valour and bravery of the ancient Britons was combined with the love of order and civilization of the classical Romans and the freedom of the Anglo-Saxons.[159] This image of a combined national origin for the English came to play an important role in imperial thought.[160] An academic context for these ideas of racial mixing was created as a result of Haverfield's reassessment of Mommsen's work.[161]

The fifth volume of Mommsen's work was translated into English and published in 1886 as *The Provinces of the Roman Empire: From Caesar to Diocletian*.[162] In developing his interpretation of Roman social change in Britain, Haverfield drew upon the idea of 'Romanising' that Mommsen had outlined in this and earlier works.[163] Haverfield was deeply influenced by Mommsen's writings and it helped him to develop what is probably the fullest explicit discussion to date of the meaning of the term 'Romanization' within his seminal work *The Romanization of Roman Britain*. This was originally published almost a hundred years ago (in 1905–6) and republished several times in revised editions. It has been the subject of a number of recent assessments.[164]

Haverfield's study drew deeply upon classical writings to explore how the civilizing mission within the empire progressed through the process of Romanization.[165] The moral purpose of Romanization is obvious from Haverfield's statement that Rome acted 'for the betterment and the happiness of the world'.[166] Significantly, in the context of the Romanization of the northern empire, the long peace made possible by Roman foreign policy and military organization created a lasting heritage. The lands protected by the legions were given Roman civilization and, as a result, the natives were 'incorporated', 'assimilated' and 'denationalised'.[167] Haverfield studied this process through the idea of 'Romanization'. He felt that Romanization resulted in a relatively fully unified empire, that 'gained . . . a unity of sentiment and culture which served some of the purposes of national feeling'.[168] In the West, Rome conquered 'races' which were not yet 'civilized' but were apparently 'racially capable' of accepting Roman culture.[169] Haverfield suggested that the use 'of things Roman' indicated that the provincial had 'realised their value . . . and ceased to bear any national hatred' towards them.[170]

Haverfield viewed Romanization as progressive, swift and uniform in the way it affected the landlords and 'upper classes'.[171] It involved various areas of life, including language, art, religion, urbanization and the construction of villas. He suggested that in the towns and among the upper classes Romanization was 'substantially complete'.[172] This indicates that Romanization was a general process that incorporated people in a fairly standardized manner. In a particularly significant passage, he states that 'We can argue from the spread of Roman material civilization that provincial sentiment was growing Roman'.[173] For Haverfield, Roman culture carried with itself Roman identity. Romanization had an effectively spiritual quality and, by adopting new items and new ideas, the whole range of provincials aimed to become Roman by abandoning an incoherent native identity.[174] Haverfield explored in explicit terms the contrast that existed in this regard with the attitude of native peoples to contemporary culture within the empires of early twentieth-century Western powers.[175] Through this argument Haverfield, in the company of other contemporary authors, reified the concept of race by universalizing its value, while also placing the responsibility for the lack of progress in the contemporary world upon the people who had been colonized.[176]

The adoption of Roman civilization was easily recognizable in the residents of the cities and villas of Britain and the Western empire, but not entirely confined to the wealthy. Although he did not possess much in the way of detailed archaeological material for the non-elite, in some of Haverfield's writings he appears to have considered these people to have been involved in the same process of Romanization as the rich. While native settlements in North Wales and on Cranborne Chase remained primarily non-Roman in appearance, the occupants swiftly adopted Roman pottery and other items of personal decoration; around these people, too, 'hung the heavy inevitable atmosphere of the Roman material civilization'.[177] Perhaps the ability of the poor to become Romanized was limited by their lack of disposable income which meant that they could only obtain Roman-style pottery and objects of personal decoration.[178] In any case, Haverfield suggested that the achievements of the empire extended into three continents the 'gifts of civilization, language, and citizenship to *almost all* of its subjects'.[179]

This led to the 'creation of a stable and coherent order out of which rose the Europe of today'.[180]

He was, however, aware that the archaeological evidence for various parts of the Western empire indicated a more complex picture than was suggested by this rather simple theory.[181] Romanization was arrested or assisted according to the various political and economic structures that it encountered in various areas.[182] Britannia provided interesting examples, as Haverfield explained that some communities did not fully adopt the trappings of Roman civilization. Indeed, the 'peasantry' were less thoroughly Romanized, although 'covered by a superimposed layer of Roman civilization'; indeed 'Celtic qualities' may have 'lingered on', especially in the military north and west.[183] This indicated to Haverfield, that Romanization was not totally triumphant.[184] In some circumstances, native identity continued well into the period of Roman rule and beyond.

Despite the attention that he paid to the regional variations in the nature of Roman culture, Haverfield followed Mommsen's example by emphasizing the unifying character of imperialism. Tacitus' comments on Britain (*Agricola* 21) were fundamental to the development of this perspective. Tacitus identified a range of innovations that were adopted by members of the Romano-British elite in the AD 70s. He mentions that the Roman style of dress – the toga – was adopted, along with arcades, baths, banquets and the Latin language. This account provides an idea of how an upper-class Roman writer envisaged that Roman administrators and officials might, on occasions, have encouraged the education (or indoctrination) of the native rulers. Haverfield's vision of Roman culture derives part of its logic from Tacitus' observations, an approach that was adopted and adapted by later writers.

It should be noted that Haverfield's contribution to Roman scholarship, within the national traditions of archaeological research that developed in the other countries of western Europe, was rather less significant than that of Mommsen. Indeed, in France, another distinct national tradition emerged at this time as a result of the highly influential writings of Camille Jullian.[185] Jullian, who had studied in Berlin under Mommsen, also used the reference to Agricola and the civilizing of the Britons from Tacitus' *Agricola* and made additional comments upon both *humanitas* and civilization. He based his analysis upon a rather more critical attitude to the benefits of Graeco-Roman civilization and a more positive assessment of Gallic culture than was the case with Haverfield's assessment of the Romanization of the native British.[186]

During the 1930s, R. G. Collingwood developed a contrasting interpretation of Romanization that gave greater emphasis to the native character within Roman Britain.[187] Despite this, many influential scholars in Britain and elsewhere during the early and middle part of the twentieth century drew upon the theory of Romanization that had been previously outlined by Mommsen and Haverfield.[188] These authors felt able to define a coherent archaeological package that identified Roman civilization. This enabled the definition of 'Roman culture' and, once identified, its spread through time and space across the empire could be mapped. Many early accounts of Romanization operated effectively on this level, by defining Roman culture and modelling its gradual but seemingly inevitable spread. In Italy, during the twentieth century, the process of Romanization has often been viewed in terms of the irresistible and pervasive triumph of a higher culture.[189] Some detailed consideration of regional cultures occurred during the course of the twentieth century,[190] and these have slowly impacted upon a dominant perspective in Roman studies, characterized by the unitary Romano-centric viewpoint derived from earlier works.[191]

Despite the power of these inherited approaches, an understanding of the variations within the archaeological information, from Italy and other areas of the empire, gradually led to increasing doubts over the unity of the Romanization process. This development of understanding emerged alongside changes in attitude to the character of colonization itself. Many of the new accounts of Romanization that developed in Italy and across Europe from the 1960s onwards began to pursue a new direction. The interest that had once been directed at the Romans and the ways that they, as incomers and colonizers, introduced civilization to much of their empire, tended increasingly to be supplemented or replaced by a more direct focus upon the native contexts within which these changes happened.[192] Landscape work, and the study of previously neglected classes of sites, helped to provide the evidence to articulate these new understandings.

Excavation and regional surveys became common in a number of western European countries from the 1960s onwards, as a result of changes in the funding of archaeological work and also of the new academic approaches.[193] Consequently, a variety of new types of settlements and landscapes were recognized, indicating a great diversity of responses to incorporation. Knowledge has gradually built up that has allowed Roman specialists to move beyond the literary and epigraphic sources and the established focus of attention upon cities, villas, forts, roads and imperial frontiers.[194]

The formation of new knowledge developed alongside, and supplemented, challenges to the dominant accounts of Romanization, both in Europe and in the USA.[195] For Italy and the Mediterranean, changes in perspective over the past few decades have, in part, resulted from the growing attention that has been paid to the rural areas. They recognize the complexity of rural settlement organization and place an increased focus upon the regional character of individual societies and their pre-Roman roots.[196] In addition, archaeologists in a number of countries have adopted ideas from social anthropology and sociology in order to create challenges to the simple models of the civilizing power of Roman imperial culture that are now seen to have dominated earlier accounts.[197] For example, in the Low Countries, an approach developed in the late 1970s and 1980s that considered the evolution of native society under Roman influence. It adopted concepts drawn from the social sciences and has continued to develop to the present day.[198] Within Britain, around the same time, challenges also emerged to the dominant perspectives.[199]

Critical assessment

The development of a global world system over the past forty years has led to the realization that the past of the West does not represent universal history and this has resulted, in turn, in trenchant critiques of what is viewed as the dominant Western perspective.[200] The period since the 1960s has been a time during which a variety of academic disciplines have become increasingly critical of the teleological and progressive accounts that characterize much modernist thought. Evolutionary theory in the social sciences, with its connected concept of progress, has given way to neo-evolutionary theory, development theory and other more critical forms; the study of Rome has seen comparable developments.[201]

Recent accounts often set themselves directly against certain aspects of modernist thought that were reviewed above. They define themselves by exploring ideas that relate to:

1. the agency that people have in their everyday lives;
2. the rejection of the centrality of the West and the development of an idea of cultural relativism; and
3. the creation of flexible or fractured identities.

Many writers reject the idea of general rules and seek cultural diversity and the breaking down of boundaries between the categories of thought that were developed in earlier accounts. In particular, postmodernism attacks the idea of teleology – that there is some overarching logic, or meaningful progress, behind historical development.[202] Much of this work is, as Ian Morris stresses, 'antithetically opposed' to the theory that has been inherent in classical studies from the late eighteenth century onwards.[203] These ideas help to define changes that have occurred in Roman studies. Critiques of earlier works have developed that aim to place modernist assumptions in context.[204]

From the early twentieth century, Romanization was able to develop as a coherent and relatively unchallenged school of thought that focused upon a monolithic image of Roman identity and its perceived natural superiority over indigenous culture. In this context, Mommsen's and Haverfield's accounts reflect modernist conceptions of progress.[205] These approaches are 'progressive' because they suggest a gradual and rather unconstrained spread of Roman culture from the imperial centre to the provincial elite and down through local society to the non-elite.[206] Such accounts fitted well with modernist discourses of imperialism and particularly with the idea that Western history had a universalizing and modernizing logic.[207]

Progress, which forms a key element of modernist thought, is a powerful image that derives in part from an origin in classical society,[208] although classical concepts of the passage to civilization from barbarism were very different from recent and contemporary concepts of progress.[209] Theodor Shanin has written that the idea of progress developed from the seventeenth century as an 'overwhelmingly simple and straightforward interpretation' which was shared by both philosophers and the general public.[210] Through time, the word for the supposed process of progress changed with fashion (from 'progress', through to 'modernization', 'development' and, finally, 'growth'), as did the legitimization (from 'civilizing missions' to 'economic efficiency' and 'friendly advice'), yet the message remained substantially unaltered.[211] Postmodern theory focuses critical attention upon the teleological character of such accounts.[212] Progressive accounts assume simple and directional changes that are conceived as inherent to the development of Western civilization, representing the secularization of Judaic-Christian notions of salvation and redemption that became transformed into progress through developments in science and technology.[213] Mommsen's and Haverfield's theories of Romanization were part of a broader image of progress that was common to many people during the later nineteenth and early twentieth centuries; ideas that were derived from the evolutionary and diffusionist theories that formed a fundamental part of modernist thought.[214]

In these terms modernity operated through the creation of clear divisions and secure understanding based on simple national, racial or ethnic categories.[215] The construction of an absolute racial difference formed the essential grounding for the conception of a homogeneous national identity, one that served a direct purpose within the imperial expansion of Western nations. The early approaches to Romanization also created binary opposites and a secure understanding on the basis of relatively coherent and monolithic cultures.[216] They share this modernist context with a variety of other concepts for social change in the modern world that are used by social scientists and others.[217] These concepts identify general processes that are felt to have occurred in the present or, in some cases, in the past. They model situations in which a form of monolithic culture that is thought to have some form of coherent existence passes from one dominant society to another subservient people. These terms, when used in a positive manner, provide historical justifications for the national and imperial actions of certain Western nations.[218]

Just as European 'civilization' was seen to be expanding and carrying new ideas and standards to those 'primitive' and 'uncivilized' cultures incorporated in the empires of Western powers, so Romanization was argued to have driven out the pre-Roman material culture in barbarian western Europe. It formed a positive step forward on a unilinear path towards modern civilization and rationality.[219] In Haverfield's words, Rome had spread its classical culture (for which we may read 'civilization') to the modern world and was, therefore, a major contributor to contemporary Western society.[220] The role of Rome in bringing civilization to the West, and the broad connections between the two processes, meant that Romanization was evidently a thoroughly good thing. The works of Mommsen and Haverfield exhibit the logic of their time, with the 'higher' culture replacing the 'lower'. This created the context for the idea of a reified and coherent category of civilization that linked the modern world with the ancient; in this regard, both authors followed common traditions of European scholarship.[221]

Romanization was used to attest to the progressive change by which barbarians in Italy and the western areas of the empire were civilized following their incorporation. In these terms, this essentialist argument enabled change from one absolute form (the 'barbarian'/the 'native') to another (the civilized Roman) through a directional form of social change which derived its logic, at least in part, from modernist conceptions of Western identity and cultural progress.[222] The context for this view that imperial control created a uniform Roman culture lies in the observation that Mommsen and Haverfield were both working with a limited, unitary concept of the empire.[223] The approaches that they adopted were conditioned by the climate of their times, the historiographical tradition out of which Roman archaeology had developed, and the limited quality and quantity of archaeological data available to them.[224] Part of the motivation of both authors was to stress the cultural homogeneity of Italy and the empire, while the cities, villas, forts and art that occurred across the empire were emphasized and standardized. At the same time, elements of local identity were either not noticed at all, or were noted but argued not to be highly significant. The less powerful were of limited importance since, in effect, these people were less Romanized (or less 'modern') than their more influential neighbours.[225]

The theory outlined by these approaches to Romanization is teleological; it assumes a simplistic and directional transition from native to Roman that reflects views of social evolution from primitiveness to civilization. The civilizing of the natives across the Western empire enabled a direct connection to be drawn between Romanized natives and 'us', thus creating a domestic link in various countries between the contemporary identity of the West and the culture of classical Rome.[226] The assumed connection between Roman civilization and modern society is derived, at least in part, from classical education.[227] In mainstream accounts the process of Romanization is viewed from the perspective of the Roman (or the Romanized native). This Romanocentric perspective characterizes much twentieth-century scholarship and has created a certain emphasis in the accounts of Romanization that have been produced to address western and eastern Europe, North Africa and the Near East.

It is imagined that modern society is based upon a range of elements that appear to derive from classical Mediterranean civilization. Roman technological innovations, in both popular and academic accounts, are effectively viewed as examples of progress from prehistory to a state that is more comparable with contemporary society, while the writings of classical authors provide relevant concepts for contemporary people. Romanization continues to provide the intellectual framework for this story, even though the focus of attention has been turning, increasingly, away from the idea of Roman civilization and towards the study of regional variations among the Romanized people of the western provinces.

Native reactions

One of the most significant developments during the 1970s and 1980s was the emergence of 'nativist' approaches with regard to two distinct areas of the empire.[228] These accounts placed a strong emphasis on the local context of identity, sometimes through the use of the results of recent archaeological research. The most extreme of these nativist approaches were defined in direct opposition to the mainstream of Romanization studies.[229] A significant school of thought developed in Britain,[230] partly as a result of the post-colonial reaction to Britain's own distinctive imperial history. A broadly comparable strand emerged in writings about Roman North Africa at around the same time.[231] It was a direct reaction to the colonial archaeology that the French and Italians had practised in these territories,[232] approaches that had played down, or ignored, the native contribution to Roman-period society while reflecting dismissive attitudes to the contemporary peoples. A comparable 'indigenous' school of thought has come, in more recent times, to have a considerable impact upon studies of the Near East, where it has evolved, for comparable reasons, in opposition to the dominating Westernizing Graeco-Roman perspective.[233]

In Britain, the nativist school of thought, which drew upon the work of Vinogradoff during the early twentieth century,[234] stressed the survival of indigenous cultural traditions into the post-conquest era, often seen as a form of resistance to Roman influence. Romanization became no more than a surface gloss beneath which native ways of life continued relatively unaltered.[235] Nativism came to influence studies of Roman towns, villas, rural settlements and ritual.[236] Richard Reece powerfully stated that 'the British way' was followed by most people before Romanization began, maintained while Romanization was in 'full flood' and returned to when Rome was no more than a memory.[237]

In Britain, the popularity of nativist perspectives in Roman archaeology was at least partly the result of the intellectual changes that resulted from the decolonization movements of the 1950s onwards. These occurred across much of the territory that had previously been incorporated within the empires of Britain and other Western nations. Nativist perspectives developed, however, differently from contemporary ideas about North Africa. These accounts reflected changing political realities and philosophies. They attempted to give a voice to the indigenous peoples of the provinces that effectively mimicked the new power that former subjects of modern Western empires were felt to be acquiring in the post-colonial world.[238] Such accounts are problematic because their increased focus upon the native position reinforced the dualistic nature of the representation of Roman and native; a dualism which was also fundamental to the mainstream school of Romanization studies.[239] The indigenous population are reified into an integrated whole, defining themselves through opposition to the dominating Roman power.[240] In this way, nativist perspectives remained modernist, since they continued to erect distinct and monolithic identities and set them in opposition to one another.[241] As such, they attacked the general approach to Romanization without challenging the overall perspective.[242]

Studies of 'localization' in anthropology and sociology have also been critiqued in recent times. They often focus upon the idea of the global and the local as dichotomies, or opposites, the local usually being viewed as providing a more pure, natural or original source of identity than the imperial or global.[243] Increasingly, it is being suggested that, far from being antithetical to one another, the local and the global are actually intricately and significantly intertwined as part of the contemporary world system.[244] Some nativist works on provincial Roman society – through a search for the authentic, genuine or legitimate – exhibited a claim to semantic superiority over the dominant imperialist accounts represented by mainstream studies of Romanization.[245] Many recent accounts of Roman-period society across the empire, however, have reacted against this position by attempting to explore the integration of local and global factors.

Few, if any, Roman archaeologists in Britain today hold to the extreme version of the nativist perspective, and this approach does not form a mainstream theory in other parts of the former Roman empire.[246] For example, most of the recent works on the Roman Maghreb show no deep influence from this approach, stressing, instead, the complexity of social change in the area (but also, from time to time, elements of the recurrence of the colonial discourse that informed earlier work).[247] The lasting legacy of nativism in mainstream Roman studies today exists in the influence that it had upon Martin Millett's significant and highly influential book, *The Romanization of Britain* (1990a). This represented an important stage in the development of the theory of Romanization.[248]

Millett's work can be seen as representing, at least in part, a post-colonial reaction to paternalistic accounts of the British imperial mission. He proposed a new explanation for cultural change in the Roman world that would be of value to members of 'the post imperial generation'.[249] His approach aimed to cater to those who are not willing to accept that 'the Britons did what they were told by the Romans because it represented *progress*'.[250] The general direction drew upon P. A. Brunt's article, 'The Romanization of the local ruling classes of the Roman Empire', which explored some of the processes by which 'Provincials Romanized themselves'.[251] Millett's interpretation differs significantly from those adopted by Mommsen and Haverfield, in emphasizing the provincial context within which social change took place.

Millett's account is nativist, since it allows agency to provincial peoples,[252] but it builds in the idea of social change in a manner that most of the earlier work of this type had not. This version of the Romanization narrative is based on a far more *laissez-faire* view of the purpose and methods of the Roman empire than earlier accounts.[253] Millett provided a more subtle picture of social change, one that was not so fully directed by the imperial centre. Earlier accounts, including the work of both Mommsen and Haverfield, suggested an imperial power that intervened directly in the lives of provincials and native societies that, in turn, reacted directly to this stimulus, while Millett sought to promote the indigenous context within which social change occurred. This had a substantial impact on subsequent writings about the Western empire.[254] A school of Romanization theory has arisen that Bill Hanson, in 1997, called the 'new orthodoxy',[255] because the basic idea of the direct involvement of the native elite in their own Romanization has become a common and significant interpretation.

This search for a native context for the adoption of Roman culture may be seen to reflect the move that has occurred towards postmodern understanding. Millett's focus upon the native and local development of Roman culture within the provinces gives agency to individual peoples. It also develops interpretation further towards the type of cultural relativism that is favoured in postmodern accounts. It assumes that the provincial elite had a direct self-interest in adopting Roman culture and identifying themselves with Rome.[256] Roman culture then spread to others in society through a progressive process of self-generation that was based upon the material benefits to everyone of Roman identity.[257]

Millett's 'post imperial' approach has, in turn, been subjected to substantial discussion. Some authors argue that this theory of Romanization remains based on simplistic assumptions that require more detailed examination;[258] others have drawn explicitly upon 'colonial discourse theory' to place Millett's version of Romanization in its historical context.[259]

The ghost of modernity

Millett's work allows agency to the native elite, while also drawing away from a strictly Romano-centric perspective on social change. It still has, however, a broadly progressive framework of analysis. To explore this issue, we can examine the way that Roman culture is felt to have spread throughout society. In Millett's most detailed consideration of Romanization, the concept is developed in terms of a model that has five parts,[260] of which the first four relate to the Romanization of the provincial elite. The final, fifth, point is that 'progressive emulation of this [Roman] symbolism further down the social hierarchy was self-generating [,] encouraging others within society to aspire to things

Roman, thereby spreading the culture'.[261] Thus, as in the earlier account of Romanization developed by Haverfield, the less wealthy and powerful are felt to have a common interest with the elite in the adoption of a 'Roman' way of life. Some explanation for change exists, however, since Roman material culture provided new opportunities to upwardly mobile natives.

Other writers explore a comparable approach to the progressive Romanization of the 'lower strata' (the non-elite). Dick Whittaker has suggested that 'cultural assimilation' occurred effectively 'by osmosis'.[262] The elites of the empire were constantly mobile and were socially entwined with their poorer compatriots and there was an infiltration of one set of values to another.[263] This allows a mechanism through which progressive Romanization of the less wealthy and powerful could occur. Ramsey MacMullen's study, *Romanization in the Time of Augustus* (2000), argues that 'Roman' goods were not confined to the rich. 'Italian pottery' could be found within the reach of people of almost every level of wealth across the empire and this is also often taken to indicate the non-elite's wish to adopt a Roman identity. Drawing upon earlier work, MacMullen argues that Romanization was a process that was carried out through imitation, 'by osmosis'.[264] In this way, 'Roman' culture is felt to have spread to a range of people within the Western provinces and is argued to have been inherently attractive. The motive for Romanization across the empire therefore lay in the 'intrinsic attractiveness of the Roman way of life seen through the eyes of the indigenous population'.[265]

This approach poses a question – why should 'Roman' culture have been intrinsically desirable to people within the Western empire? MacMullen addresses this by suggesting that it was attractive because baths, wine and other relevant innovations recommend themselves to people – they felt or they looked good.[266] But why did these innovations feel or look good to people at this time? We are asked to accept that the new material elements of civilization – including the pottery and coins in addition to the urban architecture and other 'Roman' aspects of lifestyle – were *always* preferable to alternative ways of living. This appears to be based, still, on the premise that Roman civilization was inherently superior to the ways of life that it apparently replaced.[267] The attraction of these material elements of life appears natural to the modern scholar and this desire is projected back into the past.

We are effectively asked to accept that Roman culture spread because of its inherent superiority over native ways of life and that all (or most?) within society across the empire concurred with this simple conception. This type of perspective arises naturally from the unquestioned adoption by modern scholars of the Roman concept of *humanitas* and from the development of this perspective within modern ideas of progress.[268] Both *humanitas* and progress suggest that Roman culture represented a form of material improvement for the barbarian. Modern society is seen as deriving a range of elements from Rome, introduced into western Europe by the Roman invasion, such as cities, metalled roads, a professional army, taxation, classical education, etc.[269] The Romans are perceived as bringing us closer to the way that we are today; therefore, Romanization has been developed as an early form of progress. Natives, in these terms, were effectively passive recipients succumbing to a naturally superior culture by abandoning their outmoded past.[270]

It is teleological to assume that so-called 'Roman' innovations were considered 'superior' by all within the empire, merely because they appear to be more familiar and attractive to the modern scholar. Significantly, the dominance of this progressive account acts as a continuing justification for the general failure of many Roman archaeologists to study in any detail the archaeology of the less wealthy and powerful.[271] If we follow the progressive approach, these less privileged people do not help with the understanding of the development of Roman society. If all within Italian and provincial society had a common aim of becoming Roman, why not study those who were able to realize these aims most fully in their lives? After all, the homes of these people are likely to produce far richer and more impressive finds and structures than those of people who apparently could only afford to change their ways slowly.[272]

On a more detailed level of analysis, the progressive approaches to Romanization that were developed by Mommsen, Haverfield, Millett and others are based upon an uncritical attitude to Roman culture, in which a wide range of individual elements of the archaeological record are drawn upon to represent 'Roman' identity.[273] In recent years it has been argued that the idea that so-called 'Roman' material culture was a coherent entity with some form of spiritual identity – that it carried some message of '*Romanitas*' – is unsupportable.[274] The aim of some recent studies is to pull apart the concept of 'Roman' material culture to study the complexity of the evidence for social change that lies behind it.

Philip Freeman, in an important review of Millett's book,[275] argued that the idea of a coherent 'Roman' cultural package is a modern invention stemming from the work of Mommsen and Haverfield. He contested that the definition of what constitutes 'Roman' goods has not received enough attention.[276] Roman material culture in the northern and western parts of the empire is often seen to represent the import of practices and objects from what is seen effectively as a culturally homogeneous Mediterranean Europe.[277] In fact, regional studies of the classical Mediterranean are demonstrating a very high degree of cultural variability.[278] The term *Roman* naturally focuses attention on Rome as the origin of these cultural elements; but the reality is far more complex, as many of the so-called 'Roman' items were actually drawn from various societies across the empire.[279] In addition, the adoption of this so-called 'Roman' material culture does not necessarily need to be viewed in terms of a wish by native peoples to adopt a Roman identity.[280]

Freeman explored the meaning of 'Roman' material culture by studying the example of high-status pottery in the Western empire.[281] This pottery constituted one category of material that passed around the empire through trade. The model for the production of *terra sigillata* (often called 'samian') was derived from Tuscany, but vessels manufactured in southern and central areas of Gaul were traded to other parts of the three provinces of Gaul and to Germany and Britain.[282] Imported samian pottery might therefore incorporate meanings other than that of a simple Roman identity, such as links with kin in other areas. Freeman suggests that the arrival of new 'Roman' goods and traits does not prove a clear desire to be seen as 'Roman', as it may incorporate alternative aspects of identity – ideas that were drawn from extensive geographical contexts.[283] In addition to these possible regional aspects of identity, the adoption of so-called Roman objects may also represent the arrival of technologically new goods and practices.[284]

Some new work has developed from Freeman's initiative that aims to deconstruct the idea of 'Roman' identity in so far as items of material culture, such as wheel-made pottery, are concerned. Many locally produced products supplemented the high-status wares that were imported into all provinces.[285] These provincial types featured new potting techniques and styles but were created in particular contexts using local knowledge and materials; they are called 'Roman' in archaeological works, despite their local production and the native aspects of the character of this pottery. In contrast to the position taken by Haverfield and others with regard to the, effectively, spiritual connotations of material culture, the use of these objects could be seen in a different light. Perhaps they were adopted because they were more convenient and considered to be of relatively high quality; their use may represent efficiency rather than the adoption of some form of standardized 'Roman' identity.[286] The labelling of these goods as 'Roman' is itself a simplification; these objects cannot merely, in the terms explored above, be viewed as representing native acceptance of material elements of Roman civilization.

Reintroducing power relations

In 1997 Bill Hanson argued that the dominant emphasis within Britain was upon the idea that the Roman administration had a fairly relaxed attitude and allowed the local elite a great degree of independence.[287] A lively debate has developed concerning the role of Rome in the process of social change. Did the Roman administration have an active part in 'Romanizing' the empire, as envisaged by Mommsen, Haverfield, Hanson and others?[288] Alternatively, did the native elite effectively 'Romanize' themselves under the indirect influence of Rome, as proposed by Brunt, Millett and others?

The idea of a less forceful imperial power, as Jonathan Williams has emphasized, enables 'material Romanizations of all sorts' – from samian pottery to monumental town centres – to be disconnected from Roman imperialist intentions.[289] At the same time, the Romans are stripped of any notions of cultural imperialism, while social change becomes removed from the idea of imperial imposition.[290] The Romans provided the tools, and also the models, that enabled provincials to 'Romanize' themselves. Provincials were therefore involved in progress,[291] but as a result of the fact that they chose this approach rather than because they were instructed or pushed in this direction by Rome. The results of imperial incorporation are considered to be due to the 'desires' or 'evolutionary trajectories' of the dominated societies.[292] The adoption of such a supposedly 'bottom-up', rather than 'top-down' process in the contemporary world could be seen as exonerating Western powers from any blame for their imperial actions. It resulted from post-colonial guilt derived from the recent imperial history of Britain and the West.[293]

This suggests that we need to rethink the nativism inherent in Millett's orthodoxy once more, to consider an interventionist perspective in which social change occurred under rules that were laid down by Rome.[294] We should not assume that the Roman expansion provided the opportunity for a multivocal free-for-all across the empire. Rather, it created the context for the development of a degree of cultural and political unity, symbolized in law, literature, politics, architecture and city planning.[295] John Barrett has proposed that the Roman empire is an abstraction,[296] an image that we (and others) have constructed out of a need to give a form and structure to historical events and archaeological evidence that would otherwise overwhelm us with an immense mass of detail.[297] In this way, Roman identity helps us to make sense of the world of the past,[298] providing understanding by resisting the idea that experiences are entirely fractured, random and unrelated.[299] The power and force behind Rome constituted a material reality that created the contexts within which people inhabited the various individual areas that made up the empire.[300]

There is a certain irony in these arguments, since we have seen that Millett developed his interpretation of Romanization as a direct and explicit attempt to escape from the imperial notions of progress inherent in earlier theories. The less interventionist school of thought that has developed as a result of the perspective that he outlined is now subject to criticism on the grounds of its relationship to a post-imperial guilt. As David Fredrick has stressed in another context, it would appear that one is 'damned if one does and damned if one doesn't'.[301] One solution to this apparent *impasse* is to adopt an approach to the issue of imperial control and native response that combines aspects of the two positions that are often developed in the form of opposites. We need to focus upon the commonplace imposition of order, social norms and new cultural practices in the Roman empire, but to balance this against negotiation and cultural interaction.[302] As Dick Whittaker has argued, the two positions of an interventionist Roman state and a responsive native elite need not act in opposition; direct intervention and innovation could occur alongside one another.[303]

Reconstructing Roman culture in a global context

If we abandon simple interpretations of the adoption of 'superior' Roman goods by provincials, it is necessary to think in more complex terms about the reasons for change in material cultural assemblages. Since 1998 a convergence of approaches has drawn local studies into a broadly defined but fairly consistent body of theory, providing a further new orthodoxy that builds upon Millett's perspective. Perhaps the most significant work in this convergence is the approach to 'becoming Roman' that has been outlined by Greg Woolf,[304] which looks at the nature of the Roman 'cultural revolution' and its influence upon provincial elites.[305] Woolf's perspective allows for a subtle and complex interpretation of social change and the role of Roman culture within provincial society. It is based on the observation that there are different archaeological signatures in various provinces and regions and allows for the adoption of Roman culture in more flexible ways by local peoples. Roman culture is effectively reinvented in the context of local need,[306] but a focus upon the Roman nature of this culture is fundamental.

Woolf's approach emphasizes a search for 'structuring principles', or the 'cultural logic' of empire.[307] Rome therefore becomes:

> a new, highly differentiated social formation incorporating a new cultural logic and a new configuration of power. This complex grew up from within, first, Roman and, then, Italian society, and expanded by drawing in more and more groups, individuals and resources. The process might be compared to the growth of an organism that metabolizes other matter and is itself transformed by what it feeds on.[308]

In developing and colonizing, a new imperial culture is seen to have supplanted the pre-existing culture of Rome, just as much as it did the earlier cultures of the indigenous peoples of the developing empire.[309]

Becoming Roman in this way allows for both the imperial context of social change and the local adoption of this identity to co-exist. Influential people are seen to have been keen to adopt 'Roman' culture because this helped them to negotiate their own power simultaneously in local and in imperial contexts. It offered them a 'structuring system of differences'.[310] It was also in the interest of the Roman administration actively to promote the adoption of Roman ways among provincial elites, because these were the people at the very core of the local self-government who created the stability of relations that we term the empire of Rome. In these terms, Roman identity effectively had a symbolic dimension since it served to tie influential people into the evolving imperial system. The new landscapes of culture that were created as a result formed changing and challenging physical and imaginative environments within which others were compelled to live.[311] These people will then have 'negotiated' their identities, but within the context of rules that were not entirely of their own making.

The imperial context of change is, therefore, of fundamental significance. John Barrett has suggested that:

> we might reverse Haverfield's vision of the Empire gaining a 'unity of sentiment and culture': was it not the idea of empire which made possible the desire for unity of sentiment, and gave sense and purpose to certain forms of cultural expression?[312]

Binary opposites such as 'Roman' and 'native' break down under this approach, since all are transformed by the development of Roman culture. Through local action, people were able to influence imperial culture as a whole. As Woolf has written in a study of the Roman period, Gauls were not 'assimilated' to a pre-existing social order, but participated in the creation of a new one.[313]

A complementary interpretation of 'elite negotiation' has been developed by Nicola Terrenato to account for the character of society in Roman Italy.[314] Mary Downs has assessed the way that imperial patronage encouraged the integration of the elite in southern Spain into Roman imperial society; while others have discussed the value of comparable approaches to the conquest and absorption of Britain.[315] Elite groups effectively negotiated their relationship with Rome and adopted a form of Roman identity as part of this action.

These approaches enable a general focus to occur upon the variability of imperial relations, tying these into the local context of the adoption of Roman ways of life. Two problematic issues, however, lie behind this convergence of approaches. First, – in the company of past accounts of Romanization – these new perspectives remain elite-focused. They continue to justify an approach in which the lives of the majority of people across the empire remain either excluded or understudied. Works that examine fragmented Roman identities in other ways have arisen in recent years in response to the Romano-centric legacy; they attempt to move beyond a Romano-centric perspective by considering the connectivity of members of the non-elite (soldiers, industrial workers, traders, etc.) into the imperial system.[316] Second, both the convergent approaches to elite culture and the ideas of fragmented identities highlight the relationship between the study of the classical past and our present world (pages 4-5). All these approaches relate directly to theories of globalization that have emerged in recent years within sociology and anthropology.[317] A tension between the local context of individual societies and the creation of Roman cultural coherence defines the dynamics of these accounts, while the same issue lies behind influential interpretations of the current global world system.[318] In the final chapter I shall suggest that accounts of both the contemporary world and the Roman empire address more fragmented ideas of identity, by stressing a 'less dichotomous' and more 'intricate pattern of inequality' than previous interpretations.[319]

3

ROMAN IMPERIALISM AND CULTURE

> The discourse of culture has been notorious for blending themes and perspectives which scarcely fit together in one cohesive, non-contradictory narrative.
>
> (Bauman 1999, xiii)

A convergence of interests among scholars who study Roman imperial society has therefore led to the development of a significant approach to the apparent unity of culture. This involves the re-creation of a metanarrative of Roman identity that is developed with greater flexibility than in previous accounts of Romanization. My aim is to examine a variety of recent interpretations that seek an overall explanation for the development of culture, both within the city of Rome itself and various other areas of the empire.[1] These accounts have emerged as a response to the more extensive archaeological information that has been collected since the 1960s across much of Italy and the West. As a result, they create generalized Roman identities, which nevertheless acknowledge the local contexts of identity within particular places. Such works investigate the 'globalizing' aspects of Roman culture.

The idea of 'Roman' identity will be explored in terms of the ways that culture and its material dimensions were developed through the creation and maintenance of the empire. Roman imperial expansion depended upon human labour in the form of slavery but also upon a culture, the symbolism of which needed to be read according to conventions that were passed on through the tradition of classical education.[2] The means by which people were allowed, encouraged and/or enabled to become Roman will be interpreted as one of the most significant of the ways by which imperial relations were imagined, created, extended and maintained. In simple terms that mask a wide variety of local engagements, this creation of empire emerged through a complex series of accommodations between the imperial aristocracy and the various local elite groups that gradually became incorporated.[3] Roman elite culture was part of an identity brought into being and maintained as a vital element in the creation of empire – it was an essential aspect of imperial order and stability. The power of the malleable image drew both upon the military might of the empire and the flexible ways in which imperial control was exercised in particular places.

A focal idea is, therefore, that Roman elite identity provides a useful concept when it is defined as a malleable intersection of ideas from different contexts that were used in varying ways by differing groups across the empire. A variety of powerful individuals and social groups were able to adopt Roman identity in differing ways in the context of their own local needs. The military, cultural and religious power of Rome provided some unity to these local adoptions, since one major aim of many local elites was to communicate its position of influence, both in its own regional context and also within the broader imperial system.

Defining Roman elite culture

At this stage it is important to consider one significant concept which lies behind all studies of the empire – that of Roman identity. Early accounts of Romanization reified the idea of Rome by developing the concept of a well defined and clearly bounded identity and culture. In the context of current thought, however, many writers have been looking to redefine classical Rome in more flexible ways. It would now appear that the very flexibility of the term 'Roman', and its ill defined boundaries, may have provided part of the explanation for the imperial success of Rome. Rome was able to incorporate and assimilate partly because of the flexibility of the ways in which its culture operated. The geographical extent of the empire, and its historical stability, may partly have derived from the malleability of Roman identity. This terminological flexibility, however, creates a difficulty in defining the terms 'Rome' and 'Roman'. For previous generations these terms often posed no particular difficulty, but in a postmodern context concepts are often pulled apart and 'Rome' is no exception.

Despite attempts at deconstruction, the concept of Roman culture is of use in defining how certain social forms were identified and reproduced. This culture was not a clearly bounded and monolithic entity but rather a method by which certain people constructed meaning through practices of symbolic representation. In the imperial core, Roman culture was articulated in order to combat elements of chaos within the government of late Republican Rome, by defining and communicating, both individually and collectively, a particular way of being.[4] Within the provinces of the empire it came to represent a new and powerful means by which influential people with international contacts were offered opportunities to identify themselves and communicate with others across wide areas. The disruption that resulted from the incorporation of native societies within the expanding empire placed a particular premium upon the adoption of this international culture by local elite groups, in a form of self-reinforcing order that drew upon a coordinated conception of identity.

In pursuing this theme, I shall draw upon concepts outlined in the works of contemporary writers, including Roman 'imperial ideology', 'imperial propaganda', 'Augustan ideology', 'Augustan culture', 'Roman cultural revolution' and 'imperial culture'.[5] It is argued that the idea of Roman culture can be applied to the actions of the imperial elite through the use of concepts included in these works. 'Roman' culture was brought into being through the creation of relations between peoples within the expanding empire as part of a developing discourse of imperialism.[6] It is useful to suppose that this culture was articulated as a means of imagining, creating, bounding and maintaining the empire. Ideas of Roman culture and 'imperial discourse' provided the discursive and ideological framework that facilitated the expansion, consolidation and survival of the empire.[7]

Culture

Although there is no one word in the Latin language equivalent to 'culture',[8] some scholars argue that it is of analytical value to their work and as a result, cultural studies have come to influence classical scholarship.[9] Thomas Habinek and Alessandro Schiesaro write about Roman culture as 'a dynamic process consisting of various intersecting practices and discourses' and Andrew Wallace-Hadrill has explored 'the Roman revolution and material culture'.[10]

'Culture' is a term that has been used widely and has a long history within social anthropology and sociology.[11] In the contemporary world, some use the term to refer to the arts, or an interest in what is sometimes called 'high culture' but in the context of this book another meaning is explored:[12] the identity of people as a whole and the ways in which they live their lives. Such definitions are modern and associated with the rise of the nation state and the perceived role of culture in projecting national or regional unity.[13] Consequently, there has been a modernist emphasis upon the bounded character of cultures as unified and isolated entities. Archaeologists in Britain and Germany began to use the term 'culture' from the 1920s.[14] The development of archaeological theory during the twentieth century, initially through the framework of culture-history, defined distinct material cultures within the archaeological record.[15] The boundaries of material culture assemblages were imagined to define the extent of the territories of distinct peoples. The process of the interpretation of ethnic groups, often couched effectively in terms of racial groups, formed part of the modernist project that helped with the identification of distinct nations in the landscape of Europe and the world.

Under the approach defined as the 'New Archaeology' in the 1960s and 1970s, this idea was developed.[16] Culture was now viewed as a functional method by which people adapted to their environmental surroundings.[17] New Archaeologists often argued that differing material culture assemblages defined distinct peoples. Deriving from studies in social anthropology and ideas about the character of 'primitive' human societies, an image developed of tightly bounded groups in which the surviving material elements effectively mapped the distribution of people in time and space. Under these approaches, culture is integrated, unified, settled and static;[18] it represents regularity and pattern, the way in which social groups perpetuated themselves.[19] Within these regional cultures, observed variation from the norm was played down in an emphasis upon the norm. Roman studies operated within this framework, defining one standard, well bounded culture that was felt to have spread across the empire, replacing in the process a multitude of equally well bounded 'barbarian' prehistoric cultures.[20] Within the approaches to Romanization which dominated the subject, Roman and native identity were often classified, in effect, in opposition to one another, while Romanization became a fairly simple form of 'progress' towards 'civilization'.[21]

Since the 1960s the definition of 'culture' in the social sciences has become a far more complex undertaking with the development of cultural studies as a distinct school of thought.[22] The term 'culture' has become subject to considerable discussion but has remained widely in use.[23] With the change from a dominant modernist perspective to postmodernism, cultural studies have developed a range of competing theories that show some coherence. David Howes has argued that the conclusions of cultural studies are thrown into confusion by the complex interactions that occur within modern imperial and global situations.[24] Culture itself is perceived as being in a constant state of transition.[25] In the modern world, the borrowing and lending of culture goes on across porous cultural boundaries.[26]

This growing emphasis upon malleability in cultural studies relates to the complex global interactions that constitute the contemporary world. Many recent studies contest the nature of cultures as bounded wholes.[27] It no longer appears appropriate to consider supposedly distinct cultures as self-contained entities with fixed boundaries, as distinct groups of objects or as a determinate set of traits and properties.[28] All cultures are open to influences from others. Individual cultures can have some fairly widely accepted features;[29] the formulation of a too-rigid definition, however, would lead to a level of generality that makes the concept theoretically useless.[30] For some, culture is the order of life in which humans construct meaning through practices of symbolic representation – a signifying system.[31] For others it can be understood as part of the effort to pin down meanings so that they can stay stable for a little time.[32] Culture is created in an attempt to project stability onto an unstable world. The idea of global culture in the modern world defines 'a form, a space or field, made possible through improved means of communication in which different cultures meet and clash'.[33] The interaction between different peoples leads to a situation in which cultural integration processes are occurring at a global level but in a situation that is increasingly pluralistic in terms of new levels of diversity.[34] Mike Featherstone argues that:

> If there is a global culture it would be better to conceive it not as a common culture, but as a field in which differences, power struggles and cultural prestige contests are played out. Something akin to an underlying form which permits the recognition and playing out of differences.[35]

Culture represents the ways in which people make their lives meaningful for themselves, both individually and collectively, by communicating with each other a way of life.[36] Culture is sometimes considered to be not so much about self-perpetuation as concerned with securing the conditions for further experimentation and change.[37] According to Zygmunt Bauman, it is a 'workshop' in which the steady pattern of society is 'repaired and kept in shape'.[38] It is, at the same time, just as much an agent of disorder as it is a tool of order, an aspect of obsolescence as much as timelessness.[39] It is a quest for order born out of a fear of chaos.[40] In these terms, cultures may be viewed as 'intersections', collections of ideas from various contexts, as 'processes',[41] or as matrices of possible permutations.[42]

The ideas of cultures as intersections or processes puts an emphasis on the means by which identities are created and maintained through time and also across borders. People who adopt a particular culture need to have some means of defining its boundaries or it becomes impossible to identify which items belong within and which outside.[43] Evidently, a more complex and multifaceted interpretation of culture requires the rethinking of some of the ideas that have informed earlier debates about the spread of Western identity.[44] In this context, it is possible to conceive of the 'de/territorialization' of culture.[45] Culture is no longer thought of in localized geographical terms, as 'globalization has pulled culture apart'.[46] Culture has been extracted from any concept of proscribed space to be 'reinscribed' in different cultural environments. The concept of 'de/territorialization' relates specifically to the double movement inherent in this process.[47] Culture is not merely directly adopted by the local society, it is modified and redefined in the context of local needs and projected back onto the societies from which inspiration was originally derived.

Cultures need no longer represent territorial entities, but can define certain groups within a broader society; for example elite cultures arise at some places in particular times and these can be quite widely spread in geographic terms.[48] Cultural studies also challenge frameworks of understanding based upon social hierarchy because global forces break down local structures of power and, as a result, various types of 'sub-culture' are commonly defined in the contemporary world.[49] At the same time, however, dominant individuals and institutions often establish cultural rules to organize and communicate difference.[50]

The expansion of the Roman empire during the final few centuries BC and first century AD witnessed a major increase in circulation of both people and artefacts or goods within and beyond its boundaries.[51] This was accompanied by a considerable instability across the Mediterranean, northern Europe and the Near East – a context within which conscious efforts were required to establish cultural boundaries, as people from very different backgrounds came into contact with each other in a wide variety of cultural contexts. Some of those who write about the empire have reacted to the new forms of interpretation that have been developed within cultural studies by considering the value of the concept in the context of imperial Rome.[52]

Roman culture

In both the ancient and the modern world, Rome was and is primarily perceived as a city.[53] In the second half of the first millennium BC the city-state of Rome spread through the Italian peninsular and then across much of the Mediterranean.[54] During this often violent and destructive expansion,[55] Roman armies and administrators carried ideas outwards into their expanding empire, including the concept of what it meant to be a Roman. The word 'Roman' is itself shorthand for a highly complex amalgam of variable concepts, embodying the difficulties that exist in the definition of Roman identity. Simon Keay and Nicola Terrenato have suggested that 'Rome' relates to at least two distinct cultural groupings – the original culture of the city-state of Rome itself, which was rooted in the Latin Iron Age, and the imperial culture carried across the expanding empire that came to characterize broader 'Roman' society.[56]

'Roman' culture should not be viewed as a clearly bounded and monolithic entity but as being derived from a variety of sources spread across the Mediterranean. The city of Rome was remade from the fourth century BC through the adoption of an eclectic collection of ideas and objects from a variety of places.[57] During the final centuries of the first millennium BC, elite groups across Italy developed a growing unity through a process that Nicola Terrenato has entitled 'elite negotiation'.[58] A new culture arose as a result of the benefits brought to these groups from closer contacts with the growing power of Rome.[59] Although this approach oversimplifies a complex and regional variability in the evidence and can also be subject to some criticism because of its emphasis upon consensus-building,[60] it provides a useful general way of conceptualizing the spread of Roman identity. As part of this process, other communities within Italy and Rome's growing empire became allied with Rome and incorporated precisely because they were offered, bargained for or struggled for, the privilege of retaining the core of their traditional organization within an imperial framework that was intended to guarantee order and stability.[61]

Such a coalescence of interests appears to have been more common than a mode of conquest in which the local society was subjected to radical political and social reorganization by Rome.[62] A convergence of culture may have occurred in the majority of cases as this helped to express the status of an expanding series of elites across Italy and the empire in a language that communicated their common identities.[63] The complex rules that established the relationship between Rome and these elites partly explains the variability ('cultural bricolage') that survived across Italy during late Republican, Augustan and later times.[64] Rome acted as a catalyst in the transformations that occurred across Italy and then throughout the empire by offering a widely relevant package, including light administrative control, pacification, a degree of economic intensification and, above all, from Augustan times onward, a highly powerful and flexible incorporative ideology.[65] The convergence of elite culture and values throughout the Mediterranean is a central issue in understanding the extent, durability and longevity of the empire.

In Rome and Italy the elite created their eclectic identity by absorbing the cultures of other Mediterranean peoples while trading, conquering and assimilating them; in the process, they created what has been termed by Andrew Wallace-Hadrill 'a general Mediterranean language of success'.[66] This transformation included a massive assimilation of Greek culture, particularly from the second century BC onwards,[67] a process that has sometimes been called 'Hellenization'.[68] Greece had a particular symbolic power for Romans, as it provided a language of culture that was used to exhibit the pre-eminence of the people who adopted these new ways.[69] It included a strong claim of superiority and also 'key technologies' that enabled power to be exhibited and developed.[70] Roman society was also influenced by the other peoples of Italy and of the central and western Mediterranean.[71] Indeed, as the empire expanded, people from further afield came to influence imperial culture in complex ways.

It is useful to consider that these adoptions and adaptations resulted in the creation of a 'Roman' culture that spread and, effectively, came to define a 'constellation' of cultures across the Mediterranean and parts of northern Europe.[72] This new culture was first fully 'articulated' under Augustus,[73] during the late first century BC and early first century AD, as Greek models were in effect re-projected in the context of the developing empire, to emphasize the universalizing value system of Rome.[74] During the period of imperial control, Roman identity continued to be influenced by societies on the periphery of the empire; although it has been argued that political factors limited the influence of some societies in the West upon Rome.[75] For example, the influence of the societies of the East later in the history of the empire amounted to an 'oriental revolution' which Warwick Ball has argued represents a central factor in the development of both the later Roman empire and the subsequent history of Europe.[76] As Ball has suggested:

> in order to understand Rome and appreciate it fully, it is necessary to see it in all of its breadth and richness, not just as 'European' or

> 'Western' civilisation . . . This legacy is as much eastern as western, as much oriental as occidental, both to Europe and the world as a whole.[77]

Despite such attempts to decentre the idea of Roman identity, the use of the term 'Roman' for the constellation that formed the empire is justified by the fact that these highly variable individual cultures were incorporated into an entity that called itself by this term.[78]

The topic of Roman culture – how the Romans viewed themselves and what made them distinctly *Roman* – has been defined as the key to an understanding of identity in the empire.[79] This perspective is also central to many works on the interpretation of material culture and social change – so-called imperial 'Roman' culture is often felt to have spread across a very wide area. For most ancient historians who deal with the late Republic and the empire, the defining feature of Roman identity has been the common citizenship that spread with the expansion of the empire.[80] To be fully Roman required that an individual was a citizen of Rome; a free man or woman could hold citizenship and this gave various privileges and advantages.[81] At the same time, citizens were by no means equal, as wealth, connections, gender, knowledge and the past history of a family influenced the position of an individual within the power structure.[82]

Roman identity was, therefore, not a matter of a person's ethnicity, nation, linguistic group or descent, but a status that had been inherited, achieved or awarded.[83] During the early expansion of the empire, in the Republican period, citizenship was extended to groups of allies who were often effectively incorporated into the category of Romans.[84] The creation of citizens was continued and expanded by Julius Caesar, Augustus and later emperors.[85] This enabled the elites of widely spread peoples to be incorporated into the imperial system and allotted positions within society. Other groups, such as freed slaves and, by the mid-first century AD, retired auxiliary soldiers, could also become citizens.[86] During its territorial expansion across Italy and the Mediterranean, Rome recruited its armies from both its own population and from its allies.[87] As the empire expanded, the conditions became less attractive to people from the Italian peninsula and the legions were increasingly recruited from Spain, Africa and the Danube regions. Increasingly, Rome also came to recruit auxiliary soldiers from areas within the empire that had few communities that held citizenship.[88] A free non-citizen male could join the auxiliary forces and, after a prescribed period of service, become a citizen, a right that extended to his children. The retiring soldier was also allocated land and/or money.[89] The sons of the veteran soldier, as citizens themselves, could have qualified to join a legion. Therefore the army constituted a means for men to achieve upward social mobility, especially for non-citizens.[90]

The extension of citizenship meant that, by the time that the empire had expanded to its maximum extent, many people could be described as 'Roman'.

Censuses of citizens across the empire were conducted in 28 BC, AD 47 and 73;[91] between the first and second census there was an increase from four million to nearly six million. The population of the empire is likely, however, to have been at least fifty million,[92] perhaps rather greater. This means that the citizen body was a very small percentage of the total. Citizens were also not distributed evenly, with much higher proportions in Italy and the Mediterranean core than in the northern provinces, although the presence of soldiers on the frontiers would gradually have changed this pattern. Citizens included a wide variety of peoples, from those who lived in Rome itself to those of the far-flung provinces, such as Syria or Britain.[93]

The mechanisms to create new citizens served to integrate native peoples into the imperial system and citizenship became increasingly widespread. In AD 212 the emperor Caracalla extended citizenship to almost the whole of the freeborn population of the empire.[94] If we take citizenship to signify Roman identity, by the early third century the Roman population was effectively spread very widely across the whole of the empire. By this time, however, citizenship was less of a privilege than it had been; this was because the meaning of the status changed and inequality became more of an organizing principle across the empire.[95] Redefinition of citizenship after the second century created a clear division between *honestiores* and *humiliores* that destroyed the unity of citizenship across the empire.[96]

To understand the nature of this identity and its spread across the empire, it is vital to consider in greater detail the transformations that occurred in the concept of what it was to be 'Roman' under the first emperor Augustus during late first century BC and early first century AD. It has been argued that at this time Roman identity was articulated as an international culture. A major transformation occurred at this time within both Italy and the provinces.[97] This was highly significant for the ways in which Roman identity came to be defined. Under Augustus, a local way of organizing political and social life based on that used in the city of Rome succeeded, to a degree, in becoming universal across Italy and further afield. This transformation was fundamental but at the same time it was based upon the manipulation of the Republican traditions of Rome rather than their complete replacement.[98] As part of this process, there had been a shift from a local hereditary Roman elite forming the basis of power and knowledge to a context in which a variety of specialists developed control over increasingly complex and technical fields of information and knowledge.[99] Areas of practice – including government, education, war and religion – that were once the responsibility of the elite rulers of the citizen body, became, increasingly, the preserve of specialist groups.[100]

The Augustan invention of empire, in Jas Elsner's terms, was managed by the creation of a culture – a combination of texts, art, infrastructure and propaganda – through which the first emperor established the image of a new political system that was intended to administer a vast empire.[101] The Augustan period saw the consolidation of the empire from a collection of provinces into a more unified entity.[102] The creation of this new system was the result, according to Karl Galinsky, of 'an ongoing experimentation in pragmatism and the negotiation and re-negotiation of precedents in the context of new needs and circumstances'.[103] This new imperial framework was not based on a transparent propaganda, but was a collection of familiar signs that came to be manipulated in new ways for specific purposes.[104] The result was the creation of a relatively successful new conceptual framework for thinking about, and also for governing, the empire – one that was adopted and adapted by subsequent emperors.[105] This framework had literary, governmental and material elements.

The term 'revolution', derived from the work of Ronald Syme,[106] is convenient shorthand for a series of academic arguments about the transformation of metropolitan Roman culture around this time,[107] one that focused upon the growing power and authority of Augustus. This set of transformations involved the management of various aspects of social and symbolic space in relation to time, tradition, language and law,[108] but also to changes in sexual conduct and ways of life in general.[109] The Augustan revolution reflected the development of a greater degree of coherence in the policy towards the creation and maintenance of the empire, building upon accepted and established knowledge and belief. To a degree, at least, these transformations were not confined to Rome and Italy alone – they are also evident in the imperial landscape of the provinces, which witnessed major changes from the time of Augustus onwards.[110] This cultural revolution resulted in the definition and development of a distinctive 'Augustan culture' within both Rome and the provinces – including literary, intellectual, aesthetic, artistic and architectural styles.[111]

It has been argued that the Augustan age produced a culture that transcended its time;[112] this is not to say that it remained static through history. Greg Woolf has argued that the revolution inherent in imperial expansion lasted at least 300 years, whether by imitation, reinterpretation or rejection;[113] while Karl Galinsky has defined its development in even wider terms, as 'paradigmatic' within Western civilization.[114] When thinking about the potential coherence of Roman imperial culture, it is important to bear in mind that individuals with a vested interest in the expansion and maintenance of the empire by no means all thought and acted in the same ways.[115] Indeed, it is true that this cultural revolution was the creation of various groups with differing, and sometimes clashing, interests, not purely that of those based in Rome.[116] Much of this culture was created by individuals without the direct intervention of the state. There do, however, appear to have been shared attitudes among the imperial elite about the character of their identity and also the aims of Roman imperialism.[117] These ideas were created and perpetuated through the mechanisms of education and the production and circulation of literature. People manipulated imperial culture through time – it was not a static phenomenon.[118]

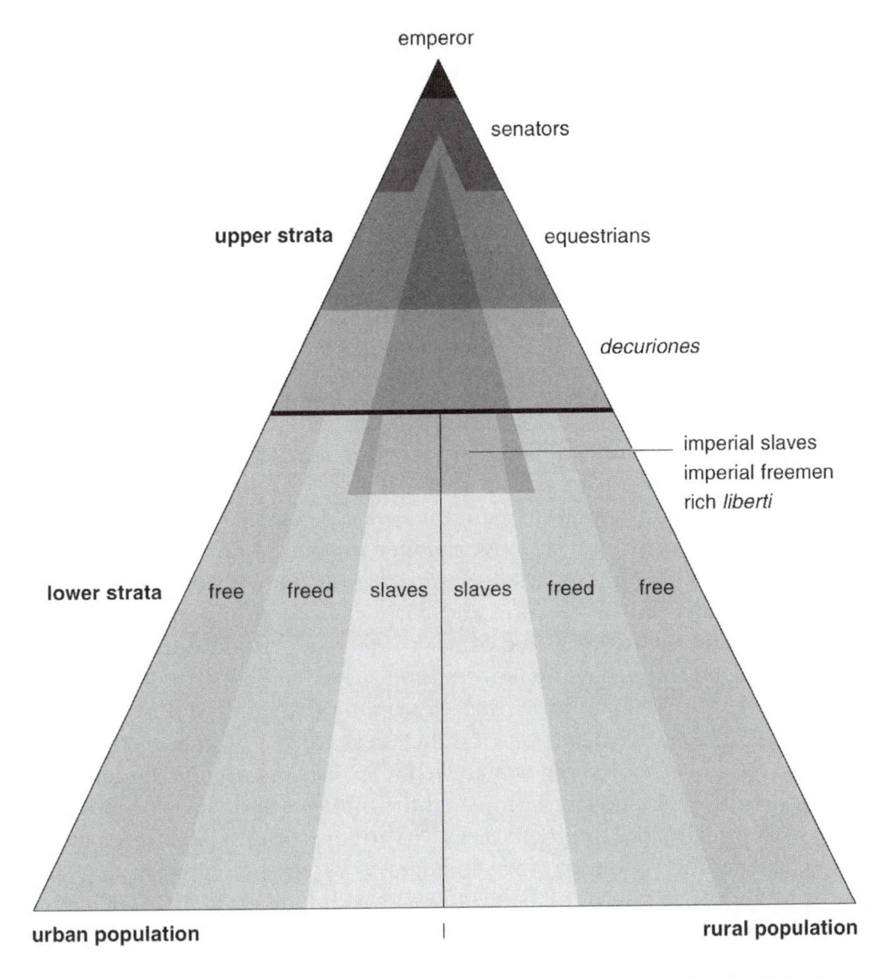

Figure 4 A schematic representation of Roman social structure under the Principate. Adapted from Alföldy 1985, Figure 1. Drawing by Christina Unwin.

I shall look first at certain literary concepts that can be argued to have formed part of a Roman civilizing ethos. Although the literary angle is highly significant, I shall not attempt to explore it in great detail, taking some observations that have been made by a number of scholars but not developing these to any great extent.

Writing about Roman elite culture

Many societies include an elite group that differentiates itself from the remainder of the population,[119] although the ways in which this is achieved differ between societies. An elite group often defines itself not only through the possession of power and its reproduction, but by a degree of self-recognition and self-consciousness, constituting a common culture.[120] The ruling elite of Rome included the senators and equestrians, who formed a single aristocratic group with many competing political sub-groups (Figure 4).[121] In the provinces, opportunities led local members of society to develop a relatively high status within their communities, but their position within elite Roman society would have depended upon the extent to which they were able and willing to adopt Roman culture.

The aristocracy of the empire used Latin language and writing to establish and police their boundaries. The formation of aristocratic behaviour in Roman society occurred through the medium of an education in Greek and Latin languages and literature and through the definition and adoption of a common culture.[122] Citizens were expected to know Latin and its use was required under certain formal legal circumstances.[123] Education performed a vital role in the socialization of the Roman elite, as Greek educational principles were refashioned in a selective manner to suit the need of an imperial governing class.[124] The knowledge imparted through this education was deeply implicated in the creation and perpetuation of imperial power and also in the critiques that occurred of such authority.[125] Education was used to create linguistic and behavioural norms and rules that defined ways of life,[126] including the ideas of authority that were so fundamental to the elite.[127] As such, it helped to instruct students to function as citizens, to rule and be ruled.

A powerful body of writing was created,[128] a 'discourse of the dominant'.[129] Classical writing pursued and projected the interests and views of the male elite, while usually stifling other voices.[130] Various works of literature participated in the formation of this aristocracy by defining, preserving and transmitting the standards of behaviour to which individual aristocrats must aspire and by valorizing aristocratic ideals and authority within a broader context.[131] During the first century BC, particular authors contributed to a developing consciousness of empire. This formed part of a cultural project that aimed to define an identity that was fitting for the new rulers of the world.[132] A set of images that often emphasized universalizing tendencies was intended to over-ride the mosaic of local diversity that formed the empire through the imposition of an image of homogeneity.[133] Relevant works include a number that were composed in the last generation of the Republic and others that were written under Augustus; these sought to define Roman identity through a shared past and also to establish the historical context for contemporary imperial destiny.[134] By the time that Virgil was writing, Latin language and writing had become an instrument of imperialism.[135]

Poetry and writing at this time were, and are, susceptible to multiple readings and should not be interpreted simply as 'propaganda'.[136] The creation of the empire as a discourse of domination, however, was backed up by an imperial ideal that was expressed by Augustan and later writers.[137] Thomas

Habinek has argued that poets, writers of histories, novelists and other artists became 'implicated in the process of constructing, refining, and promulgating the discourse that situates not just the dominated subject but the dominators as well'.[138] Early Augustan writers, including Virgil, articulated – whether with ambivalence or not – the idea of Roman superiority over subject people.[139] This idea of dominance accustomed the privileged reader to the loss of certain rights that had been enjoyed under the Republic; it helped to defuse a growing status anxiety derived from the broadening out of membership of the Senate through the putative benefits of a stable imperial system.[140] Some of this literature is explicitly imperial.[141] For instance, Virgil's *Aeneid* includes the enactment by Juno and Jupiter of a Latin myth of origin that expresses the power of Latin language and culture to establish its sway over non-Latins (12: 820–40).[142] Latin came to be expressed in this form as a civilizing force: in Joseph Farrell's words, a means for 'ordering the disorderly, standardizing the multiform, correcting or silencing the inarticulate'.[143] Other classical writers express imperial ideals, sometimes, in a less explicit fashion. In defining the formation of the Roman aristocracy this classical literature provided means by which members of native groups within the provinces could be drawn into imperial culture.

Barbarians

In drawing upon the idea of their own civilization, many societies have defined themselves through the identification of an 'other'. Greek society experienced other peoples across the eastern Mediterranean and the Black Sea area as a result of a period of colonization in the middle of the first millennium BC. Despite the fact that they were divided into a number of discrete city-states, the Greeks derived a common concept of kinship for themselves as a result of ideas of religion and ethnic derivation, but these could not, ultimately, distinguish Greek from non-Greek.[144] The measure of 'Greekness' became focused upon a common language and barbarians were identified primarily as those who could not speak Greek.[145] For elite members of Roman society, the definition of self and other was more to do with civilized behaviour.[146] Barbarians were perceived as being closer to nature, warlike and irrational. They were marked out from the civilized by strange clothing, different ways of living and aberrant (although also, sometimes, admirable) behaviour.[147] In general, however, from the Roman viewpoint, they lacked both the moral quality of civilized people and also the culture that defined the Roman elite.[148]

When defining 'barbarians', classical authors were involved in establishing their own identity. This classification was conceptualized and articulated in historical, geographical and ethnographical writings. Also of significance was the examination of the physique of prisoners from campaigns at the periphery of empire, paraded in triumphal processions through the city of Rome.

Defeated barbarians were often portrayed on imperial monumental art, on triumphal arches and trophies, both in Rome and in the provinces.[149] These images represented defeated peoples in stereotypical ways – the naked and hairy 'other'.[150] In the city of Rome they helped remind the population about the extent of the empire and the military and religious superiority of the imperial civilization. Elsewhere, such portrayals reminded certain local populations of their conquered status and barbarian origins, while also encouraging their transformation through Roman rule to a new state of civilization.[151]

The Greek definition of the barbarian was comparatively inflexible, since it often appears to have stressed the need for Greek ancestry in addition to the ability to speak Greek.[152] Within the Roman world, particularly that of the late first century BC and early first century AD, there was no direct opposition in the mind of the Roman elite between 'self' and 'other'.[153] A modest structure that was identified as the cabin or hut of Romulus (the *casa* or *tugurium Romuli*) was conserved on the Palatine Hill in Rome, where it survived until the fourth century AD.[154] This building had a complex variety of associations,[155] but served to remind Romans of the humble setting for their origins and subsequent rise to imperial greatness, while also enabling concerns about moral decline in the contemporary world to be articulated.[156] Perhaps it also served as a physical reminder of the potential kinship of the Romans with the native peoples of the imperial frontiers; indeed, Tacitus suggests that it was in these areas that some of the old virtues survived relatively unscathed.[157] Barbarians, therefore, enabled classical authors to reflect in a critical manner upon the character of their own civilization.[158]

The opportunity of conquest

Greg Woolf has recently summarized relevant works on the difficult but useful concept of '*humanitas*' and the world-view that it incorporated.[159] This term was used by Romans to describe their culture, and reflects the particular configuration of power that underlay it from the later first century BC.[160] It was a concept that developed during the period of imperial consolidation as the elite became increasingly aware of their place within the wider world.[161] *Humanitas* is usually translated to mean 'civilization' but it stood for a complex range of ideas which all served a role in contributing to the definition of the Roman self.[162] Classical Rome, in the company of many other peoples, defined its identity in contrast to a concept of 'otherness'. *Humanitas* was a significant aspect of what it was to be 'Roman'.[163] By the late first century BC, *humanitas* had been formulated in terms of cultural concepts that were regarded as the hallmark of aristocratic conduct – ideas also thought to be of relevance to humanity in general.[164] These concepts were used to define the elite as cultivated, enlightened and humane; entirely fitted to rule a wide empire and to lead others by example.

Humanitas formed a significant element in the definition of aristocratic behaviour. It included the idea that all might attempt to aspire to this ideal state and, as such, contrasted with an ancient Greek concept, *paideia*, which conceived that good education and civilized behaviour formed a Greek monopoly.[165] At the same time that *humanitas* defined an ideal state of being, it also allowed for the idea that others who had not achieved its goals might succeed, given the correct circumstances. *Humanitas* served as an effective element in Roman imperial discourse, since it enabled the empire to absorb into its structure a variety of other peoples from the societies it encountered. It did this by defining its own cultural rules in such a way that they could be adopted by others. This absorption occurred through what Matthew Roller has defined as a cultural 'mapping' that was encoded in the familiar vocabulary of the Latin language, one that allowed a charting of 'ethical space'.[166] Positive values were assigned to various moral concepts, although the exact boundaries of these categories were subject to continuous contestation and renegotiation.[167]

The idea of *Humanitas* was one conceptual element in a culture that enabled a convergence between the desires of certain provincials and the publicized aims of Rome.[168] The aristocracy's collective acceptance of this mapping, including their judgement of others according to Roman standards, and their wish to be judged positively according to the same rules, formed part of their acculturation.[169] Ethical categories were used to demarcate the boundaries of an expanding Roman elite by defining positions for people to occupy across the geographical territory dominated by Rome. As part of the drive to solidify and expand the empire, an aristocratic hegemony made use of the Latin language and literature and of an acculturative vocabulary.

An effective legitimation for rule over others was provided by *humanitas* – it served as an ideological justification for conquest and domination.[170] The concept of *humanitas*, like present-day ideas of progress, was based on the vision of a historical process. Some classical authors conceived of a state of nature that formed a common human origin.[171] Some writers felt that *humanitas* originated in classical Greece, but they presented Roman rule as being capable of providing human beings with the conditions to realize their full potential by becoming civilized.[172] By representing Greek culture as the first stage in this universal process, authors could also assert the superiority of Rome in a manner that countered cultural anxiety.[173] Rome had replaced Greece as the dominant power and had brought *humanitas* to a far wider world of barbarians in the west and north of the growing empire. The idea that Greek culture and civilization were in many ways superior to those of Rome could therefore be countered both by the latter's contemporary military and cultural superiority and its role in offering civilization to the barbarians on the periphery of imperial control.[174]

Movement towards civilization could be achieved through the conquest and incorporation of barbarians within the empire,[175] although civilization did not occur merely as a result of this. To become civilized, the barbarian was required to acquire the general moral quality of a civilized person, an identity that included the culture that defined the Roman elite.[176] Through this process of 'civilization' the barbarian could ultimately acquire Roman identity and, with the support and approval of the imperial elite, Roman citizenship. *Humanitas*, in the Roman view, was created through the adoption of civilization and it was a matter of degree and not an absolute.[177] To the elite Roman mind, categories of civilization and barbarism were not created as binary opposites.[178]

Some progress towards this idealized state from a barbarian origin may have been possible, in the mind of much of the Roman elite, for all barbarians, but it is likely that the assimilation of newly conquered peoples to full Roman identity was only considered possible for a few within the provinces.[179] Indeed, *humanitas* could be used to differentiate the civilized person, not only from the barbarian, but also from uneducated members of the empire (those of the propertied class and the vast number of those without land).[180] It consisted of a series of intellectual and moral accomplishments and qualities that were, in the West at least, the exclusive property of the elite.[181] Some classical writings, for example, suggest that the vast majority of free men even in Rome itself, where these intellectual and moral standards were more widespread, were unable to achieve virtue as a result of their lack of education.[182] It was a unifying principle but one that restricted 'the pure Roman "type" to a few thousand individuals'.[183] Being a citizen was not enough, on its own, to define an individual as cultured.

Humanitas formed part of a classification of ethical space that allowed for a continuum of 'achievement', but the top of the hierarchy was reserved for the well born, wealthy and well connected. The extension of citizenship in the early empire, reviewed above, incorporated many people within the class of citizens who are unlikely to have fully qualified as Romans in the eyes of members of the elite both of the city of Rome and elsewhere in the empire. The 'upper strata', as defined in accounts of Roman society, even excluded many of the local elites across the Western empire.[184]As such, this concept of civilization effectively continued to exclude others, as differences of wealth, education and contact meant that only a limited number of people within Rome, Italy and the provinces could achieve a full Roman identity in the view of the imperial elite.[185]

Civilizing missions?

According to some classical authors, conquest by Rome brought order, peace and stability to the natives of the subjugated provinces.[186] Explicit statements about the civilizing aims of imperial action are scarce in classical literature.[187] This does not, however, mean that there was no coherent concept of civilization behind imperial action. It has recently been argued that modern scholars have taken issue against the idea of an interventionist Roman state as a result of their own feelings of 'post-colonial' guilt. Since the decline of Western territorial empires, it has been argued that modern imperialists chose to emphasize a conscious civilizing mission that they projected onto the classical sources.[188] The scarcity of literary and material evidence for Roman cultural imperialism has been taken to indicate that this reading of the evidence was created by our forebears.[189] Bent upon their own imperial conquests, they used their readings of the Roman past to provide a historical justification for their own actions.[190] This reaction against the imperial use of classical sources has also led, as we have seen, to a new wave of archaeological research that has directed greater emphasis towards the native element of provincial culture, at the expense of the global and incorporative forces of Roman integration. Consequently, the idea of a Roman civilizing mission has been consciously excluded from many recent accounts of Romanization; these stress the *laissez-faire* attitude of the administration and the indigenous context for an acceptance of Roman culture.

We need to be aware that critical attitudes to our own recent imperial history may be driving the current agenda,[191] as it is likely that the imperial elite of Rome had a far more direct influence on the ways that provincial societies underwent change than some recent accounts suggest. The writings of two particular authors – Tacitus and Cassius Dio – about the influence of Rome upon societies in the north-west of the empire during the first century AD are sometimes used to support the idea that the administration had a deliberate policy of intervention within the frontier regions of the Western empire.[192] Although some recent authors consider that Tacitus' and Dio's comments are of only limited relevance, new research has re-emphasized their significance.

In a recent discussion of the discourse of Flavian imperialism, Rhiannon Evans explores classical writings that provide an image of Britannia as a marginal and comparatively barbaric element of the empire, one that could be tamed and brought into the orbit of Roman culture through the actions of the worthy.[193] The provincial governor, Agricola, is represented in Tacitus' writings as an educator of the provincial elite.[194] This suggests that this educative process was brought to bear upon the provincials, as they are taught Roman manners:

> he educated the sons of chiefs in the liberal arts . . . The result was that those who just lately had been rejecting the Roman tongue now conceived a desire for eloquence. Thus even our style of dress came into favour and the toga was everywhere to be seen. Gradually, too, they went astray into the allurements of evil ways, colonnades and warm baths and eloquent banquets. The Britons, who had no experience of this, called it 'civilization', although it was part of their enslavement.
>
> (Tacitus *Agricola* 4 and 21)

In this work, Tacitus makes an explicit statement of the ways in which the worthy administrator seeks to promote the civilizing of the provincials. The disorderly Britons are transformed into 'near Romans'.[195] Even though Tacitus' comments contain an ironic twist upon the value of imperial civilization, by suggesting that this process of education effectively led to the corruption of the natives, they also project the attitude that Roman culture and identity was part of a civilizing mission.[196] By the end of the Flavian era, the degree of cultural absorption of some British natives was apparently sufficient, according to the author Martial, for Claudia Rufina, a Briton resident in Rome, to have been transformed into the perfect Roman woman (*Epigrams* 11: 53).[197] To the elite mind, imperial incorporation offered the opportunity for the privileged barbarian to become Roman. As such, Britain was transformed in Tacitus' account, through the actions of Agricola, from a state of 'semi-detachment' to the empire to one of 'semi-attachment',[198] enabling individuals to accept and adopt Roman identity.

Cassius Dio records that, in Germany at the beginning of the first century AD:

> soldiers . . . were wintering there and cities were being founded. The barbarians were adapting themselves to Roman ways, were becoming accustomed to hold markets, and were meeting in peaceful assemblages . . . they were not disturbed by the change in their manner of life and were becoming different without knowing it. But when Quintilius Varus became governor of the province of Germany, and in the discharge of his official duties was administering the affairs of these people also, he strove to change them more rapidly.
>
> (Dio 56:18.2–3)

The policy of Varus created serious problems that resulted in three legions being defeated by Arminius in AD 9.[199] Dio's comments, however, suggest that a process of institutionalized social change was occurring in Germania that was recognizable from other areas that had been incorporated into the empire. Rome was bringing order to the disorderly German natives by remoulding their territory.[200] In the past, it has sometimes been assumed that Dio's comments were purely imperial rhetoric and that the area had not been thoroughly settled,[201] but recent archaeological discoveries suggest that a concerted effort was made, during the early years of the first century, to create urbanism and an administrative structure,[202] one that collapsed after the defeat of AD 9. It is implied by Dio that these actions would have led the area to become a viable part of the empire, had Varus not overstepped the mark. This reference of Dio's has been taken as an indicator that the creation of a Roman order in a new province included, where necessary, the encouragement of the towns (as he mentions markets and meeting);[203] while Tacitus refers to styles of dress, arcades, baths, banquets and language. Classical authors attributed the role to Rome of creating order – to 'impose a settled pattern upon peace' (Virgil *Aeneid*, 6: 852).[204]

Humanitas, as a tool of imperialism, represented an element in a deliberate policy towards newly conquered provincial populations. To argue otherwise would be to suppose that *humanitas* formed an unquestioned part of the Roman psyche that was spread unconsciously and inadvertently – that it had no deliberate and calculated role in expansion. The issue of whether Rome had some form of conscious policy towards conquered territory has become a highly contentious issue.[205] The fact that there are only a few direct references to deliberately planned Roman influence upon the development of native societies is not necessarily a sign that no official policy existed. Jonathan Williams has observed that much of the attitude of governors and other officials towards these issues was probably unconscious and therefore not fully articulated in the classical texts. There is certainly no evidence for an official handbook of imperial practice for generals and provincial governors, instructing them how to make natives into Romans.[206] Yet, as Williams argues, the lack of explicit written instructions does not mean the absence of a firm intent on the part of the imperial power.[207] The coherence in the efforts of British officials in their colonial actions was not the result of having access to a book of rules created by the Colonial Office, but of a shared variety of experiences derived from a common upbringing.[208] A comparable situation occurred in the Roman empire, where background, education and experience influenced the ways in which provincial governors carried out policies.[209]

It is clear that the administration sometimes interfered directly in the affairs of newly conquered territories, and this is likely to have been a common occurrence. Much of the imperial action will, however, have been less direct. In general terms, from the early first century BC, the concept that conquest enabled higher moral and ethical standards to be passed to non-Romans was developed in written form.[210] By articulating the argument of the moral superiority of Roman culture and linking this to the military might and religious identity of the empire, classical authors created a way of informing native elites about the superiority of Rome. This dominance was backed up by military successes and, apparently, by divine favour. To an extent, therefore, it may be true that provincial elite groups educated themselves with the assistance of the administration, since taking part in this mission of self-civilization was of direct value to the local elites. This does not, however, mean that it was not also a central and official initiative. Where necessary, direct force will have been used to encourage recalcitrant members of the native elite to be incorporated.

Classical education

In the modern Western world, the education of large sections of the population and mass communication have created a context in which ideas spread swiftly. The world of imperial Rome was evidently very different. There is only a very limited evidence for written texts in northern Europe prior to the Roman conquest, although some groups adopted writing prior to their incorporation within the empire.[211] After the conquest, Latin language and written texts had significant roles. We know that education formed a core element in the creation of the identity of the Roman elite and provisions were made for teaching the sons of the wealthy and powerful in Rome. Classical education also spread to the provinces.[212] Although there was no formal organization of teachers, schools or subjects of instruction,[213] the ways in which elite identity was defined resulted in a common educational agenda across certain areas of the empire.

There appears to have been a school to educate the native elite in Augustodunum (Autun) in AD 23 and similar establishments are likely to have existed elsewhere.[214] Tacitus mentions that Agricola encouraged the education of the sons of chiefs in Britain through a subtle policy rather than by coercion.[215] We do not know how widespread such schools were and there is very little physical evidence to indicate the existence of schoolrooms anywhere.[216] We do know, from classical texts, that the education of the sons of chiefs was fundamental in the spread of Latin language and Roman culture,[217] although, as we shall see, others were also exposed to Latin (for instance traders and the army). It is unlikely that classical education would have passed much further than the most wealthy in Rome and it will have been even less common within the provinces.[218] Here, such an education was probably only available to those who were destined to become senior imperial officers and administrators and to the wealthy.[219]

The education of this minority in the provinces would presumably have included the moral concepts which lay behind *humanitas*, in addition to a thorough grounding in Greek and Latin language and literature.[220] Latin writings were especially significant in this regard because of their twin characteristics of relative permanence and portability.[221] Consequently, there was an increased emphasis on the materiality of the text, enabling its use in the provinces as a tool of incorporation.[222] It is likely that literature spread widely. For instance, Martial tells us that his poetry was read by centurions in northern Thrace (among the Getae) and in Britannia (*Epigrams* 11: 3). We do not know, however, how available classical texts were in individual Western provinces. Whether the circulation of books was primarily a result of buying and selling or operated through patronage – a fundamental element of the Roman social system – is also unknown.[223] The most wealthy within provincial society will presumably have had access to significant texts, but we do not know who else had access to these.

Latin language, writing and culture were all fundamental within various provincial societies, helping to create new ways of conceiving the world and of defining status and order.[224] The learning and mastery of the Latin language itself presumably were important elements in the development of authority among provincial elites.[225] Literature also allowed acculturation through its projection of language and Roman culture.[226] As such, literary texts operated as a method for spreading the cultural revolution.[227] This process of classical education helped to create a new Roman world-view in the minds of the sons of the dominant members of provincial society by incorporating them into Roman culture, with its distinctive concepts of order, authority and identity.

Some provincials had a direct experience of Rome. The sons of the powerful native leaders of friendly kingdoms were sometimes taken to Rome itself and directly introduced to Roman ways of life.[228] The experience of the vast city and its highly stratified society must have made a deep impression on visitors from western and northern Europe, who would usually have been unaccustomed to Mediterranean urban living and political life.[229] After the conquest or absorption of new provinces, visits by members of the provincial elite to Rome continued to be one of the ways in which Roman culture and ideals were experienced and disseminated.[230] Tacitus records that, in the mid-first century AD, representatives of the Frisians (a Germanic tribe) saw the Theatre of Pompey – 'one of the sites usually shown to barbarians', where they inquired about the seating arrangements and distinctions between orders (*Annals* 13: 54).

On their visits to Rome, members of the native elite experienced urbanism and monumental architecture at first-hand and they subsequently took their impressions back home.[231] Ideas of urbanism were also communicated by the charters that were issued to some communities in the provinces of the West,[232] which set down rules by which the local community was to operate. The city of Rome came to provide a model for systems of government across the empire – one that could also be experienced directly by those upon whom Rome depended to administer local communities.[233] Visits by members of the local elite to other parts of the empire would also have helped to provide experience of alternative models of building, urban architecture and administration. For instance, the urban centres in southern Gaul and the Rhône Valley may well have had influential visitors from areas of Gaul to the north and west.[234] Language, education, travel and aspects of state religion helped to spread ideas of Roman culture and government across the empire.

Elite culture as imperial discourse

Greg Woolf has argued for a coherent and ideological civilizing ethos that was developed under Augustus and was based upon the idea of *humanitas*.[235] The idea of civilization enabled the lessons that Rome had learned from its earlier expansion across Italy and the Mediterranean to be implemented in new areas. Through the active encouragement of barbarians to become Roman, the imperial elite helped to reinforce their own conception of *humanitas* by recruiting other elite groups into a comparable understanding of the world. By adopting Roman culture, native elite groups helped to validate the beliefs that lay behind the creation of imperial power relations.

This discourse of empire was not a coherent system of thought that was established at one point in time. Rather, it was a series of ideas that developed and changed over time, drawing upon earlier roots. Paul Zanker has commented that Augustan culture can be defined as a 'thick web' of images and ideas but not as a planned system.[236] The developing Augustan discourse of empire provided an important element in the formation of Augustan culture.[237] Like Augustan culture itself, imperial discourse was a generalized ideology.[238] In a manner that is comparable to the coherence behind the strategy for conquest, the imperial discourse inherent in Roman expansion was not fully conscious, but arose from deep values that formed the mindset of a Roman elite and which spread beyond the confines of the city of Rome.[239] It was the creation of a variety of influential individuals in the imperial core rather than a centrally imposed system.[240] In addition to being experimental it was also contested,[241] both through writing and military opposition. It was, however, a frame of reference within which powerful Romans lived their lives. It helped to produce a conceptual structure within which the domination of native societies was made possible. The ideology behind imperialism can be considered to have tightened the bonds of empire, so, at the same time that it provided justification for acts of imperialism, it also assisted in the imagining, creation and reinvention of the imperial system. The idea of a civilizing mission had an ideological purpose as part of imperial discourse but, at the same time, it helped to bind the Roman elite and powerful members of the provincial population into an arrangement based upon certain basic beliefs about life that lay at the core of Roman identity.

Through an appeal to the self-interest of the native elite of the provinces, Roman culture was used to create the political and administrative systems that held the empire together for so long.[242] The small-scale nature of the administration and the absence of a system of public education meant that Rome lacked the means to impose a new culture;[243] as a result, provincial elites were encouraged to adopt Roman identity.[244] Roman policy often created political ties with elite groups in neighbouring communities, eventually absorbing them as a result of political expansion. If they resisted, it was necessary to defeat them through military conquest.[245] Cooperation was encouraged by the fact that there was a common self-interest. The incorporation of local elites into the empire gave them a clearer and more stable claim to power, one that was backed up by symbolic new ways of living and by the threat of the use of the imperial armed forces. Imperial culture provided a new language and useful sets of concepts to enable aristocrats to rule over their less 'civilized' subordinates, while also providing an inherent justification for these power relations.[246] Local aristocrats could adopt Roman ways of living that naturalized and, therefore, extended their inherited positions of power.

Roman culture did not directly replace other more localized forms of elite identity. Part of its strength lay in its malleability, which allowed it to be used to incorporate and manipulate other cultures and identities in order to define flexible joint identities that communicated on both the local and the global level.[247] Roman culture was a 'common culture' shared by a widely spread group of governing elites, but one that was always, and everywhere, vulnerable to alternative readings.[248] The dominant control of resources that underlay and maintained this system could not escape from what John Barrett has called 'deviant local readings', but this does not invalidate the exploration of the significance of the discourse that was defined to establish and maintain the coherence of imperial relations.[249] Evidently, in creating its local version of Roman identity that was relevant to its own concerns, each regional elite culture represented a deviant discourse, at least to a degree. The requirement for this local version of the culture to be recognizable (and acceptable) to elite groups based elsewhere within the locality, province and empire will have regulated the degree to which such local cultures diverged from broader concepts of what it was to be Roman.[250] Local discourses require our attention,[251] since they direct research and understanding away from dogmatic interpretations of the past as a linear and simple narrative of variable Roman identity. They also enable scholars to think beyond the research strategies that such approaches both create and perpetuate.

4

THE MATERIAL ELEMENTS OF ELITE CULTURE

> In a society that had no regular newspapers, radio, or television, the official means of communication were mostly visual: coins, statues, paintings, relief sculpture.
>
> (Bonfante 2001, 5)

In this chapter, I shall extend the perspective that derives from writings about Roman identity, and the world-view that they encapsulate, to suggest that imperialism operated through material means as well as through the writing of texts. This is explored by considering the ways in which Roman identity was projected across the empire through the adoption and adaptation of material culture. We should not apply former imperialist ideas of a hierarchy of culture, which defines European society as superior to all others. It often appears to be the case, however, that during colonial contacts, colonizing cultures have developed technologies of power and authority that are both useful and easily transferable to those with authority in the indigenous society.[1] It has been argued that the Roman elite developed methods for self-definition that helped them to establish and maintain their boundaries as a self-referential group and that they achieved this by drawing upon certain universal standards inherent in their developing culture. The nature of Roman elite identity also enabled the incorporation of the influential and well connected people within native societies. This chapter focuses upon the way that the establishment of universal standards, embodied in material culture, may have helped to create relatively uniform types of elite behaviour across the empire, standards that projected the unity and stability of the imperial system, while, at the same time, allowing for the display of local identity.

Material culture features prominently in the discussion of globalizing Roman culture. Much of the available evidence for social change concerns material goods.[2] The education of the elite has been addressed but, in Roman society, official means of communication were mainly visual.[3] Dress, appearance, monuments, buildings, architecture and space all emphasized messages of imperial unity and order. Written texts in monumental form formed part of the physical environment of Roman society, although they could only be fully interpreted by those who were both literate and educated in ways that allowed them to interpret both text and imagery.[4] Other material items – including buildings, types of dress and even the items defined by Woolf as 'bric-à-brac' – conveyed messages to the informed.[5] The meaning of these elements of culture will have varied from context to context.

A division is usually drawn between 'culture' and 'material culture'. Anthropologists and archaeologists have shown that material culture is a medium through which people create and negotiate social roles, as culture operates through material dimensions.[6] Since the 1980s, a distinct body of scholarship has developed in the social sciences (anthropology, sociology and archaeology) to interpret the relationships between culture and material culture in new ways.[7] 'Material' refers to the physical elements of society; these are usually the objects and structures that are studied through archaeological research. Human cultures create and obtain objects for many reasons. Some items are produced at a domestic level by the family group and used in their everyday lives, while others are obtained through exchange or trade with people living at some distance. Items that are exchanged or traded are sometimes called 'goods' because in many societies they were produced in one place and traded to another in which they were consumed. In this regard material culture includes portable items or possessions (such as pots, coins and personal ornaments), but also the constructed material constituents of houses, settlements and the landscapes in which people lived. Houses, buildings and settlements often incorporate materials acquired from others.

Cultures and material goods exist in relationships of complex interdependences.[8] Material items carry social meaning as a non-verbal medium that people used to communicate.[9] Material culture is not separate from other elements of the social world and we should not treat people–artefact interactions as secondary to the process of culture.[10] It is equally the case that we should not follow the path established in some previous approaches in privileging the material dimension merely because this forms the subject matter of archaeology. The traditional focus on material culture within archaeology effectively 'fetishises' material relations.[11] A more informed perspective is to consider that material culture is deeply bound up with the lives of the people who created and used it. An entirely materially based study is not a realistic perspective upon the past. This is especially true for societies, such as those of the Roman empire, for which we possess written sources which can help us to interpret how material culture was created and used.

It is necessary to form a link between definitions of culture and their material elements. Mary Douglas and Baron Isherwood have explored why people want 'goods' and have suggested that they are needed for 'making visible and stable the categories of culture'.[12] Consumption of goods firmly establishes rules and standards in 'the fluid process' of classifying people and events.[13] Goods may therefore be acquired and adopted to assist in the articulation of ideas about identity. Material culture may indicate something about the person who adopts and acquires it, his/her family, locality and place in the world.[14] Material goods therefore constitute physical elements that both structure perception and facilitate interaction.[15] Such things as clothes, pots and buildings are not merely inert materials that were created to project social ties; they are actively created constituents used to help to determine, negotiate and contest roles and relations. They have a material role in creating society.[16] Buildings, the space within and between buildings, and the goods that go into their construction also serve to substantiate life through experience and education.

Once created, material culture has a historical dimension; it takes on new meanings through human action, but it also constrains these meanings.[17] People learn about the physical environment into which they are born, experiencing the material world around them and discovering the conceptual character of their societies. Material culture can have a constraining relationship in this process that influences the succeeding generations. The uses to which pottery is put in preparing and consuming food, or the use of space in a house or monumental public building, for example, are learned through experience. People may seek to negotiate new ways of living within their inherited cultural environment, but they usually play these new actions by rules that are at least in part inherited from the materiality of the past. This may be one of the reasons that culture is often thought to 'substantiate' a particular society as this reflects the historical dimension of culture, a way of creating order and form with a temporal dimension.[18]

Projecting Roman elite identity

Images created in various media provided particularly powerful means of communication that often appear to have formed areas of particular concern to the Roman authorities.[19] According to Clifford Ando, artefacts are the surviving props of 'ceremonial dramas through which the Romans – broadly construed – endlessly reenacted their roles in the cultural script'.[20] Material culture was effectively and intimately tied into ways of life within the empire. Messages were embedded in the physical setting of the urban context and people learned about politics, religion and culture from the messages conveyed by material objects.[21] In every urban centre, displays of art, architecture and writing presented messages to those moving through the urban fabric. Movement through the urban centre also conveyed messages; for example, both daily patterns of movement and ritual parades linked together parts of the urban fabric, imbuing them with collective meanings.[22] A number of studies have explored the ways that certain forms of expression (including art, statues, architecture, buildings, inscriptions, coins and appearance) operated effectively as part of Roman imperial discourse.[23] In broad terms, it is useful to conceive that various aspects of material culture were used to create and project a sense of imperial power and beneficence – along with ideas of stability, order and permanence – that were adopted in a conscious manner by the 'upper strata' across the empire.

By drawing upon imperial inspiration, architecture and goods could be used to assist native elites to project their power and ambition both in the local political sphere and within the context of imperial power-relations. An effective unity of purpose helped to link the concerns of local provincial elites with the ambitions of the imperial administration. Rome essentially created a manner through which structuring categories, or universal standards,[24] could be established within the empire. A series of institutions and areas of cultural interaction with material dimensions were communicated within the imperial system, enabling the creation of a strong ideology of uniformity that projected elite values. This imperial unity was defined and recreated in the form of a malleable Roman cultural package, drawing upon art, architecture, language, urban space and dress or personal appearance.

It is sometimes possible to identify Roman citizens in the archaeological record through the distinctive names that they held (the *tria nomina*).[25] Such information is preserved in written texts and on inscriptions. The commemoration of Roman identity in monumental form perhaps expresses the increased anxieties about status created as a result of the expansion of the empire.[26] With the exception of burials, it is relatively rare, however, to find direct evidence to link any individual Roman citizen to a specific archaeological site or building. In order to circumvent this problem, ancient historians and archaeologists have often attempted to define a way of life that characterizes the 'typical' Roman, or citizen. For over a century, archaeologists have used the material dimensions of culture to identify 'Romans'. Consequently, within the traditions of archaeological research, the term 'Roman' is commonly used. If it were possible to identify reliable material correlates for a Roman citizen, this would enable the extent of citizenship to be mapped and comprehended.

It has often been suggested that classical literature effectively promises such an understanding. For instance, in Virgil's *Aeneid* (12: 827–30), Juno refers to aspects of culture that related to Latin identity. She does not address government or religion in any great detail, but focuses upon ordinary aspects of daily life:[27] 'native dress', what the Latin people call themselves, and their 'voice' (their language). This suggests that, to Virgil, many of the ways in which Romans identified themselves to others were fairly intimate and personal. In the *Agricola*, Tacitus mentions that the Roman style of dress – the toga – was adopted in Britain in the late first century AD, along with arcades, baths, banquets and Latin. Much of this cultural expression relates to the everyday life of the elite, since such aspects will only have been available to the powerful. These two sources suggest that in the minds of some upper-class classical authors, Roman identity was connected with such elements.[28]

Recent works have assessed aspects of life in the empire such as appearance (dress, grooming and cleaning/bathing),[29] eating and drinking (acquiring, storing, preparation and consumption) and 'public activities' (visiting the bathhouse, market, meetings, religious ceremonies, etc.).[30] These studies aim to draw a wide range of material culture into the discussion, of which a few significant areas will be discussed.

Dress and appearance

One of the ways that citizenship was represented in public life was through the dress code of the toga,[31] although status was also indicated by gestures and other attributes of appearance.[32] The toga, which originated as the national garment of early Rome was, by the time of Augustus, reserved for adult males.[33] It survived as a significant type of dress down to the fourth century AD, although it changed in various subtle ways during this period.[34] Different types of toga were worn by different sections of male elite society, in order to provide a clear-cut definition of age and status.[35] The wearing of the garment may have been declining in popularity by Augustus' time, but it was always considered to be essential for Roman citizens engaged in public business.[36] Indeed, togas may in fact have been worn only rarely, apart from by those taking part in important public occasions and at ceremonies.[37]

An important aspect of the toga was the cost of its production. The elite status of the wearer was communicated by the fact that the garment was expensive.[38] Both the large amount of cloth used and the colour of garment would immediately have said something to the observer about the wearer. The various types of toga that were worn by different status groups would have provided a clear indication of the relative importance of Roman citizens on public occasions.[39] Some elements of dress – their use controlled by law – such as the colour of the shoes or the width of the stripes, would add further information.[40] These garments are often represented on burial monuments in the provinces, indicating that the toga was adopted as a significant element in power-politics at a local level. This standardization of a particular form of dress as an elite identifier occurred despite the fact that most ways of dressing across the empire were highly variable and context dependant.[41]

The toga was valued in Rome, Italy and the provinces, because it directly symbolized the status of those who were allowed to wear it. The public acts in which those wearing the garment took part occurred within urban contexts, and formed an element in the elite projection of status. The creation of power relations among the provincial elite was also manifested by monumental architecture and by urban planning in the cities of the empire. The city of Rome was an obvious focus, but imperial discourse also operated on the broader front of the empire as a whole. From the period of Augustus onward, it has been argued, cities formed one of the instruments of imperial ideology and culture.[42]

Creating urban space

Graeco-Roman society regarded urban life as an element of civilization of peoples. In classical literature a strong division was drawn between barbarians living in an unsettled world and the civilized peoples with their cities, peace and order.[43] It has long been argued that urban life spread through the empire as a result of the incorporation of new provinces,[44] and that cities came to form an important part in the unifying of the empire.[45]

It is usually contended that, where urban communities had developed under Mediterranean influence prior to the conquest, incorporation in the Roman empire resulted in additions and modifications to the existing urban fabric.[46] By contrast, in areas where there was no strong pre-existing tradition of Roman-style urbanization, new models for urban life were introduced and used to reformat pre-existing central places.[47] This reformatting was associated with certain monumental types of building, which, through their architecture and spatial planning, expressed new ways of ordering life. These monumental forms spread widely because of their value to the resident elites across the empire.

Many of the societies that became incorporated within the empire already had forms of nucleated and organized settlement that have sometimes been defined as 'urban'. Urban centres had developed across Italy and along much of the Mediterranean coast prior to the absorption of these societies within the empire. Pre-Roman centres developed further from the Mediterranean, across much of central and northern Gaul, Germany and Britain – the so-called *oppida* and other forms of nucleated sites.[48] Although these were often significant settlements, with functions of trade and exchange, they did not contain the basic elements required to maintain a Roman-style form of government or way of life, since they did not feature the urban form or monumental architecture that characterized Roman culture. As a result, models of urban life were developed in these areas and 'cities' were created, often with regular and systematic planning.[49]

It has been suggested that it is helpful to conceive that an 'ideal' or 'typical' Roman city formed the template for the creation of these new urban forms.[50] This idea of the typical city stems from the observation that distinctive forms of urban organization and types of building spread throughout the empire as part of the expansion of imperial control. This new form of organization of space and life acted, in a highly symbolic manner, to project the character of the relationship of the individual urban community to the city of Rome. In Paul Zanker's account, the typical Roman city is seen most clearly in the form of the colonies founded by Rome on new sites during the period of early imperial expansion in the later first millennium BC.[51] These suggestions have, however, a broader relevance to the developing provincial urban centres of the late first century BC and early first millennium AD.[52]

Zanker argues that these colonies reflect how a member of the elite in the city of Rome would envisage an idealized city.[53] The significant elements of urban form were that:

- the city was built upon a major Roman road that tied it into the larger entity of the empire;
- this main road lead to (or past) the Capitolium (a structure that defined the community as belonging to Rome); and
- the gathering place of the community lay in front of the Capitolium.[54]

For the early period, this often-repeated urban form is felt to have represented a deliberate message, relating to the incorporation of territory within the empire and to the control of traffic and the local population.[55] It is a settlement type defined by a certain 'civic form', projecting a sequence of ritual actions.[56] The form and order of the city itself had direct ritual and symbolic associations, as it was often considered to represent a living and growing entity.[57]

The expanding empire was marked out and defined by the construction of roads. Indeed, it is possible to identify the expansion of Roman control during the final few centuries BC – first across Italy and then the Mediterranean and into northern and western Europe – through the extension of the road system.[58] The roads were built to dominate and divide native territories into parcels and to facilitate communication and the domination of the land.[59] Straight metalled roads across the territories that were incorporated into the Western empire were an innovation, a focal element in military control, communication and administration. As such, the roads that connected the cities to Italy and Rome carried with them a clear Roman identification. Roads assisted in the creation of imperial space, and the colonies of Rome were established as part of this developing and expanding control.[60] Colonies were nodes on the road system that helped in the process of the settlement and claiming of new territory. The road that ran through the colony expressed the fact that the local community formed part of the broader Roman world,[61] connecting it to the lands of Rome and to the city itself in an umbilical fashion.[62]

Zanker has argued that, as the empire expanded, this type of urban planning, together with a number of distinctive types of public building, were used in the construction of a variety of new cities in the provinces.[63] The idea of the city was refashioned under Augustus to develop its universal appeal across the empire.[64] A distinctive urban form, that reflected the religious and political ideology of the expanding empire, was variously developed in subsequent official foundations. The cities of the empire have been described as the 'instrument' of imperialism,[65] providing symbols of Roman identity for local use.[66] The city of Rome itself represented an evolving architectural stage on which the authority of the emperor could be communicated. Augustus reinvented the Republican city of Rome as the imperial capital, placing his image as emperor centre-stage.[67] Claude Nicolet has examined Roman imperial concepts of geography and the ways in which these operated to create and maintain imperial power.[68] In Rome, Augustus had constructed a developing range of monuments in the northern part of the city. By AD 13, these included an inscribed literary text (the *Res Gestae*) that was placed close to Augustus' mausoleum and gave an account in monumental form of his role in the domination of the people of the empire.[69] A few hundred metres away, close to the Roman forum, was Agrippa's monumental map, showing the extent of the empire and its peoples. These three monuments emphasized the ancestry of the Roman people and their domination of others in the known world. They helped to define and project an Augustan geographically conceived imperial discourse in monumental form,[70] a complex of imperial architecture that was updated and modified by later emperors.[71]

Much has been written about this continuous re-creation of the imperial capital, but I shall explore how provincial elites were influenced by these developments. The evolving ritual of Roman authority is also relevant to the ways that many urban centres throughout the West were constructed, operated and evolved.[72] Imperial relations in the provinces were created through Rome's encouragement of the building of urban centres. The spatial organization and architecture on these sites both created and monumentalized the structures of local government that were encouraged by Rome, including the local council and public cults.[73] In his discussion of urbanism, Zanker has suggested that

> The impact of the new imagery in the West thus presupposes the acceptance of a complete ideological package. Temples, theatres, water systems, and city gates, all of specifically Roman type, gave every city in the West a relatively uniform look, one which remained essentially unchanged.[74]

The spatial organization of the urban centre and its routes of communication were constructed in ways that linked it to an ideology of control. In addition to the three elements defined by Zanker (above), many individual urban centres of the late Republic and early empire had a regular plan consisting of a series of plots defined by streets.[75] This form of 'orthogonal' planning was derived initially from Greek and Etruscan society and came to be applied widely across the Western empire.[76]

The relationship between the local community and the city of Rome and its emperor was a fundamental aspect in the creation and perpetuation of imperial relations. Architecture and planning in the urban centres therefore became part of a strategy of unification,[77] providing provincials with urban amenities that were used ritually to project the superiority of Rome.[78] At the same time, this relationship projected the authority of the local elite within their own communities, by emphasizing their relationships with the emperor and the city of Rome. The significance of the local ruling classes was re-affirmed by their involvement in rituals of urban life; as the most influential people of the community they fulfilled the most significant roles in symbolizing imperial authority at a local level.

Zanker, therefore, defines the 'external characteristics that mark the "typical" Roman city'.[79] These elements effectively define how urban centres operated as architectural stages, since people performed in various ways within the infrastructure. The buildings and spatial structure were not mere images, but the medium through which life was organized and acted out in order to create forms of local authority that drew upon the powerful image of Roman control.[80] The public buildings were a monumental element in the lives of those that lived in the urban centres and also of the people who visited them.[81] They were important for the identity of the community, having a particular significance in religious life, since all public buildings were associated with religion.[82] Such public buildings were constructed according to the canons of Augustan architecture,[83] which drew upon architectural sources from Italy and across the Mediterranean.[84]

William L. MacDonald has explored the idea of 'empire imagery' in relation to the definition of Augustan architecture.[85] He has suggested that this architecture, both in Rome itself and beyond, followed a distinctly new form that was easily recognized.[86] Imperial imagery was created by the dual mechanism of a clear, strong, stable geometry and an overlay of traditional classicism that 'civilized' this geometry. These mechanisms made Augustan architecture easy to comprehend and interpret in any urban centre or province.[87] In order to project the coherence and accessibility of this new architectural imagery, distinctive buildings swiftly spread from Italy and Rome across the Western empire, as urban centres were created (or recast) in Roman form. Many of the public building programmes and sculptural commissions that were begun in Gaul and Iberia during Augustus' time were part of a larger policy that stressed the newly established unity of the West. Similar standards were utilized in provincial contexts in the Augustan period and later.[88]

Across the empire, the architecture and social use of public buildings and spaces served both to create and to perpetuate imperial control. The Augustan imperial system created an impression of a stable and monumental empire, not only through its architecture, but also through portrayals of the emperor, inscriptions, artefacts and other representations, displayed primarily in urban contexts.[89] Under Augustus, the formal worship of the emperor was instituted across the empire.[90] Part of his motivation may have been to legitimize Roman rule and to ensure that the figure of the emperor was ever-present in political life. Emperor worship was often based upon the creation of a religious observance focused upon a temple (or temples) in the provinces of the Western empire.[91] The physical influence of the emperor was not, however, restricted to the centre of emperor worship in each province. Market transactions, and the payment of taxes to the state, were made using coins that held representations of the emperor.[92] The fora, theatres and amphitheatres of many Roman urban centres were platforms for the display of power, united by the visible presentation of images of emperors.[93] These representations were produced in relatively large quantities and were fairly standardized.[94] Inscriptions, aimed at the literate population, were placed in public places,[95] on buildings, altars and milestones.[96] These often featured the name of the ruling emperor and sometimes clearly stated the relationship of the community to the wider world.[97] Under Augustus, the production of such inscriptions reached a peak,[98] and they formed part of an empire-wide vehicle of imperial ideology.[99] The fact that they are distributed unevenly may suggest that the developing tradition did not come to influence all areas evenly.[100]

The monuments, buildings, statues, inscriptions and coins which drew upon this 'empire imagery' provided influential provincials who could read the messages with a sense of being involved in a wider and integrated imperial world. The cities of the empire reflected the imperial objectives of regularity, efficiency and formal simplicity; they were 'individualised capsules of imperial purpose and identity'.[101] Architecture, space and social life helped both to create and to symbolize the internal organization of the local community and its relationship to the broader system of the empire.[102] The forum and basilica were the buildings in which local government was conducted and taxes were collected.[103] The form of these buildings divided up space to create and exhibit social hierarchies. Amphitheatres and theatres were often complex stone structures that enabled people to access different areas of seating through multiple points of access.[104] Evidence from Rome and Italy suggests that audiences in these structures were controlled by rules and regulations, while a similar situation may have occurred elsewhere.[105] Bathhouses were connected to ideas of cleanliness and civilization, and bathing was an important way of projecting social relations.[106] The baths may well have incorporated similar methods of controlled access according to different social grades, although the evidence for this is less clear-cut.[107] The bathhouse and any fountains were served by water that was brought into the urban centre by an aqueduct – a prominent symbol of the control of natural resources.[108]

This model for the Roman city is built upon a rather simple and largely traditional account,[109] but it helps us to understand the extent of Roman imperial control.[110] The emphasis upon the city as part of Roman imperial discourse focuses upon the larger and more visible architectural elements of the urban fabric and plays down aspects that relate less directly to the concerns of the elite, including domestic occupation, industry and trade.[111] We might view this approach as the expression of a powerful ideology that only informs us about urban development in a limited manner, but it does relate to the ways in which most people were forced to live their lives according to the rules of others. In Augustan and later contexts, Zanker's model accounts for how the city arose as an accommodation between the political concerns of the empire and the local interests of indigenous elites.[112] The latter took the major role in the creation of urban centres of the provinces, modifying urban form according to local interests and tastes.

Indeed, the assimilation of the idea of the urban centre in each provincial context depended upon the role of the imperial administration in the creation of the community, together with the background and interests of the people who planned and built the urban structure. The form of the city was not centrally enforced by the Roman administration. In many cases, it is likely to have been willingly adopted by local elites, as it provided a wealth of new ways by which to extend and communicate status and identity within the local, provincial and imperial context. The extent to which there was any coherent programme of urbanization across the Western empire is debatable,[113] since the development of these urban centres usually resulted from the relationship that was established between native rulers and Rome at the time of the incorporation of their territory into the empire.[114] During the time of Augustus, however, the orthogonal type of street plan and a distinct range of public buildings had become significant in marking out certain provincial urban centres in the west of the empire as new establishments connected with ordered Roman civil life.[115]

Increasingly, members of the native elite drew upon Roman concepts of architecture and spatial planning in the layout of their own urban centres. In this way they created their own local statements of power and authority. These places were developed to provide local self-government for communities both of citizens and non-citizens across the Western provinces.[116] The self-governing communities of non-citizens often developed from pre-Roman urban centres.[117] In some areas, a more direct urbanizing policy may be indicated, as suggested by Dio's comments on Germany prior to the defeat of Varus (page 66).[118] In general terms, it is inaccurate to suppose that Roman contact and conquest always brought urbanism to the provinces. It did, however, lead in many areas to types of urban form and monumentality that expressed power and authority in new ways.[119] In particular, the worship of the emperor helped to define the relationship of the provincial urban community to Rome.[120]

To explore the ways that this urban form was variously adopted, we shall examine the archaeological evidence for two particular sites, one in Iberia and the other in Britain. The Iberian site, Tarraco, was an important provincial capital with a significant centre for emperor worship. Verulamium in Britain was a *civitas* centre, or possibly a *municipium*. At both sites, the sequence of development illustrates the interplay between the inherited position of a native elite group that dominated the settlement and the new circumstances that resulted from the incorporation of the community within the empire.

Tarraco (Tarragona, Spain) was a significant pre-Roman settlement and became an important urban centre after it was incorporated into the empire during the Republican period.[121] In due course, it became the capital of the province of Tarraconensis, one of the three provinces established in Iberia

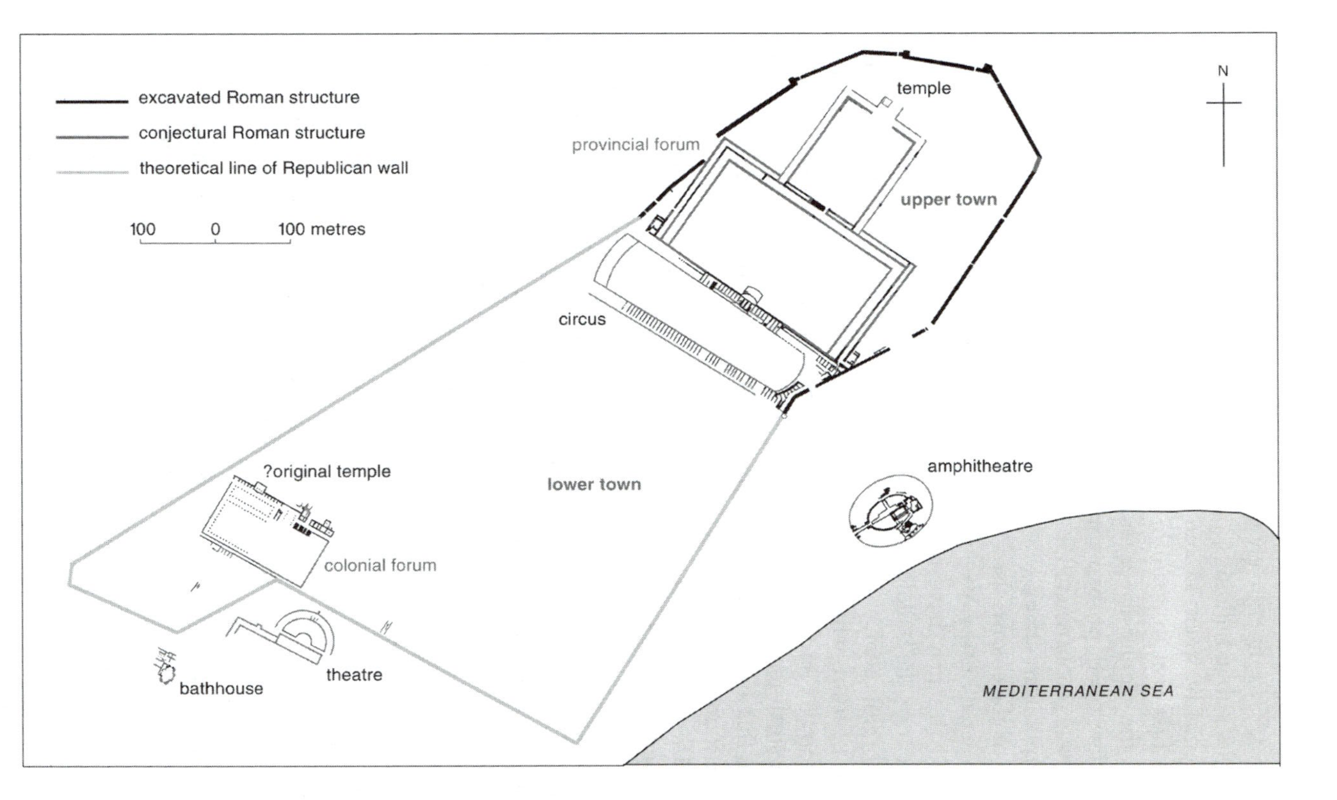

Figure 5 Taracco (Tarragona, Spain). Adapted from Ruiz de Arbulo Bayona 1998, Figures 1, 2 and 3; Remola and Ruiz de Arbulo 2002, Figure 2 and Keay 2003, Figures 6 and 7. Drawing by Christina Unwin.

by Augustus.[122] Comparatively little is known about the layout of the urban centre, or its public buildings, prior to Augustus.[123] It probably acquired its colonial status between 45 and 2 BC and was the residence of Augustus during his first visit to Spain in 26–25 BC, when it effectively acted as the capital of the empire for a short time. A centre for the worship of the emperor developed, probably in the lower town, where a large rectangular enclosure was reconstructed in the heart of what had been the Iberian and Roman Republican centre (Figure 5).[124] This complex, which was probably the forum of the colony, also included a basilica and temple,[125] while a theatre was constructed nearby. We know that an altar was dedicated to Augustus in 26 BC and this may have been placed within this forum/basilica.[126] The development of the buildings connected with the cult has been obscured by modern development,[127] but it is possible that the altar was placed in the centre of a forum, which either may have already been built or was under construction.[128] The altar may have had an axial relationship with a structure, possibly a small temple to Augustus, which formed part of the rear of the basilica. In this area, fragments of inscriptions and imperial statues and portraits were found.[129]

In AD 15, after the death of Augustus, the new emperor Tiberius agreed to an official request made by a delegation of people from Tarraco for a new temple to the Divine Augustus to be built within the urban centre. Contemporary coins issued by the colony at this time show images of this building[130] although it may in fact not have been built when the coins were issued.[131] It has been suggested that this temple may have been constructed along the south side of the forum.[132] The character of the imperial cult at Tarraco probably drew upon the formal cult to Augustus in Rome, established by Tiberius.[133] It is recorded by Tacitus (*Annals* 1.54), later in the first century, that the temple at Tarraco (and presumably also the cult practices celebrated there) served as a model for the establishment of emperor worship in other provinces of the Western empire.[134]

The layout of the urban centre is only known in part, but evidence suggests that the location of the forum influenced the positioning and orientation of the street system and the location of the theatre of the replanned Augustan urban centre. The theatre, which probably also had a role in the evolving imperial cult,[135] was embellished with images of Julio-Claudian emperors.[136] In the Flavian period, the upper town was developed into a highly impressive and monumental architectural complex that served as a provincial forum and for the imperial cult.[137] This complex lay on three terraces and appears to have comprised a temple, a monumental meeting place and a circus. The buildings performed roles in a developing imperial cult focused upon the urban centre. By the end of the first century AD, it would appear that 20–30 per cent of the entire settlement was dedicated to public buildings linked to the symbolism of Roman identity and the imperial cult.[138] A substantial amphitheatre, which also had a role in the imperial cult, was built during the second century.[139] This urban complex reflects the contemporary development of the cult of Augustus in the city of Rome and other provincial capitals in Iberia and across the Western empire.[140] Archaeological work at Tarraco has focused almost entirely upon monumental buildings and, by contrast, very little is known of the residential and commercial life of the urban centre.[141]

Simon Keay has proposed that we should view the layout of Augustan and later Tarraco in the form of a 'cognitive map'.[142] The architecture of the buildings, the layout of the urban centre and the placement of inscriptions and imperial statues provided a symbolic expression of the relationship of the community to Rome. At the same time, the day-to-day activities in the architectural spaces created rituals that embedded and communicated knowledge both to the community as a whole and between generations.[143] The development of urban space at Tarraco and in other urban centres communicated imperial power-relations, but the creation and manipulation of this imperial imagery was not imposed upon the community by Rome. Instead, the development was initiated by the influential people of the urban centre itself, with the support and encouragement of the emperors. Augustus' presence in Tarraco presumably established a personal relationship between the emperor and the dominant families that then resulted in the particular development of the imperial cult.[144] Imperial models were drawn upon in order to manipulate and perpetuate the pre-existing social order in a new situation in which established hierarchies were under some threat. The epigraphic evidence indicates the diversity of the priesthood at Tarraco,[145] suggesting that there were new pressures upon the old established families resulting from the arrival of influential incomers. Both the indigenous elite and incomers probably sought to establish new positions of authority through the special roles that they took on both within the cult and in the general running of local government.[146] The manner in which the Augustan and later urban centre developed from the pre-Roman and Republican settlement is important, but comparatively little is known about pre-Augustan Tarraco,[147] which makes this relationship difficult to explore.

Verulamium (St Albans, Hertfordshire) in Britain was a less monumental Roman urban centre. Here we have greater evidence for the development of the settlement from pre-Roman origins. Like Tarraco, Verulamium was a significant settlement prior to its incorporation within the empire. After the conquest, it probably functioned as a *civitas* capital but may have been made a *municipium* some time during the later first century AD.[148] It developed the standard elements of the Roman urban centre: a fairly rectangular street system, a central forum/basilica and a theatre. The urban form effectively developed from the pre-Roman *oppidum* (Figure 6), which may itself have been based upon Roman concepts of spatial planning.[149] The forum/basilica complex was built upon the site of a late Iron Age enclosure ('central enclosure') that may have been some form of sacred space and communal meeting

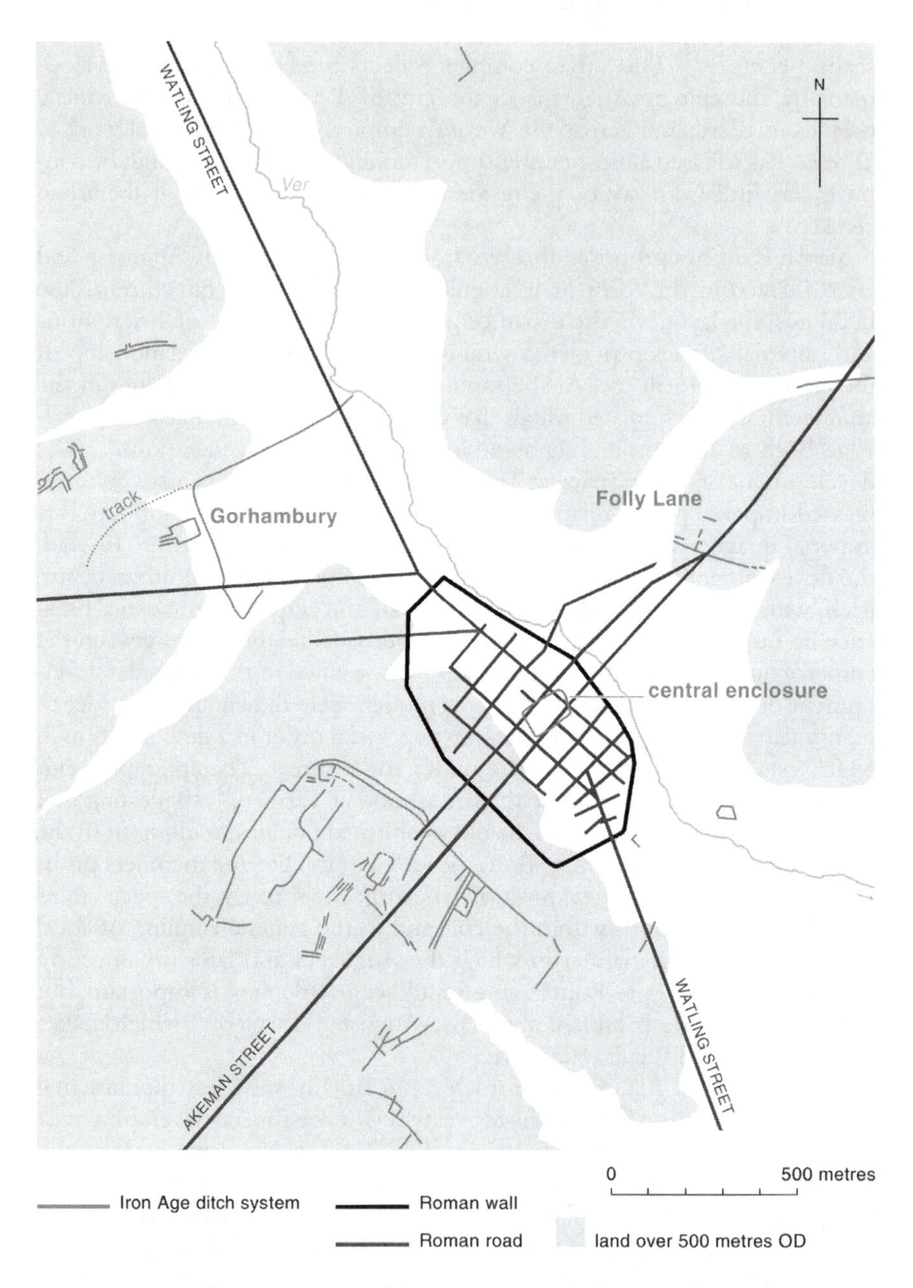

Figure 6 Verulamium (St Albans, England) in the late Iron Age/early Roman period. Adapted from Niblett 2001, Figure 19. Drawing by Christina Unwin.

place.[150] On the facing slope of the valley, a ditched enclosure at Folly Lane received an important burial very early in the Roman period.[151] In time, the Folly Lane enclosure was linked to the forum by a road, and it has been suggested that it was intended to be viewed from the centre of the emerging urban centre.[152] In the later first century a small temple was built within the Folly Lane enclosure, presumably to venerate a local person of importance,[153] possibly a tribal ancestor. Later on, possibly around AD 150, a theatre was built and the structure positioned to face across to the Folly Lane enclosure, while a road appears to have joined the two sites.[154]

At Verulamium, the elements of the Roman urban centre were fitted into the pre-existing landscape and the organization of significant features of the developing urban centre was probably designed to fit rituals connected with the cult that focused upon the tribal ancestor who was buried at Folly Lane.[155] The position of the public buildings and the creation of the road system reflected the mythical history of the foundation of the settlement and articulated these ideas to the whole community and to visitors in the new context of the incorporation of the community into the empire. It has even been proposed that the development of the ritual landscape around a tribal ancestor drew upon Julio-Claudian strategies for the creation of imperial dynasties.[156] The local ancestor may have been commemorated in a manner that drew upon concepts derived from the developing centres of emperor worship at Camulodunum (Colchester) and elsewhere.

This does not indicate a lack of interest in the cult of the emperor within the developing community at Verulamium. It is likely that the emperor was worshipped in the forum of the community but there is no clear evidence for a temple to the imperial cult, and our understanding of this area of the settlement is limited. Again, the elements of the standard Roman city were adopted by the resident elite in a way that enabled them to reinforce their pre-existing predominance within the community and the province. The possible high status of Verulamium may have reflected the relationship established between the community and the Roman administration, before, during, or immediately after the incorporation of its territory within the empire. The urban fabric at Verulamium, Tarraco and thousands of other urban centres across the empire, developed through an articulation of new concepts and practices and the manipulation of an inheritance from the past.[157] Old identities were not given up, they were recast in the context of new needs and pressures; Roman culture and native tradition were not in opposition but intricately intertwined.[158]

Creating domestic space

Individual families and households, both within and outside urban centres, occupied a wide variety of types of dwellings.[159] Societies across many areas of the Western empire developed more complex and elaborate forms of domestic architecture as new types of houses were built in both urban centres and the countryside.[160] In the countryside, 'villas' have been the focus of archaeological attention, the term deriving from Latin sources referring to the estate of the wealthy ruling elite.[161] 'Villa' has come to be applied to a wide variety of sites that differ in size, architecture, function and chronology. Nicola Terrenato has recently restricted its use to late Republican elite residences in Italy, and argued that the term is in need of a comprehensive redefinition.[162] From the end of the first millennium, high-status houses, partly deriving from the late Republican elite residences of Italy, developed both in the urban centres and in the countryside across the empire.[163]

These houses are typified by their extent, complexity and elaboration. It has often been supposed that these elaborate houses first emerged towards the end of the third or early second century BC, deriving inspiration from the Hellenistic world.[164] Terrenato has suggested, however, that villa architecture resulted from ongoing developments in Etruscan and Roman elite settlements that originated possibly as early as the fifth century BC.[165] In these houses, a number of small rooms were placed around a courtyard. Other features that became important elements of the elite housing traditions of the empire, such as stone colonnades and mosaics, borrowed in the first century BC from Greek styles of housing, were then grafted on to this architectural style.[166] Towards the end of this century, villas became more common across the Italian landscape, as a result of political and economic changes within the expanding empire.[167] They then spread across the empire and are often considered to have formed the key 'building block' of Roman social relations.[168] The individual house was the locus for the symbolism of social inequality. Its architecture and elaboration were obsessively concerned with the creation and display of distinctions of social rank, including the complex relationships between master and mistress, slaves and servants and patron and client.[169] Rural production also formed a key part in this symbolic practice, as elements of the landed estates were elaborated in a variety of ways.[170]

Some of these impressive urban and rural dwellings are likely to have been the homes of the old aristocratic families of Italy and the expanding empire, while others were constructed by people who had made a sufficient profit through agriculture, industry or trade to enable them to build an elaborate house.[171] The cultural language of elite domestic space spread to individuals who aspired to greater influence and power, as forms of architecture and decoration were adopted in variable ways.[172] Across much of the Western empire the villa was a dramatic innovation. If we view domestic architecture as providing a cultural language of domination – through the elaboration of spatial form, architectural details, decoration and furniture – the value of these new forms of building to the elite classes of the Western empire is apparent. The arrangement of space, mosaics, rooms decorated with wall plaster, hypocausts, bathing suites, etc. offered new ways of living to the wealthy.

These elaborate 'Roman' houses contrast directly with the buildings that characterized pre-Roman societies in these areas. Many pre-Roman buildings in areas of what is today western Europe were built out of locally derived materials: timber, earth and stone. On incorporation within the empire, building traditions for the wealthy and powerful changed, and increasingly both public buildings and the private residences of the elite were elaborate stone structures, built according to architectural rules derived from the common pattern defined by 'empire imagery'. Houses adopted a range of building styles that required the use of materials that had to be transported over some distance to the construction site. These materials included tiles for roofs and hypocausts, dressed stone and mortar for walls, lead for plumbing, mosaics, marble, pigment for painting wall plaster and exotic and valuable ornaments and furniture.[173]

These new multi-roomed houses would have allowed the household to be divided up in more complex ways that reflected changing ways of life. Servants, or more junior members of the family, could be allocated separate living quarters. The various elements of day-to-day life, such as eating, meeting and sleeping, could be separated in more distinct ways.[174] Innovations such as heated rooms, dining rooms, mosaic floors and decorated plaster were used to create social relations within the household. Wealthy domestic dwellings were used in the provinces to create ways of living that were associated with Roman imperial culture and, perhaps, with the new values that it represented.[175]

Standard developments?

Archaeological accounts of provincial society and the maps that are produced of individual provinces project the idea that monumental cities and villas developed in a standard way across much of the empire. In some areas of the Roman West, such an image appears to be useful but in cases in which sufficiently detailed work has been carried out, it has been found that the villas are substantially outnumbered by various other forms of settlement, while alternative urban settlements also occur. The 'becoming Roman' approach emphasizes the importance of the villas and cities of these apparently 'standard' areas,[176] but recent work suggests that many settlement landscapes developed according to different trajectories.

A far higher proportion of less monumental houses existed in both the countryside and the urban centres,[177] although these have rarely been explored in such detail.[178] It is often argued that it was not just the houses of the very rich in provincial societies that underwent a process of increasing subdivision. In Italy and the Mediterranean, many houses are thought to have been constructed by the upwardly mobile, showing elements derived from the housing of the elite. In Iberia, Britain and France, houses of the Roman period often incorporated a number of distinct rooms, often differing dramatically from the pre-Roman forms of domestic residence of these areas.[179] Innovations such as mosaics, hypocausts and wall plaster also spread fairly widely. Where houses have been studied in detail, the picture of domestic settlement is very complex.[180] Local variation in styles of building often serves to identify distinct cultures within differing parts of the Roman empire.[181] Local societies adopted new concepts of housing in their own particular ways, but conquest and incorporation appear to have offered new ways to project social relations at local levels. The extension of these ideas to serve in non-elite contexts has always formed a support for the concept of Romanization by osmosis, but I shall now turn to why this concept is oversimplistic.

5

FRAGMENTING IDENTITIES

> Rather than considering Greek culture as something simple, pure, and unproblematic – as the beginning, the source of Western civilization – we want to acknowledge, inventory, and debate the ways in which it was actively engaged in a complicated process of negotiation, conflict, and collaboration between cultures or subcultures.
>
> (Dougherty and Kurke 2003, 2)

Spreading Roman culture?

Having explored a definition of Roman culture that relates to the elites of the Western empire, we may see that this reading of 'culture' obscures a variety of complex evidence by focusing upon the identity of the 'upper strata'. Carol van Driel-Murray has suggested, for example, that recent approaches to identity in the Roman West create 'undefined, undifferentiated and apparently entirely male' elites.[1] Since the 1960s, new approaches that focus more fully on the native contribution to Roman society have emerged, sometimes focusing attention upon differing types of archaeological sites and materials. A more open research strategy is leading to some new understandings of local societies that focus less directly upon the elites (or at least, upon those who adopted the trappings of elite Roman identity). These studies of local variation, together with the evolving focus upon the centralizing idea of Roman culture, have resulted in the development of a significant disagreement. Roman specialists are divided over a particular issue – did the empire become generally Romanized, or was Roman identity merely an imperial façade that obscures far more complex provincial and local situations?[2]

It has become fashionable to suggest that 'Roman' elite identity was created within the context of the empire as a part of an imperial ideology that provides only a partial and distorted view of the complexity of societies and social relations. In other words, the idea of an integrated Roman identity is, in itself, a colonizing image that masks deeper and more complex realities.[3] Mary Downs has argued that the idea of Baetica as a highly Romanized province is a colonial image, produced by Rome and reproduced by modern scholars.[4] Another work has concluded that the idea of the Roman unification of Italy has been derived from the classical literature and imposed upon the available information from the nineteenth century onwards,[5] while a further author has analysed the 'ideology' of political unity which overrides considerations of localized ethnic identity within the preamble to Augustus' *Res Gestae*, concluding that this image has been 'practically unchallenged' until recently.[6]

These accounts emphasize that Roman identity was itself an invention of the classical authors who wrote about the empire, created for its effect as a colonizing discourse. It represents an image that has been picked up in modern times to create a particular focus of study. Roman society in general had little concern with the 'lower strata'. Modern scholars have replicated this attitude – ancient historians, through their readings of documents, and archaeologists, through their excavation and survey strategies. The Roman past has been actively created as a result of the collection, over many generations, of information that is defined as relevant through a Romano-centric discourse of the dominant. By concentrating on 'Roman' monuments, classical archaeologists have effectively used Roman culture within a Eurocentric discourse.[7] Gentlemen scholars, military officers, imperial officials and academics felt a natural association with the achievements of the Roman ruling classes, both military and civil, and this attitude has been projected into the contemporary world to affect both the archaeological approaches that we have inherited and the information that we have available. Until recently, the archaeology of the empire has been characterized by the close attention that has been paid to the settlements and monuments of the well connected, wealthy and powerful – the cities, towns, forts, frontier works, roads and villas.[8] There has been a relative scarcity of concern with the native origins of the cultures that emerged under Roman control. With the exception of villa archaeology (once again the preserve of the elite), the countryside in which the majority of the population lived has also been neglected, along with the homes of the less wealthy population in both urban and rural contexts.[9]

Social change has been regarded as a simple and directional process and, as a result, the elite and the powerful have formed the focus of attention. It has often been argued that aspects of Roman culture spread beyond the imperial and provincial elite, drawing other members of society into a coherent Roman identity. The elite of Italy and the empire was not a bounded whole and it was possible for some individuals to improve their social standing, which their children would inherit.[10] This means that the upper and the lower strata should not be viewed as clearly bounded.[11] It has been assumed that those who were less influential and wealthy were broadly emulative of the elite and were interested in new ideas and materials. At the same time, it is felt that these people were constrained in their ability to acquire Roman culture by their lack of capital and social contact. Consequently, they are seen as demonstrating their interest in Roman identity in a diluted form, which makes them less significant from the perspective of Romanization.[12] In a circular and self-reinforcing manner, the materials that have been collected have followed this elite-focused strategy, while they have, at the same time, been used to support the intellectual approach that lay behind the initial collection strategies that helped to create the material record.[13]

The changing emphasis since the 1960s has formed part of the reaction against the Romano-centric focus inherent in previous studies.[14] As a result, archaeological research now involves the study of the evolution of society from the pre-Roman period through to Roman times, together with the archaeological survey and excavation of a wider variety of sites (including native-type sites, non-villa settlements, 'small towns', 'local centres', 'secondary agglomerations', etc.). It has become clear that, across much of the Western empire, the vast majority of people lived in types of settlements that do not fall easily into the main categories (city, villa, fort) that have dominated archaeological research.[15]

This indicates that we need to look below the surface (in a literal sense, through more excavation and archaeological survey) in order to recognize and explore, in greater detail, the evidence for variations in the ways of life of people across the empire.[16] The material culture of societies provides hints of ways of life that are far too complex to be categorized through the use of Romanization theory, or even the recent approach to 'becoming Roman'.

The idea of Roman identity is useful as a concept of cultural unity that allows the exploration of power relations, but we need to accept that it is only a partial picture of the connections through which the empire was brought into being and maintained. It is an image that focuses upon the elite, while providing a very limited understanding of others.[17] Discourses of power can never operate entirely independently of the people who are dominated.[18] The Roman world did not operate according to simple and well established rules, and the ideas that we use to study it may sometimes collide and contradict. In other words, we need to think further than the useful but simplistic image of 'Roman' identity. The combination of a number of competing approaches enables us to keep a focus upon the power-relations that were used to create the empire, while considering its character as a variety of overlapping networks of power and identity. These relations will have created new stresses and opportunities within provincial society that cannot be comprehended adequately through simple emulation models.

Soldiers

The consideration of the common soldiers of the empire and their identity, which Simon James has defined as a non-elite Roman 'sub-culture', provides one useful approach to the breaking down of coherent elite and non-elite groups.[19] From the time of Augustus, soldiers, once recruited, were integrated into the society of the Roman army in a way that taught them about aspects of Roman culture, creating a particular level of imperial awareness.[20] Soldiers learnt a distinct way of life, with a particular timetable of military and religious duties that formed part of their day-to-day activities. This military culture also focused around the attachment of the individual soldier to the imperial regime.[21] The main source of unity, however, comprised a distinct military identity, discipline, routine and comradeship, rather than some overarching Roman ideology.[22] It resulted from training and enculturation within defined military ways of life that were created through distinctive, if variable, styles of military dress and the architecture of forts and fortresses.[23] Latin may have become something of a common language for many Roman soldiers, as is indicated by the documents that are found on military sites.[24] The institution of literacy in the army enabled it to operate in an effective manner across a broad geographical territory and also provided some coherence to military life.[25]

Significant numbers of soldiers were stationed in some frontier regions, far away from the main centres of Roman elite culture in the Mediterranean.[26] They would have represented a special group in these areas, both because of the power that their military identity afforded them and because they had coins to spend in local markets.[27] This may sometimes have elevated them, in Britain and Germany, into a local elite, but with a culture based upon their military backgrounds,[28] drawing, in various ways, upon Roman culture. This identity may have created a form of imperial solidarity across certain areas of the empire that extended beyond the imperial elite; indeed, military identity may be identified as another form of non-elite Roman culture, or 'subordinate' culture,[29] one shared, at least to an extent, by serving soldiers and retired veterans. Although drawing upon some common sources with elite identity, military culture was defined and manifested in very different ways.[30] When we consider members of society other than the elite and the soldiers, however, the picture is more complex.

'The empire writes back'[31]

The expansion and consolidation of the empire created new conditions that led to a variety of reactions in the provinces.[32] Latin language had a major role, not only in marking the identity of the elite but also in the administration of the empire. The exchange of written information helped to establish the relationship between the rulers and the ruled.[33] I shall examine two case studies that relate growing Latin literacy to the ways that people in particular places reacted to the administration. Latin, as a new form of communication, offered opportunities to certain groups. These two studies explore, respectively, the reaction of a rural community in Germania Inferior to the Roman army, and the response of a group of potters in southern Gaul to the new opportunities offered by the expansion in industry and trade.

Ton Derks and Nico Roymans have argued that Latin spread through the agency of the army in part of the Lower Rhine Valley. This appears to have been the homeland of a number of different tribal groupings, including one called the Batavians.[34] In this area, the development of native society is seen as aberrant or abnormal by comparison with the 'standard' development of cities and villas in many provinces.[35] It has been argued that these peoples witnessed a slower, or less thorough, Romanization than did the neighbouring areas of Gaul to the south,[36] as the result of the development of a different form of social organization that originated in the pre-Roman period.[37] The territory that has been identified for the Batavians has been defined as mainly a 'non-villa landscape',[38] one that contrasts in a dramatic fashion with areas in Gaul, where villas and successful towns became common.[39]

The dominant settlements of the Batavians consisted of one or more traditional long houses, comprising a living area and byre in the same domestic space (Figure 7).[40] The economy of this area also appears to differ from the villa zones in the emphasis on cattle-rearing rather than arable agriculture.[41] A small number of settlements developed elements of Roman architecture (such as a timber portico, stone cellar, painted wall plaster or a partly tiled roof) but these innovations did not affect the basic traditional organization of domestic space within the individual house.[42] The few villas that do occur in this area have been tentatively interpreted as the homes of veteran soldiers who had returned to the area after a period of military service.[43] It has been argued that the Roman-period urban centres of the Lower Rhine were established, as part of official Roman policy, in an area where pre-Roman societies were unaccustomed to urbanism.[44] These urban centres may have been dominated by settlers from further to the south and by the Roman army, while the local elite had, at the very most, only a limited input into their establishment, development and administration.[45] They appear to have been rather unimpressive in monumental terms and small in scale compared to some, for instance, in northern Gaul.[46]

This approach to the Lower Rhine Valley may draw too clear a division between the urban centres of the militarized zone, on the one hand, and those of non-military areas, on the other. We have seen, above, that many urban centres developed as a result of native initiatives that were encouraged by the Roman administration and it is likely that officials will have involved native elites, wherever possible, in the construction of the new urban centres. It has recently been argued that a pre-Roman tribal centre may have existed at Nijmegen, alongside which the Roman urban centre (Oppidum Batavorum) developed (Figure 8).[47] This may suggest that some frontier areas of northern Gaul and Germania followed, at least to a degree, what is viewed as the more 'normal' pattern of civil development.[48] It should be noted, however, that the Batavians probably had only a limited input into the new urban centre at Nijmegen, while most of its occupants were Gallo-Roman craftsmen, officials, soldiers/veterans and other immigrants.[49]

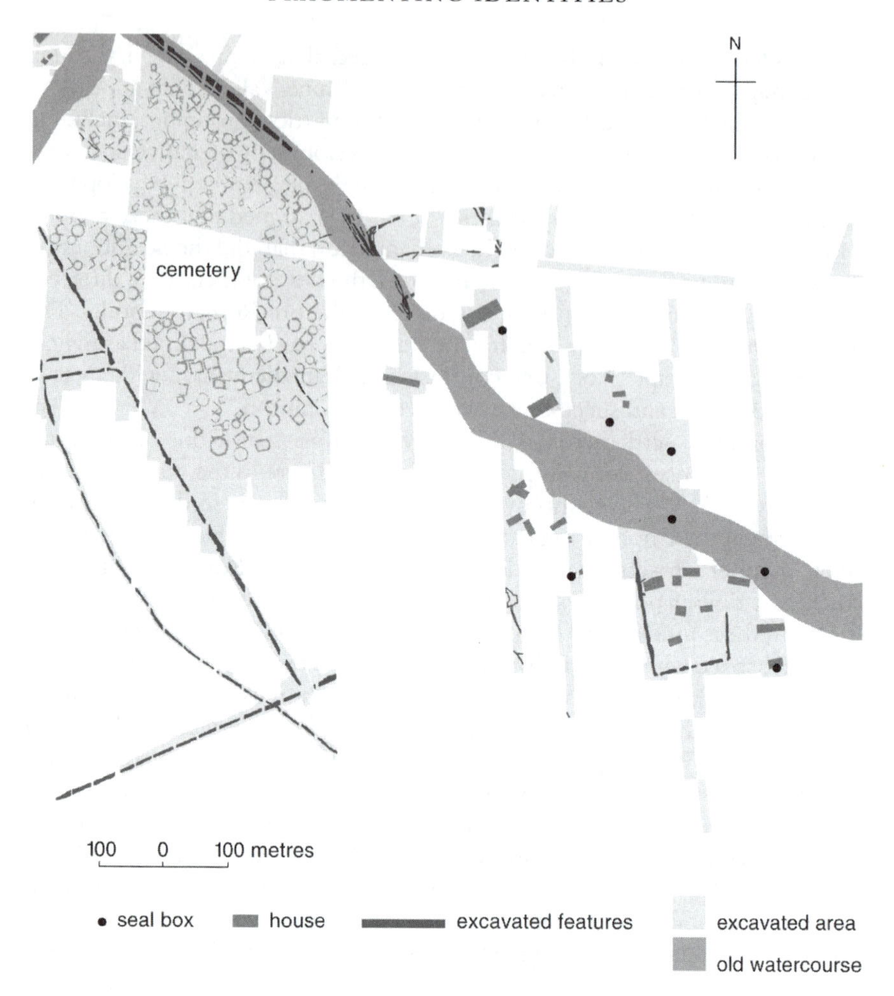

Figure 7 The Roman-period settlement at Tiel-Passewaaij (the Netherlands), showing the findspots of seal boxes. Adapted from Derks and Roymans 2002, Figure 7.10. The settlement is to the right of the drawing and individual houses are visible. Drawing by Christina Unwin.

Despite the lack of native urbanization and villas, it has been argued that considerable evidence exists for Latin literacy among the rural native population.[50] The discovery of many so-called 'seal boxes' may indicate that this occurred through the recruitment of Batavians into the Roman auxiliary. Batavians were renowned for their fighting skills and men from the community were taken in large numbers for the auxiliary units of the army,[51] perhaps by recruitment that utilized a pre-Roman native system, adapted as the result of treaties between the Roman administration and the native leaders.[52] When

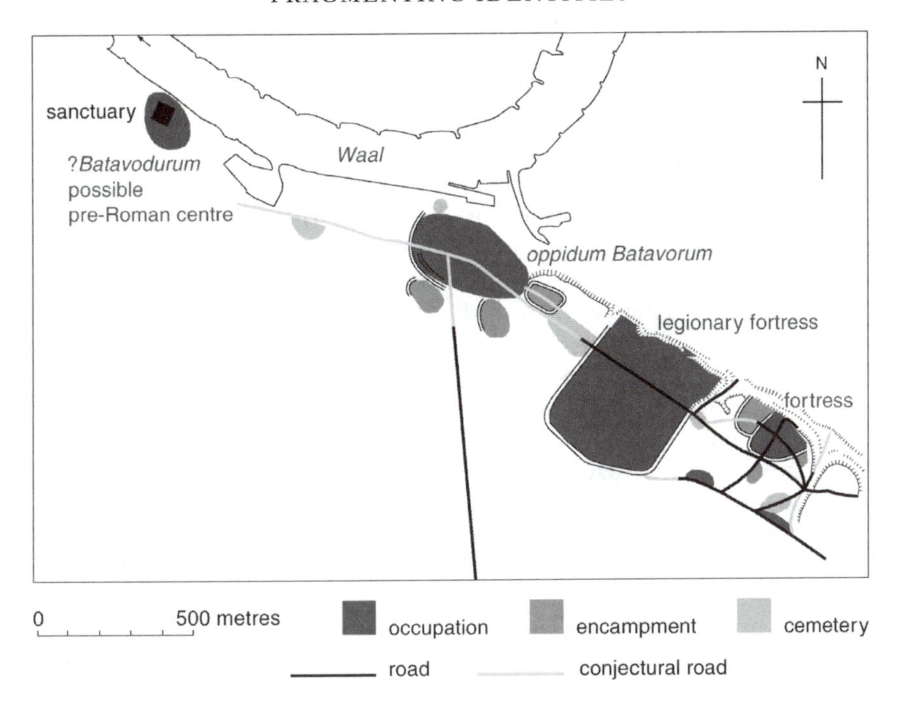

Figure 8 Nijmegen, in the early Roman period. Adapted from van Enckevort and Thijssen 2003, Figure 7.2. Drawing by Christina Unwin.

they were recruited, Batavian auxiliary units may have been allowed to serve under their own commanders, recruited from the elite families of the tribe.[53] Almost every family may have supplied one or two members for the Roman army.[54] It has been proposed that this practice of military recruitment had a major impact upon the development of society. Seal boxes are usually interpreted as containers that were used to seal a range of items, written documents in particular. The large number of seal boxes that have been found in the territory of the Batavians occur on military sites, at Nijmegen and the major temple complex of Empel, but they are also widespread in rural settlements.[55] The earliest rural contexts date to the early first century AD, but the great majority are of the later first and second centuries.[56] Derks and Roymans have taken this evidence to indicate a high degree of literacy among the people living within the non-villa settlements of this area, which appears to contrast with neighbouring areas of north Gaul, where seal boxes are rare.

Evidence for literacy among the Batavian population may reflect the fact that common auxiliary soldiers were required to communicate in Latin within their military units.[57] The acquisition of literacy may even have been one of the benefits of military service.[58] The military personnel at the fort of Vindolanda in Britannia included Batavian and Tungrian auxiliary units, for whom archaeological excavations have indicated literacy.[59] The diversity of writing styles on the writing-tablets, which date from between AD 90 and 120, probably indicates fairly widespread literacy in these military units, although it is likely that the common soldiery was unable to read and write to as high a standard as the officers.[60] The seal boxes on non-villa settlements may indicate that the population of the Lower Rhine were drawing upon aspects of Roman culture – Latin language and the technology of writing – through a creative engagement with the imperial system.[61]

Some of the writing-tablets name Flavius Cerialis as the commander (*praefectus*) of the Ninth Cohort of Batavians at Vindolanda – he may well have inherited his Roman citizenship from his father.[62] He was of equestrian rank and, if he returned home at the end of his military service, it is likely that he had considerable status within his native community.[63] The evidence from Vindolanda indicates that Cerialis had access within this fort to good food, appropriate clothing and equipment, the presence of his family and household slaves.[64] He may perhaps have been one of the people of his tribe who adopted Roman standards most fully; perhaps, on retirement, he built himself a villa in the Lower Rhine Valley. The evidence of urban and rural settlement in the territory of the Batavians suggests, however, that Cerialis was a rather exceptional member of this community.[65]

The large-scale recruitment of auxiliaries from the Batavians during the Julio-Claudian period may have led to an intensification of the martial ideology of traditional society.[66] The emphasis upon a military culture and apparent high esteem for the ownership of cattle may have resulted in a society in which many of the elements of elite Roman culture, including villa-building and urban competition, had little cultural relevance for the vast majority of the population.[67]

Derks's and Roymans's study is of particular interest because, in the past, Latin in provincial contexts has usually been associated with the imperial and provincial elites. In the elite context, the adoption of Latin could be connected with a desire to 'become Roman'.[68] The spread of the language to other less privileged people within native societies across the Roman West has then to be explained through the idea that these people wished to become Romanized. The evidence from the Lower Rhine, however, expresses the practical value of both the Latin language and the technology of writing to a broader range of people.[69] Language and the practice of writing may actually have been used widely by different members of society as a result of the potential value of the various context-dependent forms of communication that it offered to many people.[70]

Comprehension of the Latin language and an ability to write in it perhaps spread widely as a result of the recruitment of auxiliary soldiers from these communities.[71] These abilities may have been required in order for the individual soldier to function effectively in the Roman army and to communicate with distant friends and relatives. Language and literacy may also have enabled the members of the deceased soldier's family to claim his military savings.[72] The relatively low cost of the technology may have enabled the writing habit to spread. The writing-tablets at Vindolanda comprise thin sheets of wood, cut from local timber (alder, oak and birch) and written on in ink.[73] Such materials would have been both easily and cheaply available to people across the West and it is highly likely that writing on this type of media was very common, although these objects have only survived and been recognized on occasions.[74] In contrast to the relatively expensive manufactured wax stylus-tablets that have tended to dominate discussion until recently,[75] wooden tablets would have been accessible for anyone who had the knowledge and desire to write.

The adoption of Latin in this context does not necessarily indicate a direct wish to participate more widely in the culture of the Roman elite. For the Batavians, for example, it coincides with only a gradual adoption of Roman culture.[76] The adoption of Latin and writing may indicate the practical advantages of two major innovations that spread to northern Europe with the empire, a common language that enabled communication between people who were separated by great distances and the technologies that enabled this to occur. In other words, these people were not necessarily seeking their own regionally distinctive local way of 'becoming Roman', but were retaining the core of their cultural identity, with the addition of certain powerful innovations which assisted them to live in new ways under changing conditions. One way to view these developments is to argue that the Roman administrative system enabled Batavian people to adopt such an approach by providing a flexible means through which members of the tribe were recruited into the armed forces. An alternative perspective is to view it in terms of the recruitment of peripheral peoples as ethnic soldiery, a situation that kept the Batavians in a dependent position and excluded from the centres of political power.[77]

Traders are also likely to have come into contact with Latin on a day-to-day basis; the language will have had a practical value to them.[78] Many will have acquired knowledge of Latin and writing as a result of the transporting of goods across language boundaries and large-scale business activities often appear to have involved the keeping of written records.[79] The significant evidence from the *terra sigillata* (samian) pottery production site of La Graufesenque (south-eastern France) shows that potters there were adopting elements of both Latin and the technology of writing from the first century AD onward.[80] The kiln dockets were inscribed as the pottery was loaded into the kiln; they probably acted as a way of authenticating production and prices. For each firing, they recorded the names of the potters, the types of pots and their dimensions and the number of items.[81] The character of the Latin varies from docket to docket,[82] but it has been recently argued that the potters were able to distinguish between the Gaulish and the Latin that they used on the individual dockets,[83] which would suggest a certain degree of fluency in Latin.

The adoption of elements of Latin in this written form by the potters presumably reflects the fact that it was the language of business and communication within the empire. Latin enabled traders to communicate with people in different societies with whom they conducted business, while also allowing those who produced objects to communicate with traders who came to them to purchase their produce. Industry and small-scale trade are usually considered to have represented low-status professions in the empire,[84] but this evidence suggests that the potters at La Graufesenque had received a training that had taught them the Latin names for most of the objects that they were producing, alongside new methods of record-keeping.[85] The adoption of the Roman form of writing and the practice of record-keeping represent the gradual penetration of these aspects of Roman culture into native societies, presumably because of the specific roles that language played in the production and marketing processes.[86]

It is unlikely that the dockets passed beyond the local potters and the traders who sold the pottery.[87] The pots, by contrast, were intended to be sold and it has been proposed that the Latinized Gallic names adopted by the potters indicate that a Latin stamp was required for products intended for an outside market, reflecting the international character of the language and the symbolism of the pot.[88] Perhaps the potters used these Latin-style stamps because, together with the distinctive forms of pot and the decorative scenes that occurred on many, they appealed to the people who obtained and used these goods. The production and exchange of this Italian-style red pottery may therefore be seen as a 'mechanism for both spreading and defining a "Roman" material culture and indeed a Roman identity'.[89]

This distinctive pottery type was first produced in Arretium (modern Arezzo) in north Tuscany (Italy), where production probably commenced around 40 BC; the products were exported across the Mediterranean.[90] The technology to produce *terra sigillata* spread widely – workshops producing the new type of pottery have been found in Italy, Gaul, Spain and Asia Minor.[91] The major Gallic factories supplied the Roman army units that campaigned in Gaul, Germany and Britain. The pottery became very significant in both military and civil contexts within the newly conquered provinces,[92] where it has been suggested that it was adopted to symbolize new Roman identities.[93] John Hayes has written that this 'Arretine ware' developed rapidly 'into one of the flag-bearers of the regenerated Roman international culture of the age of Augustus'.[94] The pottery was made of a hard-fired clay and was sometimes decorated with motifs, including scenes from classical mythology. These derive from Hellenistic Greek imagery and ultimately from classical Athens, while some of the non-figured decoration – the floral and vegetal motifs – are also found on contemporary architecture in Rome and elsewhere and upon precious metal.[95] The delicacy of decoration and sharp angles copied the decorative styles of contemporary metalwork, especially silver plate; Arretine ware may have formed a cheaper alternative to precious metal.[96]

It is likely, however, that the identities of those who produced and consumed this pottery were not purely defined in Roman terms. Greg Woolf has suggested that this pottery was 'brought into relation with what Virgil did to epic and Augustus to public space in Rome', in other words, interpreted as a provincial contribution to the Augustan cultural revolution.[97] Woolf has proposed that *terra sigillata* represented a useful material for expressing a Gallo-Roman contribution to the new culture of the empire.[98] In this context, a specifically Gallo-Roman range of forms and iconography, in addition to the Latin form of the names of its Gallic potters, represents the acquisition of Roman culture and its reformulation in new cultural contexts.[99] The decoration on the pottery was presumably familiar to those who frequented Roman cities, while some of the mythological scenes will have been readable by those educated in classical literature, but the new ways in which these were explored communicated different ways of thinking about society.[100]

The stamps and decoration on products from centres such as La Graufesenque imply a readership fluent in both Latin writing and Graeco-Roman mythology; the choice of the language and images may well have been determined by the intended consumer.[101] If this is so, it suggests that the potters were not involved in a rather 'humble' manner within the process of 'becoming Roman',[102] but were learning and using Latin and new technologies of pottery production because these innovations assisted them in the production and marketing of their wares.

Evidence from elsewhere in the Western empire has been used to argue that Latin and the writing of the language spread throughout the social spectrum within provincial society,[103] even though the forms that were used are often 'vulgar' in character.[104] The language and the technologies of writing presumably spread because of the direct practical value that these innovations held for people in a variety of contexts. We should not imagine, however, that knowledge of Latin and writing was by any means evenly available throughout society. Despite the spread of non-elite forms of Latin, it is probable that the majority of the inhabitants of the empire, particularly away from the urban centres and forts, were unable to speak or write in Latin.[105]

The use of Latin in contexts that relate to the non-elite (or at least to the comparatively un-Roman population) is unlikely to indicate the adoption of the conventions inherent within classical elite education. In fact, education in Latin for the elite formed part of a culture of exclusion.[106] Classical education, since ancient times, has focused upon the development of the correct form of the language.[107] Latin was one element in the elite culture of classical Rome that was deliberately defined in complex ways that effectively excluded those who had not been fully educated in its vocabulary and themes.[108] In this way, the education of the elite will have served to perfect the quality of their written and spoken Latin, thus differentiating them from those with a less privileged knowledge of the language.[109] Despite this, knowledge of Latin, however 'imperfect', will have enabled certain non-elite members of society to read inscriptions on public buildings, understand public proclamations and engage in new forms of activity.

These studies of the context of the adoption of Latin assist us to counter the ancient ideas of cultural cohesion and uniformity that have dominated discussions of Roman identity and imperialism with what Maryline Parca has termed 'nuances of linguistic and cultural diversity'.[110] That is to say, they help us to think beyond the myth of the unity of Graeco-Roman culture that has dominated studies in the past.[111] Earlier forms of 'classicizations', beginning at least as early as the Roman Republic, have created simple and linear ideas of cultural evolution that have de-emphasized others which are seen as less central to the dominant theme.[112] Greg Woolf has asked whether we should reject the view of 'Latinization' in the empire as a single process, and instead view the West as a 'palimpsest' in which the language was 'written by many different hands to differing ends'.[113] The adoption of Latin in Italian and provincial contexts does not necessarily represent any direct adoption of a Roman order of values.[114] Latin will have been adopted to create a variety of new realities within local society. The use of Romanized forms of Gallic names on *terra sigillata* vessels certainly cannot be taken to project the same desires and interests as the use of Latin declamations in the forum of a Roman city, or the use of Latin inscriptions on a public building. The adoption of language and technology was both context-dependent and highly complex.[115]

'Discrepant experiences' in the landscape

These studies demonstrate the significance of archaeological work that focuses upon areas in which settlements do not develop along what is usually viewed as the 'standard' Roman trajectory.[116] They help to inform new understandings that move beyond the constraints of the centralizing images of Roman imperial culture.[117] Drawing upon the work of Derks and Roymans in the Lower Rhine, Martin Millett has considered the evidence for the native communities of north-western Iberia.[118] Villas and Roman-style urban centres appear rare in this area and native types of settlement in the form of castros (defended hill-top settlements) continued to be built and occupied well into the period of Roman control (Figure 9).[119] The basic evolution of individual castros often witnesses a gradual change to a form that has pre-Roman origins.[120] As in the case of the Batavians, the recruitment of auxiliary soldiers from these communities appears to have provided a vital supply of manpower for the Roman army.[121] Millett suggests that these soldiers may have been recruited through the use of mechanisms that left traditional forms of social structure in place and, as a result, settlement patterns changed only gradually.[122]

Other approaches to the effectively 'non-villa landscapes' of this area suggest that the large-scale mining of gold and silver by the Roman administration resulted in the development of distinctive landscapes in particular

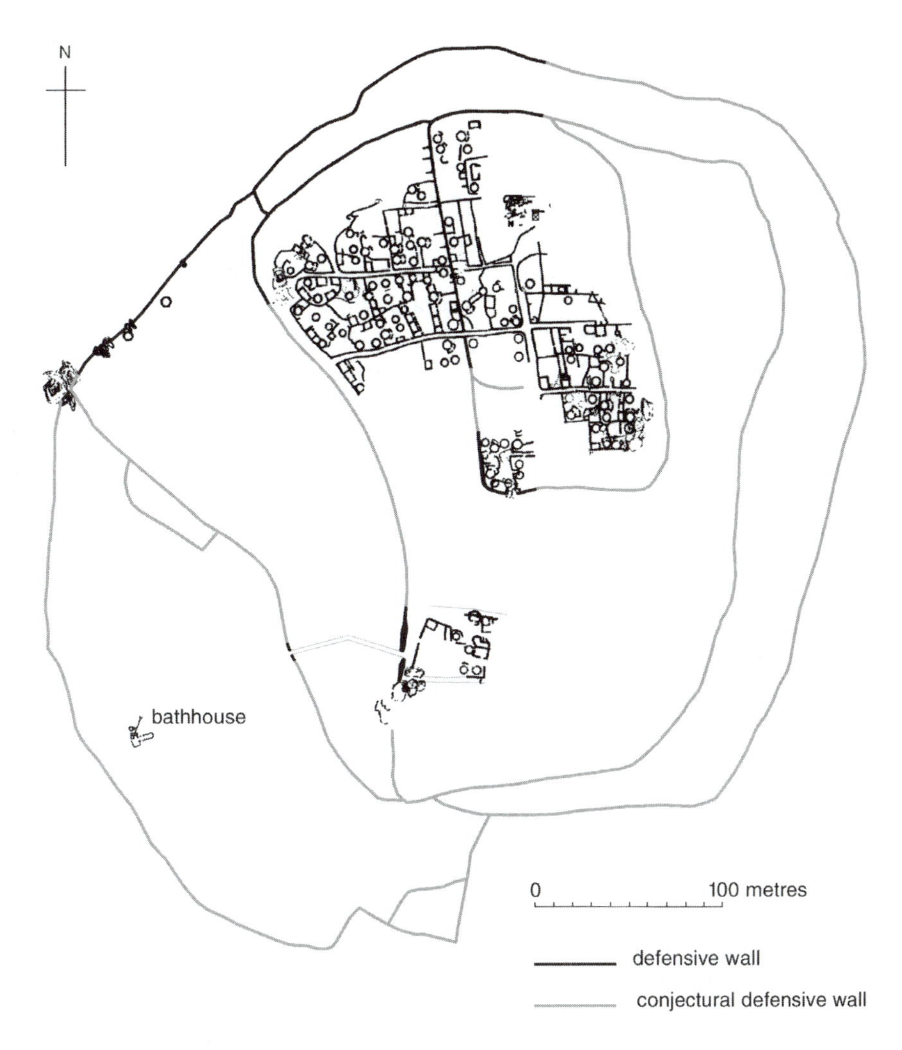

Figure 9 Citânia de Sanfins (Portugal). Adapted from Queiroga 2003, Figure 45. This extensive hilltop settlement was replanned during the early Roman period. Drawing by Christina Unwin.

areas.[123] Almudena Orejas and F.-Javier Sánchez-Palencia have proposed that these areas represent a discrepant form of reaction to Roman imperialism.[124] Highly impressive archaeological work, particularly around the major mining complex of Las Médulas (León), has resulted in the suggestion that the mining of these minerals was conducted by rural communities as a form of tribute to the Roman authorities.[125] A number of castros were built and occupied around Las Médulas during the pre-Roman period,[126] while the settlement landscape during the Roman period itself is characterized by a variety of types of sites, including open settlements but also newly established castros.[127] Some of the defended hilltop sites are broadly comparable to the pre-Roman castros, but excavation has indicated that their function had changed to a specific focus upon mining, with each site performing a particular role in the operations.[128] The native communities presumably became involved in the mining operations under the direct supervision of the Roman administration and it has been argued that members of the native elite based their power upon their position of authority in the system that was set up to run the mines. The local urban centre, Astúrica Augusta (Astorga, León), an impressive city with a highly monumental forum and basilica, may have been established to provide an administrative centre for the control of this mining, but perhaps with relatively limited input on the part of the native elites.[129]

Extensive mining occurred across much of north-western Iberia. The evidence from the inscriptions that have been found indicates the involvement of the local aristocracy in administration at the local level.[130] The development of local aristocracies across this area is demonstrated by the distinctive funerary inscriptions and the occasional villa-type building. The nucleated urban and semi-urban settlements that are now being discovered may also be related to the actions of these elites.[131] Perhaps some communities sent men to serve in the Roman army, while others directed people to work in the mines. Those areas without rich mineral deposits may have supplied auxiliary soldiers as an alternative form of taxation.

We do not know what proportion of the auxiliary soldiers, either from the Lower Rhine Valley or from north-western Iberia, returned to their homelands after the completion of military service. The interpretations that have been offered for both regions suggest that local people were incorporated into the empire in ways that resulted in features of their traditional ways of life – forms of settlement, types of building and objects in everyday use – changing only very slowly. This occurred without the wholesale importation (or imposition) of new forms of culture.[132] In this way, local societies formed their identities as discrepant local adaptations based upon the resources of their respective territories and the opportunities that arose as a result of their contact with Rome. The existence of a local governing elite group in the mining area of north-western Iberia indicates that these people became drawn into some of the aspects of the broader elite Roman culture. It would appear, however, that people in both regions became integrated in discrepant and local manners, forming identities that contrasted with the trajectory of many of the other societies of eastern and southern Iberia and southern Gaul.

The 'becoming Roman' approach indicates that people in parts of the Western empire were able to adapt to the process of imperial expansion in ways that enabled them to build upon the advantages of their new contexts, developing aspects of their pre-existing identities and the resources of their territories. The new trajectories noted above, however, do not fit with the 'standard' form of Roman identity, a form that is fundamental to the Romanization theories that have dominated studies. The number of examples of highly discrepant experiences in particular places across the empire suggests that the idea of 'standard' urban and rural settlement evolution has been imposed upon the evidence for the Roman past through the continued reformulation of a Romano-centric discourse. The gradual refocusing of archaeological attention should, in due course, provide a more balanced view about the variety of cultures that developed within the broader framework of the empire.

Consuming culture

It has been argued that people adopted the Latin language in their daily lives because of its practicality under the system that was laid down in individual provincial contexts, at least in part, by the Roman administration. Archaeologists who study prehistoric society often consider that material culture represents another form of text,[133] which raises the possibility that other elements of material culture imported by Roman contact, trade and power-relations may also have been adopted in creative new ways because of the practical assistance that they offered to individuals in the context of their own societies.

I have explored the idea that the construction of cities, public buildings and villas helped to bring the empire into being. Such arguments have been used to explore the role of the portable items of material culture that are so common on Roman settlements throughout the empire, including pottery, coins and items of dress. A broad range of new pottery types and styles spread to many, perhaps most, of the communities within the boundaries of the empire. Does the evidence for the existence of a broad range of cultural items that become common across much of the empire during the final centuries BC and first century AD indicate that Roman culture spread down through the social hierarchy, from the elite to the non-elite? This question requires us to consider whether it is appropriate to argue a Roman identity for many of these material items.

'Appearing to be Roman' had a practical value for the elite of many individual provincial societies, as it incorporated them into the power structure of the empire, where they could interact and communicate with others who drew upon the same flexibly defined culture. Can we assume, however, that the same simple explanation is valuable for the adoption of new forms of dress, eating and living that spread widely across the empire, involving many who did not represent members of the 'upper strata'? Even in those areas that appear to experience a non-standard form of development, imported items of material culture (often called 'Roman') became common on settlements. How and why did these items spread to the people in these places? Did people adopt goods, and the new ways of life in which they were involved, as part of a conscious desire to associate themselves with the power and authority of the city of Rome?

In the modern world, goods pass between regions in many complex ways that often help to determine, or define, relationships between different peoples.[134] Attempts have been made to study the rules by which goods are received into different societies – the local context of social consumption.[135] The consumption of material culture in the Roman empire has been addressed in several recent works which argue that the expansion of imperial control provided new opportunities to native peoples.[136] A powerful and emerging approach is to examine the idea of the empire as a 'consumer culture' across Rome, Italy and the provinces.[137] To explore this theme, we need to consider the character of production, exchange and consumption. The scale and character of the economy of the empire is highly contentious.[138] There is also a healthy debate upon the role of the Roman elite in industrial production and trade.[139] A lengthy debate has been under way for some time between those who see the political economy of official state trade as the only link between a series of primarily local economies, and others who see the empire as a fully integrated economic system which included a fairly unified market for industrial and agricultural products, land and labour.[140] The economic situation in the empire of the first centuries BC and AD is likely to have been somewhere between these two extremes.[141] The demands of the imperial system may, indeed, have resulted in the integration of more of the regional redistributive networks that existed across the Mediterranean than has been achieved either before or since.[142]

One recent review of some of the literary and archaeological evidence, written by an economist,[143] has concluded that the empire was an enormous conglomeration of interdependent markets. While there was no empire-wide market for all goods, local markets were linked together across the Mediterranean, while areas to the north and west also had a degree of connectivity. The evidence of pottery and amphorae, for instance, indicates the medium- and long-distance movement of goods on a considerable scale.[144] The market system appears to have been most integrated in the areas to which ships and boats had access, but trade based upon market principles could also pass further inland.[145] It is argued that even the most humble of farms were involved in the market network, obtaining the money to pay taxes and to buy other items, although most of their consumption was of home-produced items.[146] The market economy of the empire may therefore have incorporated most of its population in the expansion of production. Modest but significant economic growth occurred across the provinces, resulting from the imposition of political integration and peace.[147] This economic growth then enabled a broad range of people to change their lives through the acquisition of new objects and practices.

With the scarcity of data on prices of land, wages and interest rates, this remains a contentious argument. Such a process of economic expansion would, however, help to explain the apparent development of what we might term a 'consumer culture' across much of the empire in the period 100 BC to 100 AD.[148] Prior to this period, trade had been taking place at a significant level across the Mediterranean and within northern Europe, but the increase in the scale of the movement of goods had an intimate relationship with the expansion of Roman power. The growth of the empire coincided with a major increase in the circulation of artefacts, both within and beyond its boundaries, at the same time as it witnessed a significant increase in the movement of peoples.[149] The writings of classical authors sometimes suggest that they felt that interaction with native peoples at the frontier of imperial control through trade communicated some Roman attitudes to goods.[150] Societies that became included within the trading system of Rome were often subsequently incorporated within the empire and trade can be interpreted as intimately bound up with the growth of imperial relations.[151]

Consequently, people throughout the Western provinces and beyond the frontiers of the empire obtained a great deal of material culture that had been manufactured at some distance and transported into their areas. A proportion of production and exchange was directed specifically at the elite of Italy and the provinces; particular objects related to the construction of elite Roman identity.[152] Some of the new goods from Italian and provincial contexts, however, occur too widely to be associated merely with the richest levels of society – this is particularly the case for the pottery, coins and the other items of bric-à-brac that are found in vast quantities on many settlements.[153] A brief examination of any modern and well published excavation report for a military, urban or rural site in the Western provinces indicates the vast number of goods that were available. 'Roman' items are found at some houses and settlements that might appear, compared with the elaborate houses in cities and the villas, to have been of relatively low status.[154] Since the early twentieth century, this has been taken to suggest that the material culture that became available across the empire was used by most of its population (page 43).

The creation of the empire coincided with a considerable expansion of industry and trade that offered new ways of living. Perhaps this increase in consumer culture provided the opportunity and motivation for members of society who, in wider imperial terms, were not particularly wealthy or well connected, to transform themselves in order to exploit their new contexts within the empire.[155] An involvement in industry, trade or agriculture may have provided the surplus to pay taxes and obtain goods.[156] The character of the Roman empire as a vast network of intercommunications has been emphasized by Ray Laurence.[157] He has suggested that the study of Roman Britain should turn away from considering that the monumentalization of towns was the defining feature of Romanness and towards the view that there was a fluidity of movement of people through a network of towns connected by roads.[158] In addition to reflecting a Roman elite discourse of government, the construction of monumental town centres reflected the structure of communication (connectivity) within the empire. The construction of public buildings was based upon access to knowledge and finance (through patronage and loans).[159] The character of mobility and communication, however, went far beyond the elites of these local communities.

Movements of certain groups – including soldiers, traders and craftspeople – created a system of contacts of a quantitatively significant number.[160] Many people became bound into imperial networks of trade and military service. Subordinate cultures arose among the craftsmen, merchants and freedmen of the Roman world, who represented a range of identities that emerged as a result of the development of urban centres and trade.[161] These people may have sought a prosperity and security that had not been possible in the small-scale societies that had dominated the area prior to their incorporation in the Roman empire, thereby explaining some of the evidence for the marked increase in trade and industry. Such non-elite groups shaped provincial culture in ways that have often been played down because of an over-concentration upon elites.[162]

This explains how goods, ideas and capital may have circulated, while the geography of connectivity might have created a need for a person to define an identity outside their place of origin.[163] The establishment of identity by incomers took place when they drew upon a widespread culture that linked them into the broader identity of imperial civilization. The expanding network of relationships that was established through the increase in communication offered new ways of living to these people,[164] partly as the result of the availability of a variety of new goods created through a consumer revolution.[165] Material culture served both to create and to symbolize the relationships between peoples in various parts of the empire. Movements of, and contacts between, such 'lowly' groups transported both artefacts and beliefs between provinces and across the empire.[166] These movements and contacts at the same time helped to create new forms of identity with a relevance that extended beyond the local community, images that communicated across regional and provincial boundaries.

Recent accounts emphasize the diversity of identities that arose within the empire. As a reaction against the earlier monolithic ideas of unchanging Roman identity, some accounts have been moving towards the idea of the empire as an effective cultural free-for-all in which people were relatively free to adopt culture in constructive ways that emphasized their own contexts, feelings and desires. Steve Dyson has argued, with, I suspect, a touch of irony, that:

> Perhaps one should see ancient Rome not in French or British political imperial terms, but in those of American commercial imperialism. The Romans produced a variety of lifestyle options with appeal for all, whether it was a villa with bath, mosaic and wall-paintings or a

single African Red Slip bowl to display beside the traditional hearth. Each item produced changes big and small.[167]

The argument adopted here is that, having rejected outmoded models of Roman imperialism that drew upon the culture of the nineteenth and earlier twentieth century, we should, instead, look to contemporary theory, as expressed by works on globalization, to develop rather more decentralized and dynamic images of the Roman world. Roman culture, in these terms, could be adopted in a flexible manner to symbolize variable motivations.

Under this approach, the city takes on a rather different significance to that which it holds in the interpretation of the centrality of Roman elite-based imperial culture. It becomes the focal point for communication and connectivity within both local and imperial society.[168] It was the place at which people could meet to establish new relationships that expressed identity and was also the location in which new forms of identity could be constructed, through the involvement of individuals in industry, labour and trade. Communication and urbanism may have represented part of the means through which the 'upper strata' of the empire created its imperial unity, but it may also have offered new ways of life that bound other less privileged, but significant, groups into the structure of imperial relations.[169] The idea of connectivity should enable the avoidance of what Neville Morley has called a 'misplaced concreteness' through the study of the monumental architecture and elite buildings of the urban centres of the empire.[170] Although the urban centres emerged partly through the template provided by the Graeco-Roman concept of the city, urban trends led to many different results in varying contexts,[171] results that provided opportunities to people from different backgrounds.

Pottery and consumption

These approaches argue that the material culture that spread with Rome had a practical significance to the lives of people across the west of the empire. It is not my aim in this book to explore in any greater detail the complexity of the ways in which these material elements of culture may have been adopted in local contexts. The aim has been to examine the potential of a central, global concept of Roman culture and its relationship to the identity of the elite across the West, and also to point out the problems with such a simple discussion through a brief exploration of the opportunities that material culture offered to others. I shall, however, consider one additional case study to highlight both the potential of the perspectives that I have outlined in this book and also a significant limitation.

Pottery has a significant part to play in the discussion of identity and social change, since it is so common in the archaeological record and also because its production and circulation has been thoroughly studied by archaeologists. The consumption of pottery, however, has not received as full a discussion as its production and circulation.[172] The character of pottery as a relatively low-quality material perhaps offers the archaeologist the opportunity to examine social change at a non-elite level, but high-quality pottery will also have held significance for the 'upper strata'. Attempts have been made to argue the significance of high-quality pottery, distinctive items of 'Roman' material culture that were used in different ways in provincial contexts.

The production of *terra sigillata* has been addressed above, but it was not just the character and style of this pottery that symbolized new identities, since it is likely that the distinctive pottery types were used as part of developing lifestyles. Pottery was used to eat and drink in new ways, perhaps in a manner that was seen as 'Roman'. It has been suggested that *terra sigillata* was made and used in two distinct 'services', typical of the Augustan age, one of which appears early and the other late in the period (although there is a fair degree of overlap between them).[173] In reality, however, the use of pottery in groups may have been far more complex and subject to regional and chronological changes.[174] Formal 'sets', with matching cups and plates representing a personal set of tableware, may or may not have been popular, but, in any case, the vessels were presumably well suited to eating new food in 'Roman' ways.[175] Technology for the preparation and cooking of food may also have changed, as the spread of *terra sigillata* mortaria indicate changing methods of processing raw foodstuffs, while the widespread occurrence of amphorae across the Western empire indicates the availability of new types of food. Changes in ceramic assemblages will have offered people new ways of eating, which may in turn have been part of new social actions.[176] New ways of consuming food and drink occurred in the context of the new physical organization of social space within the domestic architectural traditions that also spread widely at this time.

The studies of language and writing present a framework for how we might think about the adoption of ceramics in the domestic environment. Perhaps new ways of consuming food were adopted in specific places because of their practical value in creating new ways of living in a variety of different contexts. Any adherence to a specifically 'Roman' way of dining is likely, however, to have been limited by resources, contacts, ambitions and world-view. The material from Britain is of particular significance in assessing these issues; it has been relatively thoroughly studied and has been the subject of substantial assessments by Steve Willis and others.[177] *Terra sigillata* was imported prior to the conquest and became part of new eating practices adopted by the elite.[178] Evidence exists to suggest that it was preferentially associated with Latin and literacy in pre-conquest contexts, as the majority of graffiti occur on imported ceramics. The use of these objects in new ways of eating and drinking wine and other exciting new foodstuffs, together with their association with writing, may suggest that *terra sigillata* vessels had a rather greater social value in pre-conquest Britain than within the Mediterranean and military frontier areas of the empire.[179] The decoration on these imported tablewares probably formed the source for some of the imagery on Iron Age coins, while the manufacturers' stamps may have provided the inspiration for the Latin inscriptions on other Iron Age coins.[180] To someone from the Mediterranean, the uses to which imports were put in late Iron Age Britain might have appeared rather peculiar, but they offered a range of new cultural opportunities within the late Iron Age for copying and adapting.

After the conquest of Britain, *terra sigillata* is preferentially represented at military sites and urban centres. It is comparatively less common at 'small towns' and roadside settlements and is rarest at rural sites, although villas often produce a higher percentage than many of the 'non-villa settlements'.[181] It is likely that samian was regarded as high-status tableware in many contexts, particularly during the early phases of conquest.[182] The military and urban sites would also appear, on the whole, to have received a higher than average proportion of decorated vessels.[183] This evidence suggests the pattern that we might expect as a result of the traditional approaches to Romanization, with high-status sites having greater access to relatively expensive objects. Nevertheless, a small number of samian vessels were obtained by people who appear, from the evidence of their architecture and possessions, to be less wealthy. In fact, the proportion of decorated samian on these sites appears rather higher than might be expected.[184] Less powerful individuals may have been able to obtain small quantities of samian to express their ambitions and intentions.

It is more important, however, to consider the context within which these objects were being adopted in order to assess whether such a simple interpretation can actually address individual actions.[185] The movement of goods and practices in the contemporary world always involves hybridization, interpretation, translation, manipulation, mutation and 'indigenization'.[186] The ways that new objects and practices are accommodated or assimilated into local cultures have come to be emphasized in recent accounts.[187] These mechanisms are not necessarily anti-globalist, rather they create a conjunction or an intersection.[188] They operate through a process that is sometimes called 'glocalization' or 'local globalization'.[189] The assimilation of objects and ideas from outside often involves transformations that reassert self-identity at a local level.[190] Adopting such approaches in the Roman context, a samian pot may have been acquired because of its symbolic value as a distinctive object rather than because of its specific 'Roman' character or its potential use in Roman ways of eating and drinking.

Information for native rural sites is relatively scarce in contrast to that for villas, military sites and urban centres.[191] Samian occurs in all sizeable rural assemblages but is typically present only in small quantities.[192] On occasions, however, the evidence holds surprises. Fairy Knowe (Stirling, Scotland), in the borderlands of Roman Britain (Figure 10), produced a far higher proportion of samian (41 per cent of the total pottery assemblage) than other rural sites in Willis's survey, together with a higher proportion of decorated

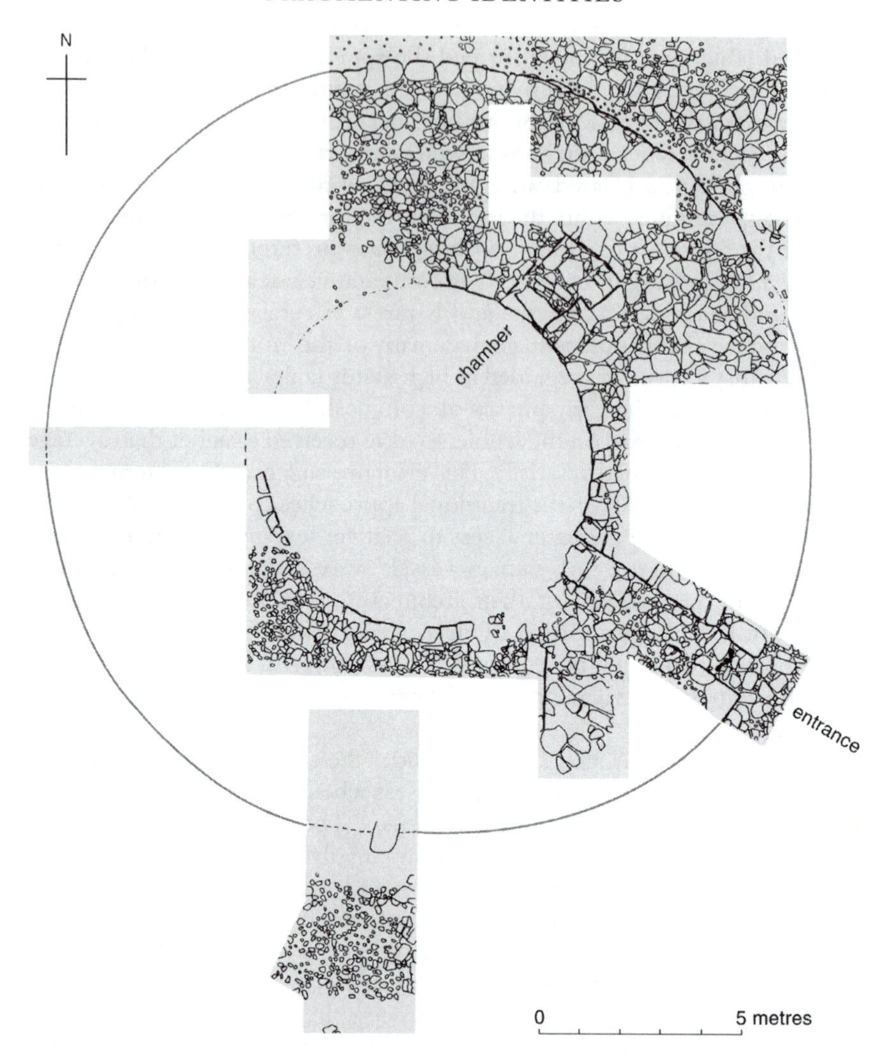

Figure 10 The broch at Fairy Knowe (Stirling, Scotland). Adapted from Main 1998, illustration 9. Drawing by Christina Unwin.

examples (36.8 per cent).[193] This is likely to reflect the character of this site – a broch – a type of site that has native origins but one which may have been the home of a powerful local individual or group that had a close relationship with the Roman administration.[194]

This assemblage, although relatively small, includes a wide but selected range of types, but the most significant information relates to the uses to which the material has been put.[195] Several pieces appear to have been deliberately trimmed down and reused, while others have worn edges, suggesting that they were used as rubbers or polishers. The trimming of a number of bases may suggest that they were being inverted and re-employed as small dishes, possibly as lamps.[196] We cannot be certain that this form of treatment relates to the initial uses to which these objects were put; they could originally have been used on this site in the creation of Roman ways of dining. Eventually, however, these objects appear to have been treated in ways that suggest a rather different interpretation and it would appear that broken pieces had some form of practical and symbolic significance that may have drawn upon the symbolism of the vessel as a high status and exotic import.[197] It would appear that, as in the pre-conquest period in southern Britain, a relatively significant type of material was being adopted in a particular context in a rather un-Roman manner.

The significance that has been placed on the production of *terra sigillata* reflects its potential importance to some of the native people who came to possess the material. Most of the pottery that is found on Roman settlement sites, however, was produced in relatively close proximity to the site at which it was consumed. It was probably usually distributed through local markets.[198] A tradition of pottery study has developed in which the object is analysed in terms of both the clay fabric out of which it was produced and its form. This type of analysis enables archaeologists to consider patterns of trade and also the chronological development of ceramic styles, assisting with the dating of archaeological contexts. Another type of analysis assesses the function of the pottery container in the acts of consumption.[199] Very little work of this type has been carried out in detail and this hampers our understanding of the ways that pottery was used in the consumption of food and drink in societies across the empire.

Some archaeologists have begun to quantify the proportions of differing types of pottery vessels (jars, bowls, cups, etc.) at particular archaeological sites.[200] It is possible that changing proportions of types of pottery vessel through time on an individual site represent varying patterns of consumption, while different sites also produce varying assemblages.[201] Jerry Evans's case study of pottery from sites in the Arrow Valley (Warwickshire, England) formed part of an archaeological survey of a range of sites of Roman date, including the periphery of a villa enclosure system and several non-villa settlements.[202] It was possible to compare the ceramic sequences on these sites to the evidence for the neighbouring 'small town' at Alcester. Changes in proportions of pottery vessel types occur, with new forms (particularly bowls) being introduced first in Alcester and then spreading to the villa. On the non-villa sites the traditional vessel form of the jar remained predominant. In southern Britain, Iron Age assemblages dominated by jars are often replaced during the early Roman period by more diverse collections, with a higher proportion of tablewares (i.e. dishes and bowls) and other types.[203] This is a change that took place at different rates on varying types of sites, while the evidence from some entire regions also demonstrates variations from the norm.

Direct evidence for the uses of distinct types of pots is difficult to obtain,[204] but presumably the new styles of ceramics indicate that new ways of preparing, serving and eating food were influencing people. The presence of amphorae also appears to reflect a comparable pattern to the samian, with military and urban sites producing far higher quantities than rural settlements.[205] The increasing quantities of tablewares and fine wares across many types of settlement, particularly the military and urban sites, indicate the spread of new forms of eating that demonstrate developing ideas of identity.[206] As with the spread of Latin language and the practice of writing, however, it is too simple merely to label such changes as 'Roman'. There may have been a value in communicating differences at a local level. In addition, perhaps new forms of pottery were adopted because they were more durable and relatively of high quality; if so, their use may represent convenience rather than the adoption of some form of standardized Roman identity.[207] The character of the changing ways of life that lie behind the ceramics (and various other types of material culture) relates to relationships that were established as a result of imperial expansion. The evidence is, however, too complex to be explained by simple theories of social change such as Romanization. Through contact and interaction, new ways of life emerged for many people, but to call these ways Roman is to oversimplify complex issues of context and identity.[208]

The evidence for the very slow rate of cultural change on some of the rural sites in Warwickshire gives us access to information about the ways that members of the 'silent majority' lived within the empire. New technologies of pottery production became available, but most of the pottery on some sites was in the jar traditions that had dominated the pre-Roman assemblages, indicating that these people may well have retained their accustomed ways of eating. Architectural traditions and ways of consuming food and drink may have changed very slowly for the majority of those who lived in rural areas.[209] These people have seldom formed the focus for the attention of archaeologists.

Evolving traditions of archaeological work focus attention on a broader range of sites than was the case in the past, but they still tend to prioritize the well connected elements of the population,[210] even when research has been extended to those living on non-villa settlements. The extremely useful studies on the Batavians, Gallic potters and people of north-western Iberia (above) focus on discrepant reactions to imperial incorporation, but they all retain a focus upon connectivity and change. Even though these studies suggest that people drew upon 'Roman' culture in fragmented ways, change remains the core issue. Incorporation into the empire of Rome will have gradually changed the ways of life of these communities, but it may well be true that many people in the Western empire did not have very much control over their own destinies outside their own households and immediate communities. If we wish to gain an overview of the complexity of the identities of the people across this vast area, those who were less well connected need to become a far more serious focus for the attention of archaeologists.[211] This consideration of the silent majority also puts the argument about the Roman consumer revolution into context.

The limits of connectivity

The extent to which conquest transformed the lives of the majority of the population is a contentious area of debate. A 'consumer revolution' suggests that, as the result of a substantial expansion of production involving many in the developing economic system embodied in imperial culture, a variety of individuals in different positions within society were able to afford, obtain and adopt the trappings of Roman civilization. Evan W. Haley has recently argued that, in Baetica, a substantial 'middle stratum' emerged during the period of the early empire, outnumbering both the ruling elite and the poor.[212] Effectively, this suggests that Alföldy's model for Roman social relations (Figure 4) requires reassessment, with the introduction of a substantial middle-income group.[213] Haley suggests that this group arose because of the economic opportunities offered by agriculture (mainly by olive-oil production) and also as a result of the specific political organization of the area and the demands of local government.[214] Such a situation would indicate widespread social mobility in Baetica; a comparable process may have been under way elsewhere.[215] These new elites may have been able to find the surplus to make significant changes to their ways of eating and dwelling across Gaul, southern Britain and other provinces of the Western empire and elsewhere.

Nevertheless, the dominant opinion in Roman studies is that the majority of the population lived at, or just above, subsistence level.[216] Mary Downs has previously argued that the idea of a highly Romanized Baetica is a piece of imperial propaganda, propagated by Rome and accepted, often without question, by modern scholars.[217] The nature of the urban pattern of the province owed much to the pre-existing character of society and many 'native towns' and 'farmsteads' apparently show comparatively little influence from Roman culture.[218] Zones of the province were Roman and urban but other areas remained grounded in indigenous and locally based networks.[219] On one side of the argument (Haley), Roman imperialism is seen as providing considerable opportunities for economic expansion. This liberated a substantial group of innovative native people from their inherited positions of subservience within an elite-focused social system that was broken down, at least to a degree, by the economic forces of Roman imperialism. On the other side (Downs), Rome had a relatively limited impact across many of the provinces, as indigenous elites continued to dominate their communities under the new circumstances of Roman control, integrating themselves into the economic system to varying degrees, but with a substantial degree of continuity from the pre-Roman pattern.[220]

The most useful perspective may be situated between the two extremes.[221] Roman imperialism created considerable opportunities for some to break out of the social situations into which they were born, through new ways of life offered by military service, trade or industry. Landowners may also have been able to expand production but, since communications and opportunities will have been more restricted for many in rural societies, the evidence for agricultural production is likely to subsume alternative responses to Roman authority. In the rural sphere, a common means of cultural expression may have been the conservation of tradition, with changes occurring only gradually.[222] This social strategy, and its relationship to resistance, comprises an important but neglected area of study.[223]

In Britain, where archaeologists have begun to examine the homes of at least some of the less wealthy within provincial society, it appears that the idea of relative continuity for large sections of the community may be broadly valid. A substantial proportion of the population remained in relative poverty, or at least relatively un-Roman,[224] while other well connected people exploited the opportunities to change their ways of life by drawing upon the new material culture that was introduced as a result of the expansion of Rome. Such may be the case for many regions of the empire,[225] but the evidence has often been sidelined as the result of a determined search for the progressive value of Roman innovation.

6

'BACK TO THE FUTURE'?[1]

Empire and Rome

> [W]e want to problematize the unity of the 'us' and the otherness of the 'other' and question the radical separation between the two that makes the opposition possible in the first place.
>
> (Gupta and Ferguson 2002 [1997], 72)

The study of Roman imperialism is a complex debate in which the present and the past are effectively interrogated together in order to create understanding. Many of the beliefs that structured the debate during the early twentieth century, and the terms that were used to develop them, are now unacceptable. This is because contemporary attitudes to identity and social change continuously influence our interpretation of the Roman past, reformatting our comprehension and the ways that we communicate. History is rewritten to reflect current ideas about the world, but the past is also drawn upon to inform the present.

Michael Hardt and Antonio Negri's study, *Empire*, provides a stimulating interpretation of the current state of the world (page 9). For Hardt and Negri, Empire in the modern world partly came into being through the adoption of models derived from classical Rome.[2] Empire is a self-generating force, creating the context at its frontiers for its own reproduction and extension. They propose that 'The Empire's institutional structure is like a software program that carries a virus along with it, so that it is continuously modulating and corrupting the institutional forms around it'.[3] This is reminiscent of Woolf's suggestions about the potentially unlimited expansion of Roman imperial culture as a form of organism that metabolizes other matter and becomes transformed in the process.[4]

Greg Woolf adopted a concept of Roman culture that views it as a new cultural logic, or new cultural configuration, that enabled provincials to transform their lives in the context of local needs; one which then fed back, at least to a degree, into the central and evolving concept of what it was to be 'Roman'.[5] The new imperial culture that developed is then seen to have supplanted the Roman culture of the capital just as it came to replace other earlier cultures of the indigenous peoples of Italy and the provinces.[6] This is a seductively inclusive image which, as we have seen, has been further developed with the discussion of the idea of an Augustan cultural revolution that spread first through Rome and Italy and then drew in some of the elites of various provinces. By adopting contemporary concepts of globalization, it is useful to conceive that Roman imperialism was effectively established through a common set of formats and structures – a culture that mediated between the societies that came to participate in it through their own local actions.[7] Roman imperial discourse may, therefore, have served to present universal categories and standards through which some cultural differences could be identified and defined. Similarities and differences could be communicated in ways that were more widely intelligible across the boundaries between regions and provinces. As a result, a global Roman hegemony developed through the articulation of 'structures of common difference'.[8]

It *is* useful to define Roman identity as a flexible but meaningful category and one that subsumed provincial elite groups across certain parts of the Western empire. To suggest that a single Roman culture – highly differentiated by region, class, social locale, age, gender – arose is, however, too comfortable a picture of consensus. Roman culture was flexible and incorporated many within its structure, but the concept loses all value if it is extended to incorporate everyone. Certain significant opportunities emerged for soldiers, traders and industrial workers who then adopted identities that drew upon new concepts and materials with which they came into contact. Many groups may have adopted some aspects of material culture and the ways of life of which it formed a part. The evidence suggests, however, that people were seeking to define their cultural identities in variable ways. Men and women may have aimed to improve their social status, both for themselves and for their children, assisted by the new circumstances consequent to the expansion of the empire. The two relatively coherent concepts of Roman identity were, however, only available to the elite and to soldiers. The 'lower strata', by contrast, will often have drawn upon new ideas and technologies because of the opportunities that these offered to in their everyday lives. In real terms, these ways of life can only be defined as 'Roman' in the broad sense that they occurred within a society that was ruled by an elite who adopted aspects of a flexible Roman identity. In addition, approaches that stress 'Roman' identity continue to sideline the poorest and those who were least well connected into the imperial system.

Enabling and imposing

The approach developed by Woolf and others to 'becoming Roman', the complementary accounts of imperial connectivity and ideas of fragmented identity, are all very much the products of the historical context in which they have developed; at the same time, they do help us to understand the Roman empire. The investigation of the variability of responses, both of individuals and societies, to the expansion of Roman control helps to define one of the significances of imperial studies today. The contemporary meaning of the Roman empire as, effectively, almost a global civilization makes its value, as a source of comparison and contrast, more direct.[9] The major differences between the ancient and the modern world allow us to view our contemporary times in a broader context by considering the ancient genealogies of the postmodern empire in which we find ourselves.[10] At a deep level, Roman imperial studies should continue to help us to interrogate our own world and the values that we hold and seek to export to others. At a 'deep level', because consideration of this issue is rarely addressed in academic works; this was true in the early twentieth century and remains so today.[11]

I have emphasized that the power of classical Rome continues to derive from the relevance that it has to ideas of Western identity. Despite vigorous attempts to deconstruct the narratives of Graeco-Roman identity, the overtly positive assessment of classical culture that formed the basis for many accounts of the nineteenth and early twentieth centuries has yet to be replaced by a more balanced position. The approaches to globalizing Roman culture continue, on the whole, to place a fairly positive spin upon the effects of Roman imperialism. The Roman elite is considered to have been involved in a series of connected political actions that enabled members of various native societies to define their identities in new and original ways. This was accomplished through the use of surplus and widespread contacts, including service in the Roman army, or involvement in industry, trade and agriculture.

Since 1990, negotiation, debate and cultural interaction have been emphasized in accounts of the Roman empire.[12] The empire is recovered and reconstructed, from the literature and the archaeological remains that it has left behind, as an imperial power with a flexible strategy of incorporation that defined relationships with its subjects in order to encourage their peaceful development along indigenous lines. These approaches have been created both through the general idea of 'becoming Roman' and also by the less Romano-centric approaches to fragmented identities. The developing consensus appears to be that the deconstruction of coherent concepts that have dominated studies, such as the myth of the unity of Graeco-Roman culture, is, in itself, a liberating exercise. Works that focus upon the variability of response within the empire, however, may develop alongside unquestioned assumptions that broadly comparable forces of regional 'emancipation' within the current world system are a force for good across the globe.[13]

Timothy Brennan has argued that the emphasis that Hardt and Negri place upon the variable new forms of identity that Empire has unleashed across the contemporary globe fits very comfortably with the inherited perception that the influence of the West has been mainly positive.[14] Whatever the intention of the authors of *Empire*, this suggests that the development of the regionally differentiated global world system is a positive development. It provides a context in which Western interests offer others across the globe the opportunity to develop and exploit their own innate abilities and the natural resources of the areas that they inhabit. Approaches to globalization view the creation of regional diversity as a highly effective tool in the spread of the global world system; the local is integrated into the global as a vital tool in the spread of its structure. Those who are critical of globalization do not support the view that the development of regional diversity represents an emancipating influence in the contemporary world, but stress that the current system continues to work in the interest of certain powerful players within the world economy.[15] Rather than breaking down power-relations, new approaches view Empire as a less dichotomous and more intricate pattern of inequality.[16]

Ancient and contemporary empires may depend on negotiation in order to come into existence and to survive, but other forces also play a part. We need a renewed focus upon Roman imperial policy in general and, in particular, on aspects that appear less palatable, but which have equal contemporary relevance. Examples include the study of the violent imposition of new order, genocide, deportation, and the exploitation of societies on the margins of imperial control, through substantial and sustained processes of enslavement and through enforced military recruitment.[17] These issues often receive scant attention in accounts of the Roman empire, but they help to balance any overtly positive image of the Roman imperial venture and its effects. We should not, however, drive interpretations to the extremes. Indeed, it is helpful to emphasize issues of negotiation and compromise in order to counter the partisan and bigoted views that help to fuel conflict in today's world.[18] Approaches that address conflict and enslavement therefore should not entirely replace the current emphasis upon negotiation and accommodation, since a complex range of processes defined the discrepant experiences of various individuals and groups within the empire.[19]

I have provided an account that reacts against the idea that one coherent interpretation *could* provide an adequate explanation for the complex evidence. An alternative approach is to consider that our writings about social change should create a wider arena to accommodate debate and variable interpretations,[20] since dissent is an integral part of the dynamic that drives knowledge forward.[21] By adopting approaches to fieldwork and interpretation that reflect the evolving understandings of Empire and globalization, our studies of the world of classical Rome will continue to provide new and valuable insights into our present situation.

NOTES

1 THE PAST IN THE PRESENT

1 From 76 to 75 BC the symbol of the globe, reflecting 'universal' domination, appears on Republican Roman coins (Lintott 1981, 53; Nicolet 1991, 35–6). For the 'sphere of Billarus', its removal from Sinope to Rome, and the possible significance of this object, see Clarke (1999, 236–7). The persistent idea was that Rome had subjected the entire world to its rule, an image often symbolized through the globe or sphere (Hartog 2001, 192; Mattern 1999, 169 and Nicolet 1991, 35–41). In 29 BC Augustus arranged for an image of Victoria, carrying a wreath in her right hand and racing over the globe, to be placed on the new Curia within Rome, at which time the same image appeared on a variety of coins (Zanker 1988, 79, 81–2). An earlier statue of Octavian, which was in turn based on the one of Caesar, shows the leader with a foot propped up on a sphere explicitly symbolizing his *oikoumene* (sole power; Dio 43.14.6; see Zanker 1988, 40–1; for a rather different interpretation of this statue, see Nicolet 1991, 39–40). Classical ways of portraying the world were complex and flat maps may have provided a more common form of representation than spherical images (see Mattern 1999, 44–66; Nicolet 1991, 99–100).

2 Edwards and Woolf (2003, 3) discuss authors who, from the time of Cicero onward, drew upon the analogy.

3 See Edwards and Woolf's comments (*ibid.*) on the writings of Ovid, Aelius Aristides and Rutilius Namatianus and the equation of *urbs* and *orbis* through the mechanism of the extension of Roman citizenship across the empire.

4 Toner (2002, 14). It should be noted that, despite its rhetoric, the Roman empire failed to become truly global and it has been suggested that the failure of Rome to incorporate groups on the margins of imperial control into its power structure represents one of the reasons for the ending of imperial expansion (Groenmann-van Waateringe 1980; Hanson 2002 and Whittaker 1994, 85–91).

5 Tsing (2002 [2000], 457).

6 For a variety of perspectives see Featherstone (1995), Friedman (1994), Hardt and Negri (2000), Haugerud *et al.* (eds) (2000), Holton (1998), Inda and Rosaldo (eds) (2002), Legrain (2002), Petras and Veltmeyer (2001), Robertson (2003) and Tomlinson (1999).

7 Many accounts of globalization divide into those that argue that it is a positive force for good (e.g. Legrain 2002) and others that conceive it in a negative manner as an offshoot of Western imperialism (for example, Petras and Veltmeyer 2001).

8 Hingley (2003), Sturgeon (2000) and Witcher (2000) provide brief explorations of the issues behind this topic.

9 Sturgeon (2000, 663). For relevant accounts within anthropology and the human sciences in general, see Friedman (1994), Haugerud *et al.* (eds) (2000), Howes (ed.) (1996), Inda and Rosaldo (2002), Knauft (ed.) (2002), Miller (ed.) (1995) and Wilk (1995, 111). The value of various anthropological works upon globalization lies in the manner in which they approach the experiences of particular societies; by contrast much sociological analysis deals with very large-scale economic and political processes (for this general point, see Inda and Rosaldo 2002, 4). For comparable approaches to the ancient worlds, see Benton and Fear (2003), Clarke (1999, 39–40), Cooley (ed.) (2002), Hingley (2001a, 2003), Laurence (2001a), Parca (2001), Terrenato (2001a, 3) and Witcher (2000).

10 Hingley (2000, 112) provides further discussion of these issues.

11 Although it should be noted that some of the material considered below dates from the early second century and later. For the changes that occurred to imperial culture during this time, see Boyle (2003) and Dench (2003).

12 Sturgeon (2000) argues that approaches that address the East and West together are particularly valuable, but a thorough study of this type is beyond the scope of this work.

13 As observed by Cartledge (1998, 20), Harrison (2001, 1–5) and Toner (2002, 2).

14 Funari *et al.* (1999, 2), M. Johnson (1999, 150) and Moreland (2001a, 10).

15 Renfrew (1995, xvi).

16 For the (relatively) unquestioned status of classical texts in previous ages, see Farrell (2001), Kennedy (1992, 37), Stray (1998, 11–12) and Wyke and Biddiss (1999). For the ways in which archaeology has operated, see Beard and Henderson (1995, 44), Dyson (1995, 27), Small (1995, 1–3) and van Es (1983, 3).

17 Moreland (2001a, 10).

18 Funari *et al.* (1999, 2); for the origin of this concept see Storey (1999, 206).

19 Beard and Henderson (1995, 44).

20 The tendency of Roman archaeologists to categorize all ancient historians and linguists within a single amorphous group of classicists should be resisted. For a discussion of the relationship of classical and ancient history in Roman studies see Beard and Henderson (1995) and Toner (2002).

21 For postmodernity see Anderson (1998). For the development of theory within classics and ancient history, see Fowler (2000, 115), Galinsky (1992), Hardwick (2003), Harrison (2001), Heath (2002, 16–21), Morley (1999) and Toner (2002). Harrison (2001, 1–2), in particular, has reviewed the 'theory wars' in classics from a balanced perspective. See Kennedy (1992), Martindale (1993, xiii) and Morley (1999, 13–14) for more pessimistic reviews of the degree of influence of discussions of theory upon the study of ancient literature and classics, and Cartledge (1998) for some concerns about the influence of postmodern theory upon classics.

22 M. Johnson (1999a) provides a useful summary of the use of theory in archaeology, with a short summary of its adoption within Roman archaeology. See Barford (2002) for post-processualism and postmodernism. Dyson (1993; 1995) and Storey (1999) have focused in greater detail on the influence of theory upon Roman archaeology (see also papers in Small [ed.] 1995). Morris (1994a; 1994b) and Whitley (2001) have considered classical Greece. For a variety of other viewpoints upon theory and classical archaeology, see Renfrew (1995, xvii), Small (1999, 122), Snodgrass (1983, 148) and Spencer (1995). For the origins of the Theoretical Roman Archaeology Conference in England, see Scott (1993).

23 Hardwick (2000), Harrison (2001, 4), Heath (2002), Jenkins (1995) and Martindale (1993).

24 Cartledge (1998, 18) and Heath (2002, 11). For the origin of the idea of the canon see Parrinder (1999). Potter (1999, 33–5, 42) discusses the canonical status of classical literature. Martindale (1993, 25–36) considers the role of classical knowledge in the creation of images of 'the West'. Cartledge (1998, 17–8, 20) discusses canons and postmodern critique.
25 Martindale (1993, 19) and Morley (1999, 15) discuss the context.
26 Martindale (1993, 19). For a more detailed consideration of this argument, see page 7.
27 For a review of such work in ancient history see Morley (1999); for Roman studies, see Toner (2002); for the context see Jenkins (1995), Harrison (2001) and Golden and Toohey (1997a, 5).
28 Martindale (1993, 22).
29 Toner (2002, 14). Laurence (2001a, 99) and Terrenato (2001a, 87) also consider relevant issues.
30 Benton and Fear (2003, 268).
31 *Ibid.* Cartledge (1998, 28) makes comparable points about the potential of classical studies to become part of a general shift of intercultural studies towards the contested edges of cultures, nations and identities. *Arethusa* 36 (2003) contains studies that draw upon classical literature and material culture.
32 Ferrary (1994, 45) notes that the Roman empire effectively gave Europe a predetermined dominance over the Orient, since parts of the latter were conquered and incorporated by Rome. My comments have also been informed by Hall (2004, 24) and Vasunia's (2001) writings on the reception in the modern world of the ancient Greek plays which deal with issues relevant to the relationship between the East and the West.
33 Giddens (1984, 239).
34 Tomlinson (1999, 36).
35 Hardt and Negri (2000, 237–9), Saller (2002, 253) and Witcher (2000, 216). For the scale of the contemporary world system, see Appadurai (2002 [1996], 46–9) and Petras and Veltmeyer (2001).
36 Giddens (1984, 236).
37 Tomlinson (1999, 36).
38 *Ibid.*, 37.
39 *Ibid.*
40 See Laurence (2001a) and Woolf (2001a).
41 See Whittaker (1994). It is felt that the Roman administration did not have the facility to monitor and police the frontiers in a fully systematic manner (Campbell 2002, 16–18; Isaac 1990; Mattern 1999, 21–2; Whittaker 1994, 62–9).
42 Horden and Purcell (2000, 372).
43 Golden and Toohey (1997a, 1), Holton (1998), Konstan (1997) and Robertson (1992, 2003). See Frow (1997, 3–5) for the modernist creation of dualities and the problems this causes.
44 Holton (1998, 8) and Robertson (1992).
45 Holton (1998, 9) and Robertson (2003).
46 Golden and Toohey (1997a, 1).
47 Galinsky (1992, ix) and Golden and Toohey (1997b, 13–15).
48 Holton (1998, 9) and Friedman (1994).
49 For studies of the body, behaviour and architecture in classical Rome that draw in an explicit fashion upon the work of Michel Foucault and other contemporary scholars, see Fredrick (2003), Habinek (1997), Kilmer (1997) and Richlin (1997).
50 See Potter (1999, 152) for this concept.
51 Galinsky (1996). See Galinsky (1992, 74–92) for additional discussion.

52 For the general context of this work in the tradition of studies of Virgil, see Stahl (1998, xxvii–xxviii).
53 Galinsky (1996, ix).
54 *Ibid.*, 237.
55 *Ibid.*, 245.
56 *Ibid.*
57 Galinsky (1992, 74).
58 *Ibid.*
59 Heath (2002, 111–16). Morley (1999, 79–80) discusses some of the problems with such an approach.
60 Galinsky (1992, 74). For some recent works on reception, see for instance Beard and Henderson (1995) and the papers in Edwards (ed.) (1999) and Wyke and Biddiss (eds) (1999).
61 Galinsky (1996, 3).
62 Alföldy (1993), C. Wells (1972, vii–viii) and Galinsky (1996, 3) discuss the context of Syme's work. For recent reassessments of both Augustan culture and also Syme's contribution to the debate, see *La Révolution Romaine* (2000).
63 C. Wells (1972).
64 *Ibid.*, viii.
65 Galinsky (1992, 154–70) also provides an interpretation of the contribution of classical Roman to society in the USA.
66 Galinsky (1996, 5).
67 *Ibid.* and Galinsky (1992, 114 and 154–70).
68 Galinsky (1996, 6–7).
69 Stahl (1998, xxvii–xxvii).
70 Kennedy (1992, 37).
71 Isaac (1990, 1). For works of the early twentieth century that argued a comparable point of view, see comments in Woolf (1998, 4) and Hingley (2000, 41–52).
72 Isaac (1990, 1).
73 Stahl (1998, xx).
74 Kennedy (1992, 39–40) and Stahl (1998, xxvii). See Gregory (2004) for some of the connotations.
75 Potter (1999, 152).
76 Habinek (1998, 169).
77 For the value of classical cognitive models, see Kennedy (1992, 37–9). For the reuse of these in modern times, see Pagden (1995, 11–28), J. Richardson (1991, 1), Stray (1998) and Woolf (1997, 339; 2001b, 312).
78 Clarke (1999, 45, 192), Nippel (2002 [1996], 296–301) and Romm (1992, 215–22).
79 Kennedy (1992, 37–8).
80 For Britain and France in the nineteenth and early twentieth centuries, see Dondin-Payre (1991), Hingley (2000) and Mattingly (1996); for the contemporary situation, see Kennedy (1992).
81 Dondin-Payre (1991).
82 Betts (1971), Hingley (2000) and N. Vance (1997).
83 Mouritsen (1998).
84 Hardt and Negri (2000). See Balakrishnan (2003, xiii) for the suggestion about ancient genealogies.
85 Balakrishnan (ed.) (2003) and Passavant and Dean (eds) (2004) contain reviews of Hardt and Negri's work, while Rofel (2002) provides a critique of the work as a 'masculine fantasy'.

86 For the use made of Polybius by these authors, see Hardt and Negri (2000, 163, 314–16). For a consideration of Polybius' work, see Walbank (1979).
87 See C. Johnson (2004) for an analysis of the contemporary uses of imperial Rome in the USA. For other examples of the drawing of parallels from the classical world, see Alcock's (1993, xvii) discussion of the – at least superficial – conceptual parallel between ancient Greece and Rome on the one hand and modern Britain and the USA on the other, and Galinsky's account (1992, 53–73, 154) of decline and fall as a contemporary analogy. P. Richardson, in his book, *City and Sanctuary* (2002, 1), recalls lectures that he presented in Canada in the aftermath of 9/11, during which he drew a comparison between imperial Rome and the contemporary USA. He argues that this relationship should not be explored in too blunt a fashion, but evidently feels the comparison to be both relevant and interesting. Benton and Fear (2003, 268) also explore the significance of Roman studies in the context of globalization and the 'War on Terror'.
88 Gellner (1988, 11).
89 *Ibid.*
90 Harrison (2001, 8).
91 For the importance of being explicit about ideological agendas, see Harrison (2001, 8), Morley (1999, 94) and M. Johnson (1999a, 5–6).
92 For some uncertainty over this point, see Stahl (1998, xxviii).
93 Potter (1999, 154) and Raaflaub and Samons (1990).
94 Grafton (1992, 254).
95 Torelli (1995, 141).
96 Although Torelli also observes that documentation, archaeological and historical evidence are rarely studied together.
97 Beard and Henderson (1995, 55). Wallace-Hadrill (2000, 291) has made comparable comments about the role performed by archaeology in illuminating the degree of local diversity among the regions of Italy and the timing of the move towards the homogeneity of culture. See the comments of Alcock (1993, 5) about the role of archaeology in illuminating the ways of life of the non-elite.
98 M. Johnson (1999b); see also Moreland (2001a).
99 For discussions of the complex ways in which boundaries between archaeologists and ancient historians have been erected, see Curti (2001), Dench (2003), Dyson (1991), Torelli (1995, 141), Wallace-Hadrill (2000, 284–5, 289) and J. Williams (2001, 91–3).
100 Moreland (2001a, 77). For a critical discussion of the context, see Barrett (1997a, 1).
101 Barker (1991, 1), Cherry (1998, ix), Dyson (1993; 1995), Hingley (1989; 2000, 150–1) and M. Jones and Miles (1979). Funari *et al.* (1999, 12) make comparable comments about historical archaeology. A counter-argument, however, which is picked up below, is that much of the detailed work that is carried out by classical archaeologists, especially excavation, retains a focus upon the lives and monuments of the elite.
102 As observed, for instance, by Habinek and Schiesaro (1997, xvi), Laurence (1998a, 1), Small (1995, 1), Snodgrass (1983, 139) and J. Williams (2001).
103 M. Johnson (1999b, 31).
104 Snodgrass (1983, 142).
105 Parca (2001, 64). For the context of the survival of writing tablets and other perishable forms of text in the archaeological record, see Bowman and Woolf (1994, 5).
106 For the additional division within classical studies between papyrologists and epigraphists and the issues that the division entails, see Bodel (2001, 3).

107 See, for example, Bodel (2001, 3), Parca (2001, 64, 72), articles in Bowman and Woolf (eds) (1994) and Cooley (ed.) (2002).
108 Mattingly (1997a, 15), who is pursuing the idea of material culture as text. Dyson (1995, 39) and A. Gardner (2003, 1–2) discuss the complexity of the relationship between the material remains that are studied by archaeologists and various postmodern approaches to textual analysis.
109 Hingley (1997). See pages 36–7 for a study of the impact of archaeological discoveries upon knowledge of the classical past.
110 Mouritsen (1998, 174).
111 Clarke (1999, 3); see also Morley (1999, 142). Saller (2002, 257–8) applies some ideas that are derived from modern economic theory to the Roman economy as a way of 'making explicit the frame of reference', while Martins (2003) does much the same with regard to consumer theory and Roman villas.
112 Although Roman concepts of geography differ dramatically from contemporary map-based concepts. See Clarke (1999), Dilke (1985), R. Evans (2003), Purcell (1990, 8–9), Mattern (1999), Nicolet (1991) and Whittaker (1994, 12–30) for images of the world and the Roman mind.
113 Clarke (1999, 3, 338).
114 *Ibid*, 3–4; Morley (1999, 80–1).
115 For the relative absence of critical and self-reflective discussions of parallels between the ancient and contemporary world in the early twentieth century, see Freeman (1996, 23); for the comparable situation in the contemporary world, see Hingley (2003), Terrenato (in press) and Witcher (2000).
116 Galinsky (1992, ix–x).
117 Morley (1999, 94).
118 See Cartledge's (1998, 26) comments upon the 'liberating effect' of a comparative, interdisciplinary approach within classical studies.
119 Barrett (1997b, 58).
120 R. J. Evans (1997, 125), Galinsky (1992, ix), Moreland (2001a, 114) and Toner (2002, 36–7).
121 Morley (1999, 51–2).

2 CHANGING CONCEPTS OF ROMAN IDENTITY AND SOCIAL CHANGE

1 See Alcock (1997a, 1), Barrett (1997b, 51), Beltrán Lloris (1999, 132), Crawley Quinn (2003), Fear (1996, 275–6), Freeman (1993; 1997a, 28), Hingley (1995; 1996; 2000, 112), Laurence (2001a; 2001b), López Castro (1992, 161), Mattingly (2002), Merryweather and Prag (2003, 5), Trimble (2001) and Woolf (1998, 7; 2001a, 173).
2 M. Johnson (1999a, 167) and S. Jones (1997, 29–39, 129–34).
3 As, it should be noted, is the Roman empire itself (Barrett 1997b, 52). See Delanty's discussion of the meaning of 'Europe' (1995).
4 Including Romanisation, Romanization, romanisation and romanization (Alcock 1997a, 1). The use of the lower case 'r' perhaps sometimes focuses upon a more critical evaluation of the significance of the term than the use of the upper case letter. The variant Romanization will be used to refer to the use of the concept in past works, but I will adopt the author's version of the word in quoting from the works of others.
5 Mouritsen (1998, 60).
6 M. Johnson (1999a, 167).
7 Freeman (1993), Hingley (2000, 111) and Mouritsen (1998, 59).

8 Syme (1988 [1983], 64) quoted by Keay (2001, 122).
9 For the final two centuries BC in Italy, see David (1996, 1); for the Augustan and later empire, see MacMullen (2000).
10 Huskinson (2000a, 21) and Woolf (1997, 339; 1998, 54–67).
11 Desideri (1991), Hingley (1995; 2000), Laroui (1970, 47–9), Sheldon (1982, 102–3), Terrenato (1998a, 21) and Mattingly (1997a, 8).
12 Woolf (1997, 339).
13 Freeman (1997b), Goudineau (1998) and Mouritsen (1998).
14 Desideri (1991), Freeman (1996; 1997a; 1997b), Hingley (1995; 1996; 2000; 2001b), Laroui (1970, 47–9), López Castro (1992, 158), Mattingly (2002), Mouritsen (1998), Terrenato (1998a; 2001b) and Woolf (1998, 4–7).
15 Desideri (1991) and Hingley (2000).
16 Differences of opinion exist as to whether we now live in a post-colonial, or post-imperial world. Many argue that the current world system is no longer an imperial one (Hardt and Negri 2000), while others argue that imperialism never went away and has reared its head in powerful new ways in the past few years (see, for instance, Brennan 2003, 93; C. Johnson 2004; Petras and Veltmeyer 2001 and Said 2003, xiii–xvi). For the use of the concept of the 'just war' in the Roman world, see articles in Rich and Shipley (eds) (1993) and Webster (1995); for the idea in the contemporary world, see Hardt and Negri (2000, 12, 36–7) and Petras and Veltmeyer (2001).
17 See, for example, Alcock (ed.) (1997), Blagg and Millett (eds) (1990), Keay and Terrenato (eds) (2001) and Metzler *et al.* (eds) (1995). Dench (2003, 328) has, however, suggested, with regard to the Keay and Terrenato volume, that the results of what could have been an extremely useful exercise are undermined by the division of the book into three sections that reflect the usual divisions in the subject.
18 As argued by Keay and Terrenato (2001, x). For Italy and the Mediterranean core, see Mouritsen (1998) and Terrenato (1998a); for the significance of the north-western empire, see Mattingly (2002) and Woolf (2001c, 579).
19 David (1996, 2).
20 Giardina (1994), Häussler (2002), Terrenato (1998a, 21) and Wallace-Hadrill (2000, 294), for example, argue that considerable regional diversity of settlement and culture survived into the time of Augustus and beyond.
21 For a highly influential account of this approach, see Woolf (1998). This draws deeply upon earlier work, including that of Millett (1990a; 1990b).
22 Alcock (1993, 1–2; 1997b). See also articles in Alcock (ed.) (1997) and Hoff and Rotroff (eds) (1997).
23 Woolf (2001a, 173).
24 For criticisms of this position that also quote some examples of works that argue in this way, see Ball (2000, 7), Cherry (1998, vii), Crawley Quinn (2003, 8), and Laroui (1970, 47–9).
25 Hanson (1994, 149).
26 For reviews that take a variety of different perspective to Romanization, see Alcock (1997a; 2000; 2001), Barrett (1997a; 1997b), Beltrán Lloris (1999, 131–4), Blázquez (1989), Champion (ed.) (2004, 214–77), Cherry (1998, 75–100), Curchin (2004, 8–14), Curti *et al.* (1996, 181–8), Dench (2003), Derks (1998, 1–9), Desideri (1991), Freeman (1993; 1997a; 1997b), Hanson (1994; 1997), Hingley (1995; 1996; 2000, 4–5, 111–13), Keay and Terrenato (2001), Laurence (2001a), López Castro (1992, 161), Mattingly (2002), Merryweather and Prag (2003), Millett (1990a; 1990b), Musco Mendes (2000), Reece (1988, 1–12), P. Richardson (2002, 7–24), Savino (1999, 13–46), Slofstra (2002), van Es (1983),

Webster (1996; 1999; 2001), Whittaker (1995; 1997) and Woolf (1998, 4–7; 2001c).

27 See, for example, Bergemann (1998), Blázquez (1989), Blázquez and Alvar (eds) (1996), Brandt and Slofstra (eds) (1983), Delplace (1993), Hoff and Rotroff (eds) (1997), *La Romanisation du Samnium* (1991), Millett (1990a), Santos Yanguas (1991), Savino (1999), Torelli (1995) and Wood and Queiroga (eds) (1992). The volume edited by Metzler *et al.* (eds) (1995) derives from a conference titled 'The Romanization of the early Roman West'.

28 Haffner and von Schnurbein (eds) (2000).

29 See note 1.

30 Alcock (2000, 222).

31 Curchin (2004, 8).

32 Lomas (1995, 109).

33 See, for instance, Keay and Terrenato (2001, ix), MacMullen (2000, xi), Slofstra (2002, 17) and Terrenato (1998a, 20).

34 A comparable situation is apparent with those who conduct aid work in the modern world (K. Gardner and Lewis 1996; Iggers 1997), where social change has, for some, continued to be understood in terms of 'modernization', despite knowledge of the limitations of the concept (Iggers 1997, 143–4).

35 See for instance, Beltrán Lloris *et al.* (2000), Curchin (2004), *Digressus* (2003), Dondin-Payre and Raepsaet-Charlier (eds) (2001), Fentress (ed.) (2000), Gorges and Nogales Basarrate (eds) (2000), Keay and Terrenato (eds) (2001), Lee (2003), MacMullen (2000), Noelke (ed.) (2003) and Pollini (2002). Slofstra (2002) also argues for the continued use of the concept.

36 Barbanera (1998, 3–48), Barkan (1999), Greene (1995, 23) and Schnapp (1996, 57).

37 Barkan (1999) and Schnapp (1996).

38 Greene (1995, 30).

39 Betts (1971), Stray (1998) and Toner (2002, 2).

40 Dyson (1993, 195; 1998, 1).

41 Meskell (1999, 3). For the relationship of the East to the West, see Said's (2003 [1978]) seminal work.

42 Latouche (1996, 119–20). See also Parrinder (1999, 270–3), Shohat and Stam (1994, 13) and R. Williams (1981, 333–4).

43 For the ironic relationship, see Herrin (1987, 295); for post-war divisions, see R. Williams (1981, 334) and, for recent developments, Gross *et al.* (2002 [1996], 198–200).

44 Babic (2001) and Janik and Zawadzka (1996). For concepts of Europe in general, see Chakrabarty (2000, 3–23) and Pagden (2002).

45 Shohat and Stam (1994, 1).

46 A. Smith (1986, 180–1) and S. Jones and Graves-Brown (1996, 6).

47 See Kennedy's (1992, 38) discussion of classical literature and literary theory and Vasunia's (2003) account of Hellenism. See also articles in Edwards (ed.) (1999) and Hingley (ed.) (2001).

48 Barford (2002, 77) and Kristiansen (1996, 138).

49 Beard and Henderson (1995, 6).

50 *Ibid.*, 6–7.

51 *Ibid.*

52 *Ibid.*, 32. Such an approach sidelines other contributions to Western identity.

53 Dougherty (1993), Dyson (1995), Habinek (1998, 15–20), Morris (1994a), Turner (1981, 1989) and Vasunia (2003).

54 Farrell (2001, 28) and Toner (2002, 12). This theme is so common in Latin and later literature that Farrell (2001, 28) titles it 'the poverty topos'.

55 Morris (1994a; 1994b; 2000), although see Vasunia (2003) for the need for a fuller study of these issues within the archaeology of classical Greece.
56 Morris (1994b, 11) and Whitley (2001, 16).
57 For the appropriation of the Greek past, see Lowenthal (1988); for the significance of this to scholarship see Morris (1994b, 11). For particular studies, see Malkin (1998) and Vasunia (2001).
58 Edwards (1999, 2–3), Farrell (2001), Hingley (2001c), Potter (1999), Thompson (1971) and Wyke and Biddiss (1999) consider various aspects of this relationship.
59 Herrin (1987, 295) and Moreland (2001b).
60 Struck (2001, 94).
61 Terrenato (2001b, 74–5).
62 Desideri (1991) and Grafton (1992).
63 Mora (2001, 34).
64 The literature is vast, but for a few studies of architecture, literature and politics from the sixteenth century on, see Hingley (2000), Mora (2001), Pagden (1995), Too (1998a) and Struck (2001).
65 Farrell (2001) and Stray (1998). For the place of Latin, grammar and rhetoric in the medieval period, see articles in Lanham (ed.) (2002). For the uses of Latin by European elites since the Renaissance to create cultural dominance and ideas of Western identity, see Waquet (2001); for the nineteenth century, see Stray (1998).
66 For the USA, see Dyson (2001), Linderski (1984, 145–9), W. Vance (1989) and Chapter 1, note 87.
67 Bahrani (1999), Bernal (1987; 1994), Hingley (2000), Patterson (1997) and Vasunia (2003).
68 Amin (1989), Bernal (1987), Shohat and Stam (1994) and Patterson (1997, 22).
69 Shohat and Stam (1994, 2).
70 *Ibid.*
71 For the Near East, see Bahrani (1999); for Greece, see Said (2003 [1978], 55–8) and Vasunia (2003).
72 For contemporary American imperialism, see C. Johnson (2004).
73 Shohat and Stam (1994, 2).
74 Desideri (1991), Hingley (2000) and Majeed (1999).
75 Bahrani (1999), Bernal (1994) and Hingley (2001c, 15).
76 Morris (1994a; 1994b), van Dommelen (1997, 306) and Vasunia (2001; 2003). Martindale (1993, 25–36) considers the role of classical study in the definition of what it is to be 'Western' or 'European'.
77 Said (2003, xv–xvi) and Seth (2003, 47).
78 Kristiansen (1996, 138).
79 For Italy and the Mediterranean, see Curti (2001, 22), Curti *et al.* (1996), Mouritsen (1998) and Terrenato (2001b, 71); for the Near East, see Shahîd (1984, 157) and for north-western Europe, see Hingley (2001c, 8–9).
80 Malkin (1998) and Nippel (2002 [1996]).
81 Habinek (1998, 157), W. Jones (1971), Mattern (1999, 71–8), Nippel (2002 [1996]), Romm (1992), Shahîd (1984, 157), Shaw (1983) and Webster (1996).
82 Nippel (2002 [1996], 297).
83 Curti (2001, 22), Deletant (1998), Díaz-Andreu (1998, 201), Hingley (2001c, 9) and Ruiz Zapatero (1996, 179).
84 Clarke (2004) and Mattern (1999, 78).
85 Hingley (2001c, 9) and Patterson (1997, 94–102).
86 Smiles (1994, 26).
87 A. Smith (1986, 180).

88 For Viriatus, see Pastor Muñoz (2000; 2003); for Vercingetorix, see A. King (2001) and *Vercingetorix et Alésia* (1994); for Arminius, see Roerkohl (1992), Struck (2001) and P. Wells (2003); for Boudica, see Hingley and Unwin (in press) and Smiles (1994); for Civilis, see Hessing (2001).
89 Kristiansen (1996) and Rowlands (1987).
90 A variety of national and regional studies have explored the extent and character of these peoples. See, for example, Curti (2001, 22) for the Etruscans, Díaz-Andreu (1998) for the people of Iberia and Cunliffe (1991) for those of Britain.
91 For archaeology and nationalism, see Atkinson *et al.* (eds) (1996), Díaz-Andreu and Champion (eds) (1996) and Meskell (ed.) (1999).
92 A. Smith (1986, 180).
93 Deletant (1998), Díaz-Andreu (1998), Hingley (2001c), Hessing (2001), Struck (2001) and Ruiz Zapatero (1996, 180).
94 Härke (2000), Kristiansen (1996, 139), Struck (2001, 101) and Trigger (1984, 360).
95 Härke (2000, 16), S. Jones (1997, 2–3) and Díaz-Andreu (2001).
96 Clarke (2004, 50–1) explores the way that Tacitus in the *Agricola* portrays the ancient Britons as in some ways more Roman than the Romans themselves.
97 For example, for sixteenth-century England and the Dutch Republic see Mikalachki (1998, 4) and Hessing (2001); for late nineteenth- and early twentieth-century England and France, see Hingley (2001b) and Goudineau (1998).
98 Desideri (1991, 586) and Woolf (1997, 339).
99 For race relations, see Betts (1971); for decline and fall and frontiers, see Hingley (2000); for international politics, see Purnell (1978).
100 Hingley (2001b, 154).
101 Hingley (2000; 2001b).
102 Woolf (1998, 54–60). See further discussion on pages 62–3.
103 *Ibid.*, 57.
104 Bernal (1994, 119) and Hingley (2000, 162; 2001b, 154; 2001c).
105 Desideri (1991, 611–21).
106 Hingley (2001b, 156).
107 Desideri (1991).
108 Hingley (2001b, 153).
109 For civilizing missions, see Bernal (1994, 119), Desideri (1991, 586), Hingley (2000), López Castro (1992, 158), Mattingly (1996) and Sheldon (1982).
110 Bernal (1994, 119).
111 Hingley (2000).
112 Hingley (2001b).
113 Grafton (1992), Nippel (2002 [1996]), Patterson (1997, 94–102) and Shaw (1983).
114 Nippel (2002 [1996], 296–310) and Romm (1992, 215–22). Grafton (1992, 3) has studied the process by which, by the early seventeenth century, knowledge derived from colonial experience of the New World had 'burst' the bounds of the library.
115 Grafton (1992, 254).
116 Clarke (1999, 69–70), Helgerson (1992, 243), Malkin (1998), Olivier (1999, 177) and Piggott (1968, 128–9; 1989, 60–86).
117 Olivier (1999, 177) and Piggott (1989, 61). See MacCormack (2001) for the directly contrasting way that the Spanish conquerors used the Roman empire as an analogy for the Inca society that they encountered and destroyed during the sixteenth century.
118 For imperialism and racial definition, see Hardt and Negri (2000, 103); for colo-

nial definitions of 'otherness' and their perpetuation into the contemporary global world system, see Gupta and Ferguson ([1997] 2002).

119 Nippel (2002 [1996], 297).

120 Hingley (2000, 51) and Mattingly (1996, 56).

121 Hingley (2001b, 154).

122 Mattingly (1996, 51, 56), Quartermaine (1995), Segrè (1974, 3–18), Sheldon (1982, 102–3), M. Stone (1999, 217), van Dommelen (1997, 307) and Wyke (1999, 190).

123 Mattingly (1996).

124 Desideri (1991, 621). Gilkes and Miraj (2000), Manacorda and Tamassia (1985), M. Stone (1999) and Terrenato (2001b, 80).

125 Crawley Quinn (2003, 10) and Mattingly and Hitchner (1995, 169).

126 For examples of works that make such claims, see Mattingly (1996, 51–2, 56) and Sheldon (1982, 103). See van Dommelen (1997, 307) for J. Boardman's comparably colonial view of the context of Greek colonization in the Mediterranean.

127 Most notably by Bénabou (1976; 1978), but also by other writers, including Le Bohec (1989) and Mattingly (1996; 1997b).

128 Shahîd (1984, xxiii).

129 Ball (2000, 448).

130 Ball (2000, 447), Isaac (1990, 20), Mattingly (1996, 52) and Said (2003 [1978]). For the classical context of this type of perspective see Nippel (2002 [1996], 297).

131 Isaac (1990, 20–1) provides several examples of dismissive modern accounts, while Shahîd (1984, xxi, 157) and Isaac (1990, 21) consider the way that these have drawn upon ancient writings. Alston (1996) discusses the significant ways in which Roman writings differed from the works of writers of the nineteenth and twentieth centuries.

132 Cherry (1998, vii), Mattingly (1996), Shahîd (1984, xxiii) and van Dommelen (1997, 308).

133 For the impact of Rome upon the East, see references discussed by Mattingly (1996, 59) and Ball (2000, 444); and for influence passing in the opposite direction, see P. Richardson (2002, 21–2) and Shahîd (1984, 149). See further on pages 54–5.

134 Hingley (2001c).

135 Bernal (1994) and Hingley (2001c).

136 Alcock (1993, 3).

137 Frow (1997, 1–3).

138 See van Dommelen (1997) for the context.

139 See Featherstone (1995, 6, 10) and Tomlinson (1991, 26–7; 1999, 32–47).

140 Featherstone (1995, 7), Friedman (1994), Knauft (2002), Miller (1995) and Ritzer (1998). Knauft (2002) argues that an approach that allows for contrasting modernities in various contemporary cultures characterizes anthropological approaches in the early twenty first century. For a variety of contrasting views, see Knauft (ed.) (2002).

141 Featherstone (1995, 10).

142 This list, and the one on page 37, are modified from Ritzer (1998, 81–2). For consideration of the creation of binary oppositions between modernist and postmodern understandings, see Frow (1997, 16–17).

143 Mouritsen (1998, 23, 59), see also Linderski (1984); for the general context of Mommsen's work, see Demandt (1990) and Freeman (1997b, 30–1).

144 Demandt (1990, 287–8) and Linderski (1984, 134). See Barbanera (1998) and

Terrenato (1998a; 2001b) for fuller discussions of the history of the development of classical and Roman archaeology in Italy.
145 Mouritsen (1998, 23).
146 *Ibid.*, 11.
147 *Ibid.*, 8.
148 The fourth volume of the combined work of five volumes was never completed and published (Demandt 1990, 290). For the context of the fifth volume, see Freeman (1996, 31–2).
149 Mommsen (1886, 4).
150 *Ibid.*, 4–5.
151 See Demandt (1990, 288–9).
152 Forcey (1997, 16) and Hingley (2000, 113).
153 Mommsen (1886, 193).
154 Freeman (1993; 1997b) and Mouritsen (1998, 57–8).
155 Mouritsen (1998, 59–86), Horsfall (2001) and Terrenato (1998a, 20) consider the situation in Italian scholarship.
156 Mouritsen (1998, 24–6) and Terrenato (1998a; 2001b). For Italian unification and the role of Roman archaeology, see also Barbanera (1998, 49–118), Manacorda and Tamassia (1985), Moatti (1993, 122–43), Ridley (1992), M. Stone (1999) and Wyke (1999).
157 Quartermaine (1995), M. Stone (1999) and Gilkes and Miraj (2000).
158 Hingley (2000; 2001b) and Trigger (1984, 364).
159 Hingley (2000, 94–5).
160 Trigger (1984, 364).
161 Hingley (2000; 2001b).
162 Mommsen (1886).
163 Freeman (1997b) and Hingley (2000, 113–14).
164 See, for example, Freeman (1996; 1997b), Hingley (2000, 111–29), Laurence (1994a) and Webster (2001, 211).
165 It is also necessary to examine others of Haverfield's works to view how the theory operated.
166 Haverfield (1912, 9–10).
167 Haverfield (1911, xviii); see also Haverfield (1909, xii).
168 Haverfield (1915, 11).
169 Haverfield (1905 186).
170 Haverfield (1915, 20).
171 Haverfield (1905, 210–11).
172 *Ibid.*
173 Haverfield (1915, 20).
174 Haverfield (1915, 14, 20); see Hingley (2000, 120).
175 Haverfield (1905, 188).
176 See the comments of Majeed (1999, 105) on the writings of Bryce and Lucas; see also Hingley (2000, 50–1).
177 Haverfield (1905, 203).
178 Hingley (2000, 119).
179 Haverfield (1909, xii), my emphasis.
180 *Ibid.*
181 Webster (2001, 211).
182 *Ibid.*
183 Haverfield (1905, 210–11).
184 Webster (2001, 221).
185 See Jullian's *Histoire de La Gaule* (1929, 531–2).

186 Goudineau (1998, 7–32) and A. King (2001, 119–21).
187 Collingwood (1932); see Hingley (2000, 132) for a review.
188 Relevant works in Britain included those that were produced by S. S. Frere and A. L. F. Rivet (Hingley 2000, 131–49).
189 Terrenato (1998a, 21).
190 Lloyd (1991, 233) and Torelli (1995, 141).
191 Horsfall (2001, 39), Lloyd (1991, 233), Mouritsen (1998, 174) and Terrenato (1998a, 22–3).
192 Wightman (1975, 585).
193 See, for example, C. Thomas (ed.) (1966) for an early synthetic summary of excavation work in England and Bloemers *et al.* (1981) for the Netherlands. For the influence from the 1960s onwards of field survey on understandings of settlement systems in Italy, the Mediterranean, Iberia and parts of northern Europe, see the papers in the volume edited by Barker and Lloyd (eds) (1991) and Alcock (1993, 5–6, 33–48), Downs (2000, 197–8), Dyson (1991; 2003, 36–54), Greene (1986, 98–141), Mattingly (1997b, 126–30), Vallat (1987), van Dommelen (1993) and Wallace-Hadrill (2001, 106–10). Derks (1998, 4) provides a detailed discussion of the influence of excavation on ideas of Romanization in the Netherlands, while Wightman (1975, 584–5) considered developments in Britain and France in the 1960s and early 1970s. Hingley (2000, 149–52) contains an assessment of the development of settlement studies in Britain.
194 Dyson (2003, 53).
195 For instance, Brandt and Slofstra (eds) (1983), Burnham and Johnson (eds) (1979), M. Jones and Miles (1979), Millett (1990a; 1990b) and Terrenato (1998a, 22–3).
196 See, for instance, Alcock (1993, 221), Downs (2000), Giardina (1994), Lloyd (1991, 235), Terrenato (1998a; 2001b, 82–3), Vallat (1991, 11–12), van Dommelen (1993) and various papers in Keay and Terrenato (eds) (2001).
197 For a very important but somewhat neglected paper, see Sheldon (1982). This paper explores the power of the idea of acculturation in the context of Roman North Africa to solve the impasse created by the reverse stereotypes of Romanization and resistance.
198 A comparable approach to that adopted by Sheldon informed the papers in a survey of Romans and natives in the Low Countries that emerged the following year (Brandt and Slofstra (eds) 1983). For the more recent development of Romanization theory in the Netherlands, see Derks (1998, 4–8), Roymans (1996) and Slofstra (2002). For the initial adoption and subsequent partial rejection of these approaches to Romanization (*Romanisierung*) within the large-scale *Deutsche Forschungsgemeinschaft* project in Germany, see Krausse (2000, 1; 2001). For recent publications on this major project, see Haffner and von Schnurbein (eds) (2000) and Creighton and Wilson (eds) (1999, 35–124).
199 See, in particular, some of the papers in Burnham and Johnson (eds) (1979).
200 Featherstone (1995, 88); see also Patterson (1997). Galinsky (1992) contains a discussion of postmodernism and the classics, as do a variety of the works listed in Chapter 1, note 21.
201 Cartledge (1998, 24) and Woolf (1997, 340).
202 Knauft (2002, 24).
203 Morris (1994b, 41).
204 Examples include Hingley (1995; 1996; 2000), Mouritsen (1998), Terrenato (1998a; 2001b) and Webster (1995; 1996; 2001).
205 Hingley (2000). See also Woolf (2001c, 578).
206 See Hingley (1995).

207 Featherstone (1995, 87). See also Chakrabarty's (2000, 7–11) comments on historicism and imperialism.
208 Pollard (1968), Rist (1997) and Shanin (1997).
209 Veyne (1993, 344).
210 Shanin (1997, 66).
211 *Ibid.*
212 Hingley (2001b, 145).
213 Pollard (1968), Featherstone (1995, 87) and Rist (1997).
214 Hingley (2000, 144). For an account of progress and Victorian society, see Bowler (1989).
215 Featherstone (1995, 10).
216 'Essentialism' in Huskinson's terms (2000a, 10–11).
217 Including, for instance, modernization, Anglicization, Europeanization, Westernization and Americanization; see Featherstone (1995, 9) and Ritzer (1993; 1998).
218 The idea of 'McDonaldization' focuses upon more negative aspects of the modern world order that are often linked to the idea of cultural imperialism (Ritzer 1993; 1998; see also Brennan 2003 for the current global influence of the USA).
219 Terrenato (1998a, 20).
220 Haverfield (1909, xii; 1911, xix; 1912, 11).
221 Hingley (2000, 121–3) and Freeman (1996, 45–7).
222 Hingley (2000, 144).
223 Freeman (1993, 443) and Terrenato (1998a, 21).
224 Freeman (1993, 443).
225 For a parallel situation in the world of the recent past, see Chakrabarty (2000, 9).
226 Hingley (2000, 124; 2001b).
227 Hingley (2000, 9) and Stray (1998).
228 This trend roughly coincided with the publication of Dyson's influential article (1975).
229 Forcey (1997, 16–17), Sheldon (1982) and Webster (2001, 212).
230 See, for example, M. Jones and Miles (1979), Hingley (1989) and Reece (1980; 1988).
231 Most notably in the work of Bénabou (1976; 1978); see also Laroui (1970; 1977) and Leveau (1978).
232 Crawley Quinn (2003, 8), Mattingly (1996), Mattingly and Hitchner (1995; 170), Sheldon (1982) and van Dommelen (1997).
233 Butcher (2003, 16–17).
234 Forcey (1997, 16).
235 Webster (2001, 212).
236 For towns, see Reece (1980; 1988); for villas, see J. T. Smith (1978; 1997); for rural settlement, see Hingley (1989) and for ritual, see Scott (1991).
237 Reece (1988, 74).
238 Wightman (1975, 585).
239 Crawley Quinn (2003, 8), Mattingly and Hitchner (1995, 170) and van Dommelen (1997, 308); see also Butcher (2003, 17) and Whittaker (1995, 19–20).
240 See Curchin (2004, 9–10) for a discussion of the problems behind this type of approach.
241 Forcey (1997, 17), Sheldon (1982, 103–4) and Webster (2001, 212–13). Sheldon calls them 'reverse stereotypes' (1982, 103). Dougherty and Kurke (2003, 3) make comparable observations about attempts by Bernal and others to reinterpret the classical Greek past.

242 Woolf (1997, 340).
243 Hardt and Negri (2000, 44–5).
244 *Ibid.*; Gupta and Ferguson (2002 [1997], 75) and Knauft (2002, 25).
245 For semantic superiority, see Butcher (2003, 16).
246 For critiques of the perspective, see Thébert (1978) and Sheldon (1982, 103–4). Some accounts of the Roman empire contain assessments of the significance of Bénabou's work: see, for example, Blázquez's writings about Spain in the Roman period (1989, 99) and Février's (1990) work on the Maghreb. It has also been argued that one contemporary approach to indigenous development in Near Eastern archaeology mirrors this perspective (Butcher 2003, 16–17), but the work that is quoted (Ball 2000) actually takes a balanced, thoughtful, and consciously post-colonial, approach.
247 Mattingly provides an example (1996, 59–61); see also Mattingly and Hitchner (1995, 170).
248 Webster (2001, 212–13).
249 Millett (1990a, xv).
250 *Ibid.*
251 Brunt (1990 [1976], 268).
252 Hanson (1994, 149).
253 Whittaker (1995, 20).
254 See, for instance, the influence of Millett's account on some of the papers in the volumes edited by Hoff and Rotroff (eds) (1997), Keay and Terrenato (eds) (2001), Metzler *et al.* (eds) (1995) and Wood and Queiroga (eds) (1992). Downs has argued that many recent approaches build upon the results of field surveys to argue the 'multiple cultural and ethnic experiences' that occurred across the empire (2000, 198).
255 Hanson (1997, 67).
256 Millett (1990a; 1990b, 38).
257 Millett (1990b, 38).
258 See, for instance, Freeman (1993) and Hanson (1994).
259 Hingley (2000, 6–7, 142–3) and Webster (1996; 2001, 213–15).
260 Millett (1990b, 38).
261 *Ibid.*
262 Whittaker (1995, 155).
263 *Ibid.*, 149.
264 MacMullen (2000, 128, 137). See Pflaum (1973, 67) for the earlier example that MacMullen draws upon.
265 MacMullen (2000, 134).
266 *Ibid.*
267 For an earlier example, see Brunt's comments (1990 [1976], 268) on Roman culture as 'a world of thought and beauty and enjoyment'.
268 Hingley (2001b, 153).
269 Hingley (2001c, 11).
270 Curti *et al.* (1996, 181).
271 Hingley (2000, 143), James (2001a, 199) and Webster (2001, 216).
272 Hingley (2000, 148).
273 Freeman (1993).
274 See, for instance, Creighton (2000, 217), Freeman (1993), Hingley (1996) and Reece (1988, 6–7). In fact, the term *Romanitas* does not appear in Roman writings prior to the third century AD (Woolf 2001a, 183).
275 Freeman (1993).
276 *Ibid.*

277 *Ibid.*, 443
278 See Storey (1999, 207–12); see also articles in Alcock (ed.) (1997) and Keay and Terrenato (eds) (2001) for useful summaries.
279 Freeman (1993, 443).
280 *Ibid.*
281 See also Freeman's discussion of Spanish amphorae (1993).
282 Freeman (1993, 444).
283 See also Creighton (2000, 82).
284 Freeman (1993, 444).
285 See Willis (1995) and Cooper (1996) for the situation in Britain, while Roth (2003) considers Gaul and Italy.
286 Cooper (1996, 89) and Eckardt (2002, 27). For some potential problems with the continuing colonial aspects of this debate, see Hingley (1999, 143).
287 Hanson (1997, 67)
288 For modified forms of this view, see Hanson (1994; 1997), Häussler (1999), Whittaker (1995; 1997) and Woolf (1992a).
289 J. Williams (2001, 94).
290 *Ibid.*
291 In Millett's terms (1990a, xv).
292 Vallat (2001, 103). For some comparable developments in the humanities in general, see Knauft (2002, 3) and Tomlinson (1991, 143).
293 Hanson (1994, 49); see also Beltrán Lloris (1999, 131–2) and Dyson (2003, 88).
294 Beltrán Lloris (1999, 131–2) and Woolf (1992a, 352). Note that Fear, in a study of Rome and Baetica (1996, 16–17, 22), takes a directly contrary approach in order to argue that Rome had no strongly ideological conception of a civilizing mission. He places the explanation of the nineteenth-century imperial civilizing mission in the development of Christianity within Western society (*ibid.*, 23). Following the writings of Woolf (1998), a rather different approach has been taken in this work, one that aims to balance imperial direction and local adoption.
295 Beltrán Lloris (1999, 132–3) and Mattingly (1997a, 11). Beltrán Lloris (1999, 132) refers to the need to focus upon the political as well as the cultural aspects of Romanization.
296 Barrett (1997b, 52).
297 *Ibid.*
298 *Ibid.*, 58.
299 *Ibid.*
300 See Barrett's (1997a, 4) rather more general comments on Romanization, which I have adapted here.
301 Fredrick (2003, 204).
302 Curti (2001, 24) and James (2001a, 198); see also Veyne (1993, 354–9) for the violence of Roman conquest.
303 Whittaker (1995, 21).
304 Woolf (1997; 1998; 2001a).
305 It should be noted that Woolf remains unhappy with the use of the concept of 'Romanization' itself (1998, 4–7); see also Creighton (2000, 217).
306 Creighton (2000, 217) and Woolf (1997; 1998).
307 Woolf (1997)
308 *Ibid.*, 347.
309 *Ibid.*, 341.
310 *Ibid.*
311 Woolf (2001a, 179). See Sewell (1999, 56) for comparable comments.

312 Barrett (1997b, 52), including a quote from an earlier work by Haverfield.
313 Woolf (1997, 347).
314 Terrenato (1998a; 1998b; 2001c).
315 Downs (2000, 203–5). For Britain, see Creighton (2000) and James (2001a).
316 For example, Derks and Roymans (2002), James (2001a, 199–205) and Laurence (2001a; 2001b).
317 Hingley (2001a; 2003).
318 See Chapter 1, note 9.
319 See Balakrishnan's (2003, x) comments upon Hardt and Negri's book *Empire*.

3 ROMAN IMPERIALISM AND CULTURE

1 Including, Barrett (1997a; 1997b), Beltrán Lloris (1999), Elsner (1996), Galinsky (1996), James (2001a), Keay and Terrenato (2001), Terrenato (1998a; 1998b; 2001a; 2001b), Wallace-Hadrill (1997; 2000), Whittaker (1997), Woolf (1997; 1998; 2001a; 2001b) and Zanker (1988; 2000).
2 Barrett (1997a, 6). For the role of labour in the Roman world, see Brunt (1987).
3 For a general definition of the concept of the elite, see Shore (2002, 4). The Roman elite did not form a single undifferentiated group. Lendon (1997, 43–7) explores the network of various overlapping 'communities of honour' within Roman society, while Keay (2002, 582) has considered the argument against the idea of a single reified concept of the Roman elite (see also Hopkins 1983, 44). The concept of the elite will be used in a flexible manner in this book, to address various powerful groups across the empire.
4 Wallace-Hadrill (1997).
5 For some works that use these concepts see Alston (1996), Ando (2000), Beltrán Loris (1999), Desideri (1991), Elsner (1996), Galinsky (1996), Gruen (1990; 1996), Häussler (1999), Kennedy (1992), Mattingly (1997a, 10–11), Moatti (1997), Nicolet (1991), Roller (2001), Wallace-Hadrill (1989; 1997; 2000), Whittaker (1997), Woolf (1998; 2001a) and Zanker (1988; 2000).
6 Habinek (1998), see also Alston (1996), de Souza (1996) and Webster (1995; 1996). I will not address areas that have been discussed recently, including the way in which the imperial policy of Augustus was based on a projection of military vigour, expansionism, triumph and dominance (Gruen 1990, 416; Mattern 1999; Woolf 1993, 183), the ideological character of the idea of the *pax Romana* (Cornell 1993; Woolf 1993) and the development of geographical concepts of empire (Clarke 1999; R. Evans 2003; Nicolet 1991; Pomeroy 2003 and Woolf 2001b, 317–18).
7 See Vasunia (2001, 248) for comparable observations upon Alexander's conquest of Egypt.
8 Wallace-Hadrill (1997, 8).
9 For instance Galinsky (1996), Miles (2000), Roller (2001, 9), Wallace-Hadrill (1989; 1997), Whittaker (1997) and articles in Habinek and Schiesaro (eds) (1997). Dougherty and Kurke (2003, 1–2) apply the concept of culture to classical Greece. For the political context of the use of the term in the contemporary world, see Cartledge (1998).
10 Habinek and Schiesaro (1997, xx) and Wallace-Hadrill (2000).
11 For example, see Bauman (1999, x–xiii), Geertz (1973), Sewell (1999) and Miller (1985, 2–3).
12 For 'high culture' see Huskinson (2000a, 5).
13 Gellner (1983).
14 Díaz-Andreu (2001, 4819) and S. Jones (1997, 16–17).

15 S. Jones (1997, 16–17).
16 M. Johnson (1999a, 22) and Morris (2000, 20–1).
17 Miller (1985, 2–3).
18 *Ibid.*, 13.
19 Bauman (1999, xvii).
20 S. Jones (1997, 34).
21 Hingley (2000, 113–15) and Woolf (1997).
22 For relevant works, see Bauman (1999), Featherstone (1995) and Tomlinson (1999, 18).
23 Bauman (1999), Featherstone (1995) and Sewell (1999).
24 Howes (1996a, 2).
25 McCracken (1988, 71).
26 Howes (1996b, 156), Tomlinson (1999, 29) and M. P. Stone *et al.* (2000).
27 See Sewell's useful distinction (1999, 39) between culture as a theoretical category and culture as a concrete and bounded body of beliefs and practices.
28 Howes (1996b 156).
29 See Adam and Allan (eds) (1995) and Tomlinson (1991, 3–5; 1999, 18).
30 Tomlinson (1991, 5).
31 For symbolic representation, see Tomlinson (1999, 18); for signifying system, see Tomlinson (1991, 6).
32 Douglas and Isherwood (1996 [1979], 43).
33 *Ibid.*
34 *Ibid.*, 13–14 and Knauft (2002).
35 Featherstone (1995, 14).
36 Tomlinson (1991, 5).
37 Bauman (1999, xx).
38 *Ibid.*
39 *Ibid.*
40 *Ibid.*
41 Howes (1996b, 156).
42 Bauman (1999, xxix).
43 *Ibid.*, xxi.
44 Tomlinson (1991).
45 Inda and Rosaldo (2002, 10–12).
46 *Ibid.*, 11.
47 *Ibid.*, 12.
48 Shore (2002).
49 Dougherty and Kurke (2003, 11, 16) discuss subcultures and the application of the idea to the classical Greek past.
50 Sewell (1999, 56).
51 Fulford (1992), Greene (1986), Temin (2001), Wallace-Hadrill (2000, 309–12) and Woolf (1992b).
52 In addition to works in note 9, see Huskinson (2000a, 5) and Woolf (1998, 11–14) for detailed discussions of the value of culture in the context of Roman society and Woolf's updating of these ideas (2001a). Beltrán Lloris (1999, 131–2) considers how approaches to Roman culture can result in a lack of attention to the political factors behind Roman control of native societies.
53 For a recent review of the evidence for the ancient city of Rome, see Coulston and Dodge (eds) (2000) and for a collection of papers, see Edwards and Woolf (eds) (2003); for the variety of images that the city has provided, see Edwards (1996, (ed.) 1999) and Moatti (1993).

54 For the Italian peninsula see David (1996), Keaveney (1987), Pallottino (1991) and Torelli (1995).
55 Curti *et al.* (1996, 183).
56 Keay and Terrenato (2001, ix).
57 David (1996, 45).
58 Terrenato (1998a; 2001c).
59 Terrenato (2001a, 3); see also Wallace-Hadrill (2000, 311).
60 Berrendonner (2003) critiques Terrenato's model for the region of Volaterrae on the basis of a detailed study of the evidence of inscriptions. Mouritsen (1998, 42) discusses the way that such consensual models of the voluntary surrendering of authority draw upon nineteenth-century interpretations of the harmonious fusion of Italians into Romans. This suggests that we need to allow for greater force and less consensus (James 2001a, 198).
61 Terrenato (2001a, 5).
62 Terrenato (1998b, 113).
63 Wallace-Hadrill (2000, 311).
64 Terrenato (1998a, 20; 1998b, 112–13; 2001a, 5).
65 Terrenato (1998a, 26).
66 Wallace-Hadrill (2000, 311).
67 For material culture, see David (1996, 6, 109), Galinsky (1996, 332–63), Huskinson (2000b, 98–102), Wallace-Hadrill (1998) and Woolf (2001a, 183). For the incorporation and adaptation of Greek, native Italian and other ideas into Roman literature in Republican times, see Kraus (2000).
68 For discussions of the complexities and contradictions behind this simple term, see Curti *et al.* (1996, 181–8) and Wallace-Hadrill (1998). Bowersock (1990, 7) describes Hellenization as a combination of language, thought, mythology and images. As a flexible medium of expression, it was not necessarily antithetical to local adoption and adaptation.
69 David (1996, 109) and Farrell (2001, 28).
70 Wallace-Hadrill (1998, 85).
71 Keay and Terrenato (2001, ix) and Pallottino (1991, 160–1).
72 Keay and Terrenato (2001, ix).
73 Wallace-Hadrill (2000, 313).
74 Woolf (2001a, 183).
75 For the relative limitation of borrowings from the West, see Beltrán Lloris (1999, 133) and Woolf (2001a, 183).
76 Ball (2000, 7) and Shahîd (1984, 149).
77 Ball (2000, 449–50).
78 Beltrán Lloris (1999, 131–3).
79 Laurence (1998a, 2).
80 For Roman citizenship see Finley (1985), J. Gardner (1993), Hassall (1987), Nicolet (1993, 17–22) and Sherwin-White (1973); although see also the comments of Giardina (1993a, 6).
81 J. Gardner (1993).
82 *Ibid.*, 133. Indeed, we shall see that many citizens were not members of the 'upper order' of imperial society.
83 Laurence (1998a, 2).
84 Curti *et al.* (1996, 185), Keaveney (1987, 1), Laurence (1998b, 103–4) and Sherwin-White (1973).
85 Hassall (1987) and Sherwin-White (1973, 221).
86 For a brief review of the ways that citizenship could be awarded, see Hassall (1987, 693–6).

87 Campbell (2002, 22) and Rich (1993).
88 Campbell (2002, 25–9) and Haynes (2001). See Carrié (1993, 106–8) for a detailed discussion.
89 Campbell (2002, 34), Hassall (1987, 694) and Mattern (1999, 85).
90 Campbell (2002, 34).
91 Nicolet (1993, 19–20).
92 *Ibid.*
93 Huskinson (2000a, 6).
94 Giardina (1993a, 6).
95 For the dismissive views of the imperial elite to the soldiers of the empire, see Carrié (1993).
96 Nicolet (1993, 21–2).
97 For relevant works, see Galinsky (1996), Habinek and Shiesaro (eds) (1997), Wallace-Hadrill (1989; 1997; 2000), Woolf (1998; 2001a) and Zanker (1988).
98 Eder (1990), Habinek (1998, 140) and Wallace-Hadrill (1997, 12–13).
99 Wallace-Hadrill (1997, 20–1).
100 Hopkins (1978, 74–96).
101 Elsner (1996, 35).
102 Galinsky (1996, 6).
103 *Ibid.*, 363.
104 Kellum (1990, 276).
105 Ando (2000), Boyle (2003), Galinsky (1996) and Mattern (1999, 5).
106 Syme (1939).
107 Woolf (2001a, 175). See Wallace-Hadrill (1997, 3–8) for a fuller discussion of the concept.
108 Nicolet (1991) and Wallace-Hadrill (1997, 20–1).
109 Culham (1997) and Habinek (1997).
110 For Italy, Wallace-Hadrill (1997, 20; 2000, 292); for Gaul, see Woolf's 'experiment' (1995; 2001a) and also Whittaker (1997, 157–8). For the relatively slow change in the provinces prior to the period of Augustus, see Merryweather and Prag (2003) and Woolf (1995).
111 Galinsky (1996), Habinek and Schiesaro (eds) (1997) and Woolf (2001a). For literature, see Habinek (1998, 45), Hardie (2000), Kraus (2000) and L. Morgan (2000); for architecture and material culture, see Wallace-Hadrill (2000), Woolf (2001a) and Zanker (1988).
112 Galinsky (1996, 4).
113 Woolf (2001a, 175).
114 Galinsky (1996, ix). See Boyle and Dominik (eds) (2003) for recent accounts of the ways in which the Flavian emperors recreated Rome on the basis of what came before.
115 Roller (2001, 63).
116 Feeney (1992, 3) and Habinek and Schiesaro (1997, xxi). See Habinek's discussion of the exile poetry of the author Ovid (1998, 151–69) and also Woolf's (2001a) discussion of Gaul, including his thought-provoking ideas about *terra sigillata* (for which see page 101).
117 Lendon (1997, 38).
118 J. Williams (2001, 98). Boyle (2003, 37–40) considers the strong development of imperial knowledge, based upon mapping and conquest, during the Flavian period.
119 Shore (2002, 3).
120 *Ibid.*
121 See Alföldy's (1985, 147) model for society in the first two centuries of the

Roman empire. For discussions of the organization of the Roman elite, see Alföldy (1985) and Hopkins (1983, 44–5); see also Hope (2000), Huskinson (2000b, 95–7), Lendon (1997, 37, footnote 31), MacMullen (1974, 88–120), Mattern (1999, 14–17) and Roller (2001) for the character of the Roman ruling classes. The 'upper strata' in Alföldy (1985, Figure 1) include the *decuriones* of the local communities in addition to senators and equestrians.

122 For education, see Fantham (1996), Hopkins (1978, 76–80), T. Morgan (1998); for education and culture, see Huskinson (2000b, 114–16).

123 J. Adams (2003a, 185–8). The same author reviews the complexity of the uses to which Latin was put across the empire. It is important not to view Latin in simple terms as a national language, since this introduces concepts drawn from the role of languages in the formation of the modern nation-state (for this issue, see J. Adams 2003a, 185 and Cooley 2002, 12).

124 Atherton (1998), Corbeill (2001, 261–2) and Too (1998a; 1998b).

125 Too (1998b, 8).

126 Corbeill (2001, 283–4).

127 Atherton (1998, 217).

128 J. Adams (2003a, 193–4), Farrell (2001), Habinek (1998, 45), T. Morgan (1998, 74) and Potter (1999, 8). For alternative, less elite-focused contexts for the spread of Latin and writing, see Cooley (2002), Parca (2001) and discussion on pages 94–102.

129 Or 'discourse of domination' (Potter 1999, 152–4). Potter considers the complexity of Latin literature and stresses that people could opt out as well as in (*ibid.*, 154).

130 *Ibid.*, 8, 42, 154. Potter considers some alternative non-elite 'histories of Rome' that existed in classical times and the way that the elite discourse has dominated these (*ibid.*, 154–5). Culham (1997) concludes that the reforms of Augustus provided new opportunities for elite women in the Roman empire, although they constantly had to reassert their stake within Roman society. For further discussion of women and citizenship, see J. Gardner (1993, 85–109).

131 For the nature of the 'publication' of literature at this time, see Potter (1999, 29–35); for the formation of aristocratic behaviour, see Habinek (1998, 45), Jenkyns (1998, 655) and Roller (2001, 7).

132 Woolf (2001b, 315).

133 See the comments of Parca (2001, 57) on the preamble to Augustus' *Res Gestae* and the success of the ideology that these images projected.

134 Farrell (2001, 2–4) and Woolf (2001b, 315).

135 J. Adams (2003a, 195) has studied the evidence that suggests Latin became less exclusive from the mid-first century BC. At that time, he suggests that there was a change from a more formal to a less formal system of pronunciation (*ibid.*, 193–4). See also Hardie (1992; 2000), Kennedy (1992), L. Morgan (2000) and Taplin (2000, xxii) for the context of Augustan literature and its relationship to imperialism.

136 Galinsky (1996, 229).

137 Habinek (1998, 13–14) and Kennedy (1992).

138 Habinek (1998, 14).

139 *Ibid.*, 164; Jenkyns (1998) and Stahl (1998). For the complexity of the various readings of Virgil's work that are possible see, for instance, Hardie (1992), Powell (1992) and R. Thomas (2001).

140 Habinek (1998, 164). See also Roller (2001, 264–72), Habinek and Schiesaro (1997, xvii–xviii) and Wallace-Hadrill (1998, 85). L. Morgan (2000) discusses the crisis of the late Republic and the response of authors.

141 Farrell (2001, 1).
142 *Ibid.* See also Kraus's (2000, 27–8) comments on Livy's back-projection of an integrative function onto the Rome of Romulus.
143 Farrell (2001, 1).
144 Nippel (2002 [1996], 280–1).
145 For discussion of the Greek definition of their own identity and the image of the barbarian, see Eckstein (1995, 119), Hall (1989), Hartog (2001), Malkin (1998), Nippel (2002 [1996]), Shaw (1983) and Vasunia (2001). Nippel (2002 [1996]), Malkin (1998, xi) and others have stressed that Greek definitions of self and other were not as exclusive as has sometimes been argued, but has also explored the ways that such images hardened from the time of the wars with Persia.
146 See Clarke (2004), Dauge (1981), Ferris (2000), Habinek (1998, 157), Huskinson (2000a, 14–15), W. Jones (1971), Mattern (1999, 71–3), Romm (1992), Shaw (1983) and Webster (1995).
147 Woolf (1998, 60).
148 For the way in which Tacitus turned this image around in order to project *humanitas* onto various free 'barbarian' leaders in the West, see Clarke (2004).
149 For barbarians in sculpture and art, see Conte (1994), Ferris (2000, 3) and Gergel (2001).
150 Ferris (2000, 1).
151 For barbaric origins, see Mierse (1990, 320) and Ferris (2000, 44); for transformation, see Woolf (1998, 75–6.)
152 Woolf (1998, 59).
153 Clarke (1999, 214–15). Of course the Roman attitude to the barbarian was not simple or timeless. For the apparent hardening of Roman attitudes to barbarians from the first and second centuries AD onward, see Veyne (1993, 359–61), and for the use of the concept of the barbarian in civic rivalries, see Nippel (2002 [1996], 296).
154 Edwards (1996, 33–42) and L. Richardson (1992, 74.) A second example, a duplicate of the first, was maintained in the *area Capitolina* (Edwards 1996, 35–7; L. Richardson 1992, 74).
155 Edwards (1996, 32–42).
156 *Ibid.*, 37–9.
157 Clarke (2001, 106) and O'Gorman (1993, 146–9) examine relevant works of Tacitus.
158 O'Gorman (1993, 135).
159 Woolf (1998, 54–60). See also Moatti (1997, 95, 293–8) and Veyne (1993).
160 Woolf (1998, 55; 2001a, 183).
161 Ramage (1973, 143).
162 Veyne (1993, 343) and Woolf (1998, 54–60). Wallace-Hadrill (1997, 8) defines *humanitas* as the combination of education and the humane behaviour of a civilized man. Veyne (1993, 342) defines it as 'literary culture, the virtue of humanity, and the state of civilization'. This work contains a summary of the origins of the concept and its context within Roman society.
163 Giardina (1993a, 4).
164 Woolf (1998, 55); for the general context, see Habinek (1998, 45) and Farrell (2001, 2–6).
165 Wallace-Hadrill (1997, 8).
166 Roller (2001, 21).
167 *Ibid.*
168 Ando (2000, 68).

169 Roller (2001, 21).
170 Woolf (1998, 56–60).
171 *Ibid.*, 56–7. Woolf mentions Cicero and Vitruvius.
172 Woolf (1998, 57); see also Clarke (2004). These writers consider works by Caesar, Strabo, Tacitus and others.
173 Woolf (1998, 57–8).
174 See Woolf (2001a, 185) for a further discussion of the connotations.
175 Ferris (2000, 4).
176 Woolf (1998, 59).
177 *Ibid.*
178 Although, for the complexity of the situation, see Clarke (1999, 214–15) who explores the relationship between this transformative idea of Roman identity and the fixed territorial boundaries that were felt to define the margins between the empire and the barbarians.
179 Hope (2000, 134).
180 Veyne (1993, 342).
181 Woolf (1998, 59).
182 See Roller (2001, 281–4) for a discussion of the writings of Seneca.
183 Giardina (1993a, 8). According to Alföldy (1985, 147) the 'upper strata' of Roman society formed no more than 20,000 adult males, together with their wives and children. This forms no more than 1 per cent of the total population of the empire and, in addition, the top level of the elite was far more restricted than this.
184 Including the governing groups of the local cities that were not allocated a particular status within the empire and also the substantial military communities that developed on the northern frontiers of the empire from the time of Augustus onward.
185 Hope (2000, 134).
186 R. Evans (2003) and Hartog (2001, 194).
187 Fear (1996, 17–23). Woolf (1998, 57, 68–71) discussed relevant examples; see also Dueck (2000, 116) for the writings of Strabo.
188 Fear (1996, 23) and Millett (1990a, xv).
189 J. Williams (2001, 93).
190 Hingley (2000, 48–51). See above, page 26.
191 Hingley (2001a).
192 See, for example, Hanson (1997, 75).
193 R. Evans (2003, 275). Evans (*ibid.*) and Clarke (2001, 94–5, 105–6; 2004) note that in Tacitus' writings, Britannia formed a theatre for the opening up of alternative positive and critical perceptions of Roman imperialism, while O'Gorman (1993) applied a broadly comparable approach to Germany. For critical conceptions of Roman imperialism in classical literature, see also, for instance, Veyne (1993, 434).
194 R. Evans (2003, 266).
195 *Ibid.*, 267.
196 *Ibid.*, 269 and Woolf (1998, 68–71).
197 Quoted by R. Evans (2003, 268).
198 Clarke (2001, 103).
199 P. Wells (2003).
200 O'Gorman (1993, 137).
201 For the context of Dio's statement, see Carroll (2003, 28); for a review of previous suggestions that the area had not been settled, von Schnurbein (2003, 94).
202 Carroll (2003, 28) and von Schnurbein (2003) note the results from excavations

at Haltern, Anreppen and Waldgirmes, where a number of urban centres appear to have been under construction, a situation that may also have been occurring upon the lower Rhine (Carroll 2003, 28). For Haltern, see Kühlborn (2000, 30–2) and von Schnurbein (2003). For Waldgirmes, see Becker (2002), Becker and Rasbach (1998), Rasbach and Becker (2000) and von Schnurbein (2003). Note Fear's (1996, 13–27) rejection of the idea that Rome had a direct policy of promoting urban life in Iberia. His alternative suggestion, that deliberate encouragement of urban centres was part of an imperial desire to control unruly natives, is not counter to the type of explanation proposed here.

203 See Woolf (1998, 71) for a consideration of the Roman general Corbulo's later activities among the Frisians.
204 See Whittaker (1997, 143) for an alternative translation of this section.
205 For instance, Fear (1996, 17), Hanson (1994; 1997), MacMullen (2000, 135), Millett (1990a, xv), Whittaker (1995; 1997), J. Williams (2001, 94) and Woolf (1994).
206 J. Williams (2001, 94).
207 *Ibid.* See Lendon (1997, 194–222) for the relationship between governors and the governed.
208 J. Williams (2001, 94). See also Whittaker (1997, 156–7). Some of this shared experience and knowledge was actively derived from the reading of classical texts that formed a staple element in the education of the British ruling classes (Hingley 2000, 9–11).
209 Veyne (1993, 362–3).
210 Galinsky (1996, 133–4) and Woolf (1998, 57).
211 J. Williams (2002) and Woolf (1994, 93).
212 For education in Rome and the Roman provinces, see Fantham (1996, 3–4, 26), Huskinson (2000b, 114–16), T. Morgan (1998) and Woolf (2000a, 879).
213 T. Morgan (1998, 25–6).
214 J. Adams (2003b, 692), Balsdon (1979, 122), Fear (1996, 18–19) and Woolf (1998, 72–3).
215 J. Adams (2003b, 691–2).
216 T. Morgan (1998, 28–9).
217 J. Adams (2003a, 189), Balsdon (1979, 122), Derks and Roymans (2002, 101), Hanson (1997, 77), Noy (2000, 16) and Woolf (1998, 72–5; 2000b).
218 Hopkins (1978, 77).
219 Balsdon (1979, 122).
220 Woolf (1998, 72–4).
221 Habinek (1998, 45).
222 *Ibid.* See Woolf (1998, 126; 2000a) for the potential impact of some of this imperial literature on the new Gallo-Roman elite within Gaul and Cooley (ed.) (2002) for some provincial reactions to the spread of writing.
223 For a discussion of some of these issues, see Fantham (1996, 14–15).
224 Fantham (1996, 10) and Farrell (2001, 2–3).
225 R. Evans (2003, 267–8).
226 Habinek (1998, 45).
227 Woolf (2001a).
228 Braund (1984, 15) and Creighton (2000, 89–92).
229 Creighton (2000, 92).
230 Griffin (1991, 21), Woolf (2000b, 121). For example, see Ando (2000) and Noy (2000, 100–5).
231 Woolf (2000b, 121).
232 *Ibid.*, 70.
233 Griffin (1991, 22).

234 Woolf (2000b, 121).
235 Woolf (1998, 56–60).
236 Zanker (1987, 171), translated by Wallace-Hadrill (1989, 159).
237 Elsner (1996, 35).
238 I shall not address in detail whether it is realistic to suppose this degree of rationality and logic in constructing our approaches to Roman identity (see Isaac 1990, 5–6 and Mattern 1999, 21). While not feeling too constrained about the ways that we use ideas derived from works about the contemporary world, we need to keep a critical eye on the nature of the theories that we use. It is often argued that modern scholars attribute a degree of rationality, intentionality, complexity and sophistication to the Roman empire that is likely to be anachronistic. In classical studies there is no firm consensus about the uses to which such approaches should be put; some authors consider them to have direct value, while others feel that they introduce anachronistic thought. Much recent work on Roman imperialism articulates (whether in an explicit manner or not) ideas that derive from the works of Michel Foucault and Edward Said. The relevance to classical Rome of these works has been explored by a number of authors (including Ando 2000, 20; Fredrick 2003, 204; Golden and Toohey 1997a, 5–6; 1997b, 13–14; Habinek 1997, 43; Mattingly 1997a, 10–12; Vasunia 2003 and Webster 1996, 8). For the adoption of colonial discourse theory within classical studies, see Malkin (1998, xi), Vasunia (2001, 248; 2003) and Webster (1995; 1996).
239 Mattern (1999, 215) and Wallace-Hadrill (1989, 159).
240 Galinsky (1996, 121, 245).
241 See Raaflaub and Samons (1990) for opposition to Augustus, and Potter (1999, 152–4) for resistance in general.
242 Ando (2000, 48).
243 Brunt (1990 [1976], 268).
244 Millett (1990a; 1990b).
245 See J. Williams (2001) on northern Italy, Purcell (1990, 17–20) on Cisalpine Gaul and James (2001a) on Britain.
246 Woolf (2000a, 874).
247 See Huskinson (2000b, 107–8).
248 Barrett (1997a, 6).
249 See the use that Potter (1999, 9) makes of Foucault's concept of 'small narratives', the stories of those who were not fully bound in the grand narrative of the Western tradition.
250 Barrett (1997a, 6).
251 *Ibid.*, 7.

4 THE MATERIAL ELEMENTS OF ELITE CULTURE

1 Wallace-Hadrill (1998, 85).
2 MacMullen (2000, x).
3 Bonfante (2001, 5).
4 Literacy would include both knowledge of language and the concepts behind the Roman elite view of the world (Miles 2000, 48–50; Woolf 2000a, 875–6) and the material ways in which such culture was represented.
5 Woolf (1998, 171–2). Bric-à-brac includes, for example, decorated glass vessels, pottery and other highly portable material goods.
6 Howes (1996a), Miller (1987) and Schiffer (1999).
7 Examples considered below include Barringer and Flynn (eds) (1998), Douglas

and Isherwood (1996 [1979]), Haugerud *et al.* (eds) (2000), Howes (ed.) (1996), McCracken (1988) and Miller (1987).

8 Howes (1996a, 1).
9 Douglas and Isherwood (1996 [1979], 41).
10 Schiffer (1999, 6).
11 Graves-Brown (2000, 3), Miller (1987, 3) and Tomlinson (1999, 83).
12 Douglas and Isherwood (1996 [1979], 38).
13 *Ibid.*, 45; see also McCracken (1988) and Howes (1996a, 2).
14 Douglas and Isherwood (1996 [1979], 45).
15 Howes (1996a, 2).
16 Graves-Brown (2000).
17 Appadurai (1985) and Gosden and Marshall (1999).
18 Howes (1996a, 2).
19 Ando (2000, 209–11).
20 *Ibid.*, 210–11.
21 Favro (1996, 6–7).
22 *Ibid.*, 7 and Laurence (1994b).
23 See, for instance, Ando (2000), Bruun (1999), Fishwick (1999), C. King (1999), Levick (1999), MacMullen (2000), Woolf (2001a) and Zanker (1988).
24 For these concepts, see Wilk (1995, 118) and Woolf (1997).
25 Hope (2000, 132).
26 Woolf (1996).
27 Bonfante (2001, 3) and Farrell (2001, 2).
28 Huskinson (2000a, 7).
29 Hill (2001) and Woolf (2001a).
30 For consumption, see Meadows (1994; 1999) and Woolf (2001a); for 'public activities', Haüssler (1999), Laurence (1994b) and Whittaker (1997).
31 S. Stone (2001, 13).
32 Bonfante (2001, 5). For example, see Stout's (2001) discussion of jewellery.
33 For exceptions, see S. Stone (2001, 13).
34 S. Stone (2001).
35 Croom (2000), Hope (2000) and S. Stone (2001, 15).
36 S. Stone (2001, 13).
37 Croom (2000, 13) and S. Stone (2001, 21).
38 Croom (2000, 145).
39 S. Stone (2001, 15).
40 *Ibid.*
41 Croom (2000).
42 Whittaker (1997, 144–5).
43 Goudineau (1980, 66–7), Rives (2001, 118) and Woolf (2000b, 120).
44 Wallace-Hadrill (2000, 295); for a discussion of the history of the adoption of these ideas within Roman studies, see Laurence (1994b, 12–17). For a clear introduction to urbanism in the Roman empire, with an explanation of the different categories of Roman cities and some examples, see Nevett and Perkins (2000). For other relevant recent works on Roman urbanism, see Parkins and Smith (eds) (1998) and Fentress (ed.) (2000).
45 Hanson (1994, 154).
46 Mierse (1990, 312).
47 Burnham *et al.* (2001), Ward-Perkins (1970) and Woolf (1998, 117).
48 For a review of such sites in Gaul, see Woolf (1998, 107–12); for Britain, Burnham *et al.* (2001) and Laurence (1994a). Discussions of nucleated pre-Roman sites (castros) in north-west Iberia include Da Silva (1995), Peralta Labrador

(2003), Queiroga (2003) and additional references in Chapter 5, note 119. Some of the most impressive developments at the Iberian sites actually occur after the Roman conquest of these areas. Cherry (1998, 83) makes a comparable point about the pre-Roman urban sites of North Africa.

49 Ward-Perkins (1970).
50 Zanker (2000, 25).
51 Zanker (2000); see also Gargola (1995, 51–174). For recent accounts that suggest that Republican colonies were not all standardized in the way explored by Zanker, see, for example, Bispham (2000, 158) and Gargola (1995, 82). Bispham (2000, 158) suggests that the rigid pattern evident, to an extent, in colonies developed from the late third and early second centuries BC were recast in a much more formal manner under Augustus. Ideas of regularity in the early period may well, therefore, often project an anachronistic concept of order. For the colonies from Augustus on, see Campbell (2002, 100–4).
52 Zanker (2000).
53 *Ibid.*, 27–8. For the role of the senate in the setting up of colonies during the Republic, see Gargola (1995).
54 See Zanker's (2000, 27) fuller description.
55 *Ibid.* This regularity includes informative differences between individual sites, deriving from the particular circumstances of each community (Curti *et al.* 1996, 173).
56 Gargola (1995, 85, 111).
57 See Favro's discussion of Rome (1996, 8); Rykwert (1988) also discusses symbolic order and the Roman city.
58 Laurence (1999).
59 Curti (2001, 19), Purcell (1990) and Witcher (1998).
60 Purcell (1990, 16) and Zanker (2000).
61 Zanker (2000, 28–9).
62 Purcell (1990, 13).
63 Zanker (2000). See also the legally based definition of Roman urbanism in Fear (1996, 6–11), which also focuses upon public buildings and amenities.
64 Whittaker (1997, 144).
65 *Ibid.*, 145.
66 Zanker (2000).
67 Favro (1996, 3, 19) and Kellum (1990).
68 Nicolet (1991).
69 Elsner (1996).
70 Nicolet (1991, 9).
71 See Boyle (2003, 29–35) and Fredrick (2003) for the Flavian reconceptualization of the Augustan mapping of the city of Rome.
72 For Rome, see Zanker (1988, 307–33) and Favro (1996); for Italy and the empire see, for instance, Häussler (1999), Laurence (1994b), Wallace-Hadrill (2000) and Whittaker (1997, 145).
73 Rives (2001, 118).
74 Zanker (1988, 332). For Iberia, see the recent summary in Mierse (1999); for Gaul see Février *et al.* (1980) and Woolf (1998, 116–18); for Germany, see Carroll (2001; 2003); for Britain, see Millett (2001a) and Wacher (1995).
75 As exemplified by the examples at Luni and Aosta that are illustrated by Zanker (2000, Figures 3 and 4).
76 For the planning of streets, see Ward-Perkins (1970, 5–6); see Owens (1991) for an account of city planning and street systems in the Greek and Roman world; for the cities of the empire and street systems, see Fear (1996, 12) and Woolf (2000b, 123).

77 Häussler (1999, 3).
78 *Ibid.*
79 For the concept of the 'typical city', see Zanker (2000, 25).
80 Whittaker (1997, 145); also see Favro (1996).
81 Laurence (1994b, 20).
82 *Ibid.*
83 MacDonald (1986).
84 See Wallace-Hadrill (2000, 299–303) for a brief discussion of the complex history of the development and identity of public buildings.
85 MacDonald (1986).
86 *Ibid.*, 146.
87 *Ibid.*, 147.
88 Mierse (1990, 309).
89 Ando (2000, 40), Elsner (1996), MacMullen (2000, 129) and Nicolet (1991).
90 Ferguson (1987).
91 Fishwick (1999).
92 C. King (1999).
93 Whittaker (1997, 149).
94 MacMullen (2000, 131).
95 Ando (2000), Bodel (2001), Elsner (1996) and Woolf (1996).
96 Bodel (2001, 7). See Ando (2000, 96–8) and Rives (2001) for further discussion.
97 Woolf (1996).
98 MacMullen (1982), Prag (2002) and Woolf (1996).
99 Bodel (2001, 7).
100 Bodel (2001, 8), Prag (2002) and Woolf (1998, 81–2).
101 Orr (1983, 93).
102 Häussler (1999) and Whittaker (1997).
103 Haüssler (1999).
104 Rawson (1991 [1987], 510) and Whittaker (1997, 146).
105 Rawson (1991 [1987] and Zanker (2000, 38). See also page 69.
106 Woolf (2001a, 181).
107 Fagan (1999).
108 Purcell (1995) and Hingley (1997, 90).
109 Hingley (1997, 90–1) and Woolf (2000b, 123).
110 Alcock (2000, 224).
111 For the focus of this perspective upon monumentality, see Laurence (1994b, 20) and Zanker (2000, 25); for the general critique, Nevett and Perkins (2000, 217) and Millett (2001a, 64).
112 Alcock (2000, 224).
113 Millett (2001a, 60).
114 Morley (1997, 48) and Laurence (2001b, 89).
115 Woolf (1998, 116–17; 2000b, 123).
116 Hassall (1987, 687–9) discusses the *civitates* (or 'foreign' states) of the empire, while Drinkwater (1987) and Wacher (1987, 104) introduce the evidence for urban sites.
117 Burnham *et al.* (2001) and Woolf (1998, 117).
118 Hanson (1994, 154; 1997, 76), Laurence (2001b, 69) and Whittaker (1997, 154).
119 Woolf (2000b).
120 Whittaker (1997, 149–50) and Zanker (1988, 307–33).
121 For Tarraco see, Aquilué *et al.* (1999) and Ruiz de Arbulo Bayona (1998). For convenient summaries in English, see Keay (1995, 308–10; 1997,197–205; 2003, 175–9) and Mierse (1999, 141–9). For the recent discovery of a public bathhouse, see Remola and Ruiz de Arbulo (2002, 48–51).

122 For the Roman history of Iberia, see Keay (1988) and, for recent archaeological research, Keay (2003).
123 Keay (1997, 198).
124 Keay (2003, 175–6). The exact extent, form and development of this building complex will only emerge when further excavation is carried out. For discussions, see Aquilué *et al.* (1999, 31–2, 65–74), Mierse (1999, 146–7) and Ruestes i Bitrià (2001, 98–112). For pre-Roman occupation, see Miró (1998).
125 Aquilué *et al.* (1999, 65) and Ruestes i Bitrià (2001, 98).
126 See Fishwick (1983, 224–5) and Keay (2003, 176). Mierse (1999, 129–31) provides further discussion and references.
127 Keay (1995, 308).
128 Keay (1997, 200–1). For alternative interpretations of the sequence in this area, see Mierse (1999, 145–8) and other works listed in this work.
129 Aquilué *et al.* (1999, 65–74) and Ruestes i Bitrià (2001, 100, 102–5).
130 See Fishwick (1999, 102–12). Mierse (1999, 132, 135–49) also discusses this building in some detail.
131 Fishwick (1999, 105).
132 Keay (1997, 201). The evidence, however, appears far from clear.
133 *Ibid.*
134 Mierse (1999, 132).
135 Aquilué *et al.* (1999, 59–65), Fishwick (1983, 232) and Keay (1995, 308–9).
136 Keay (1997, 202). Two statues were found during the excavation (Aquilué *et al.* 1999, 60).
137 Aquilué *et al.* (1999, 33–40), Keay (1997, 202; 2003, 176) and Ruestes i Bitrià (2001, 112–22).
138 Keay (1997, 203).
139 Aquilué *et al.* (1999, 94–100).
140 For Rome, see Favro (1996); for Spain, see Keay (1995) and Mierse (1999, 128–72); for Gaul, see Goudineau *et al.* (1980).
141 See Keay (2003, 177) who gives the explanation that later nineteenth-century development of the lower part of the modern town has obliterated much of the evidence.
142 Keay (1997, 203–4).
143 *Ibid.*
144 Fishwick (1983; 1999) and Keay (1997, 198).
145 Mierse (1999, 133–4) discusses the evidence and also the diversity of the population at Tarraco, which is likely to have included the native elite, successful Italian immigrants and members of the governor's entourage.
146 See Mierse's comments (1999, 133) on the ways in which the community at Tarraco may have drawn upon the example of the people of Mytilene who petitioned Augustus while he was resident in Tarraco.
147 Keay (1995; 1997).
148 Niblett (2001). For some doubts about this suggestion, see Laurence (2001b, 88).
149 Niblett (2001, 60–3).
150 Niblett (1999, 408, 411).
151 Niblett (1999).
152 *Ibid.*, 411.
153 *Ibid.*, 413.
154 *Ibid.*, Figure 118.
155 *Ibid.*
156 Creighton (2000, 191, 196–7). For comparable suggestions that emperor worship in Iberia drew upon earlier native ideas of the worshipping or honouring

through dedication of powerful warriors and leaders, see Mierse (1999, 133) drawing upon the work of R. Étienne.

157 Gosden and Lock (2003, 79).

158 See Knauft (2002, 25) for a parallel situation in the contemporary world.

159 Ellis (2000).

160 *Ibid.*

161 Percival (1976, 14).

162 Terrenato (2001d, 5).

163 Ellis (2000, 11, 22–72), Hales (2003) and Percival (1976).

164 Terrenato (2001d, 18).

165 *Ibid.*

166 *Ibid.* Wallace-Hadrill (1998, 90–1) considers the Greek origins of elements of the form and decoration of Roman houses and also the way that these structures were reconfigured to represent key Roman values.

167 Terrenato (2001d, 28) and Ellis (2000, 37–40).

168 Wallace-Hadrill (1998, 90). For detailed discussions, see Hales (2003) and Wallace-Hadrill (1994, 4–5).

169 See the discussion of the connotations of Vitruvius' writings about domestic architecture in Hales (2003) and Wallace-Hadrill (1994, 10–1).

170 Purcell (1987).

171 Wallace-Hadrill (1994, 14). This account discusses the way that insecurity of identity inherent among the freedman and the *novus homo* caused them to draw upon the cultural language of the dominant class.

172 Hales (2003, 245).

173 Ellis (2000) and Wallace-Hadrill (2000, 309–12).

174 See Ellis's discussion (2000, 170–4) of *salutatio* and the dinner party; see also Wallace-Hadrill (1994).

175 Hales (2003, 193).

176 It is not clear how far the 'standard' development came to influence particular areas and provinces, since publications and summaries usually emphasize the more 'Roman' classes of monuments. Even detailed and well researched maps of the empire emphasize cities, forts and villas. Alcock *et al.* (2001, 455, 459–60) have explored the Barrington Atlas's categorization of 'significance' and the dangers of feeding 'a Eurocentric, colonialist view of the ancient world'. A comparable observation can be made about maps of provinces and regions that mark villas, cities, temples, forts and frontier works while ignoring the vast mass of rural settlements that occur in all contexts. The mapping of the empire and the individual provinces is a political undertaking (*ibid.*).

177 Ellis (2000, 73–113) considers some of these.

178 See, for example, the emphasis upon high-status housing in the recent works by Hales (2003) and Perring (2002).

179 Ellis (2000, 99–102) and Hingley (1989, 35–45).

180 For an example, see Hingley (1989), and Taylor (2001) for discussions of the evidence from Britain.

181 Ellis (2000, 89–103), Percival (1976, 51–105), J. T. Smith (1997) and Terrenato (2001d) consider some of this variation. Numerous accounts of housing and rural settlement in individual provinces exist, but almost all the discussion at an inter-provincial level has been of villas, with very little consideration of 'non-villa', 'native' or other forms of settlement.

5 FRAGMENTING IDENTITIES

1 van Driel-Murray (2002, 200). Rofel (2002) labels Hardt and Negri's work as an example of 'modernity's masculine fantasies' and many accounts of the Roman empire appear open to a similar critique. Gender critiques are relatively rare in Roman archaeology (for examples that address this issue, see Scott 1998 and van Driel-Murray 2002).
2 P. Richardson (2002, 17–18) has observed this division. For the general Romanization of the empire, see MacMullen (2000).
3 These suggestions reflect Tacitus' observations, in the *Agricola*, that Roman civilization incorporated servility, by building upon the idea that the civilizing process was an ideology propagated within the empire that deceived the Roman ruling classes more than it did anyone else (Woolf 1998, 246–7).
4 Downs (2000, 209). Other authors have argued similar points. Cherry suggests that in North Africa there was a world of 'unromanized' people, forming an area of research that has not received adequate study (1998, 79). See Hingley (1997) and Hingley and Miles (2001, 161–4) for comparable suggestions about Roman Britain.
5 Mouritsen (1998, 81, 174–5) feels that the process of cultural integration was complete 'in most areas' of Italy by the time of Augustus (*ibid.*, 81). Other authors appear less certain about the homogeneity of Augustan and later Italy (e.g. Pallottino 1991, 164; Terrenato 2001c).
6 Parca (2001, 57).
7 Hingley (2000; 2001c).
8 Cherry (1998, ix), Hingley (1989), Laroui (1970, 27), Lloyd (1991, 233) and Mattingly and Hitchner (1995, 170). For the long history of research into the villa, see Dyson (2003, 13–19).
9 Hingley (1997), Mattingly (1997b, 126) and Mattingly and Hitchner (1995, 170).
10 For example, Hope (2000, 142–6) and Lendon (1997, 89–90, 97). Freedmen are often felt to provide the best evidence for an upwardly mobile group, but MacMullen (1974, 101) has argued that, as these people may have been more common in Italy than elsewhere, our understanding may exaggerate the amount of social mobility.
11 Joshel (1992) discusses some of the problems with our sources for Roman social organization, including the focus on the elite for information about status and the ways in which this is based on a 'culture of exclusion' of the non-elite (*ibid.*, 5). Some writers have attacked the division drawn between the 'upper' and 'lower strata'. Haley (2003, 4–9) has suggested that imperial expansion created the context for a fairly substantial 'middle stratum' of people who profited from the opportunities of Roman imperialism by expanding agricultural production (see further on page 115).
12 Hingley (2000, 151).
13 *Ibid.*, 149–55.
14 For example, see Downs (2000) on Spain and individual articles on the Netherlands in Brandt and Slofstra (eds) (1983). For Germany, see Haffner and von Schnurbein (eds) (2000); for Britain, see James and Millett (eds) (2001).
15 For examples of provincial landscapes that do not appear to be dominated by cities/towns and villas, see the non-villa landscapes of the Lower Rhine Valley discussed by Derks and Roymans (2002) and Roymans (1995; 1996), the studies of mining landscapes in north-western Iberia (Sánchez-Palencia (ed.) 2000) and those of non-villa settlements in Britain (Hingley 1989, 95–100; 2004; Taylor 2001). For the complexity of the urban landscape in Britain, see Burnham *et al.* (2001) and Millett (2001a); other provinces have at least equally complex urban situations (e.g. Pérez Losada 2002).

16 Mattingly (1997a, 15).
17 James (2001a, 199) and Webster (2001, 209).
18 Mattingly (1997a, 13).
19 James (2001a, 200–1) has proposed that soldiers and also traders may have formed 'sub-cultures' within the empire. The higher ranks of the Roman army was filled by imperial aristocrats, but the common soldiers came from the 'lower strata'. It is often argued that these lower ranks became drawn into a Roman military culture (Campbell 2002, 32) – one that varied significantly from the culture of the elite (Carrié 1993, 126–7).
20 James (1999) and Campbell (2002, 36–46). For imperial awareness see Carrié (1993, 112).
21 Campbell (2002, 38) and James (1999, 16).
22 Campbell (2002, 45).
23 James (1999).
24 Bowman (1994a; 1994b). Although it should be noted that these do not indicate mass literacy among all ranks (J. Adams 2003a, 200; 2003b, 760; Bowman 1994a, 95–6; 1994b, 121; Carrié 1993, 128–9 and Woolf 2000a, 880). Despite this, the use of the language within the army is likely to have been significant to the spread of literacy (J. Adams 2003b, 761).
25 Bowman (1994b, 122).
26 Campbell (2002, 33, 45). See also Carrié (1993, 112), who draws upon Cassius Dio and other classical writers.
27 James (2001b, 95).
28 James (2001b), Campbell (2002, 94–6) and Carrié (1993, 109–10).
29 See Carrié (1993) and James (2001a, 197–200).
30 Campbell (2002, 33), Carrié (1993) and Hope (2000, 141). For the Roman army as 'the plebs of Rome in arms', see Lendon (1997, 237).
31 This heading is adapted from the title of a film in the *Star Wars* series but is also used by Ashcroft *et al.* (1989).
32 An approach to 'discrepant experiences' in the Roman empire has been explored by Mattingly (1997a), who draws upon a framework derived from Said (1993, 35–50). Various papers in Mattingly's edited volume (1997) and other works reviewed below explore the concept.
33 Ando (2000) and Miles (2000, 44–8).
34 In an area that now forms part of southern Netherlands, northern and western Belgium and the most northern part of the German Rhineland. See Derks (1998), Derks and Roymans (2002) and Roymans (1995; 1996). van Driel-Murray (2002, 204) discusses problems with the identification of the Batavians.
35 For the idea of the 'standard' development, see pages 89–90.
36 Derks (1998, 55–66) and Roymans (1995, 48).
37 Derks (1998, 64).
38 Derks and Roymans (2002, 88).
39 Roymans (1995, 48).
40 Derks (1998, 63–4) and Roymans (1995, 49–50).
41 Derks (1998, 64–5). van Driel-Murray (2002, 205) stresses the economic poverty of the region and the limited possibility for surplus accumulation.
42 Roymans (1995, 50–3).
43 *Ibid.*, 53.
44 Carroll (2003, 22).
45 Roymans (1995, 55–8) and Carroll (2001, 60–1; 2003, 28). See van Enckevort and Thijssen (2003, 64) for the limited evidence for integration of the Batavian elite into the urban structure of Nijmegen in the pre-Flavian era. After its

destruction in AD 69–70, the site was not rebuilt until the early second century AD (*ibid.*, 65). The Ubii, with their impressive city of Cologne, form an interesting contrast to the other tribes of this area (Carroll 2001, 61; 2003). See also Derks's (1998, 70) comparison of Nijmegen, Voorburg and Xantern to Tongres for the evidence of the apparent lack of native input into these tribal centres.

46 Carroll (2003, 22).
47 van Enckevort and Thijssen (2003, 60).
48 von Schnurbein (2003, 105) has recently reviewed the relationship of the Roman fort/town at Waldgirmes to the important neighbouring Iron Age *oppidum* at Dünsberg. Although the close relationship of the developing town to the pre-existing community requires further analysis (*ibid.*), it may indicate that an attempt was being made to use a native elite group to encourage the development of urban society.
49 van Enckevort and Thijssen (2003, 64).
50 Derks (1998, 228–30) and Derks and Roymans (2002). Some potential problems exist with this interpretation because we are uncertain about the exact function of seal boxes (*ibid.*, 90). Additionally, the information does not suggest that all areas of the empire that were subjected to auxiliary recruitment on a substantial scale developed widespread literacy (Hanson and Conolly 2002 discuss the need for further research).
51 For fighting skills, see Campbell (2002, 30); for the recruitment of Batavians, see Bowman (1994a, 26–7), Carroll (2001, 65), Derks (1998), Haynes (2001) and Roymans (1996).
52 Roymans (1995, 58). See also van Driel-Murray (2002, 200) for a more critical approach which stresses the asymmetrical nature of the relationship between Batavians and Romans and argues that 'ethnic soldiers' represented an aspect of imperial relations.
53 Bowman (1994a, 26–7).
54 Derks and Roymans (2002, 87–8) and Willems (1984, 236).
55 Derks and Roymans (2002, 94–7). These authors (*ibid.*, 99) discuss some potential biases in the recovery and recording of seal boxes, which they argue do not affect the overall picture that they describe.
56 *Ibid.*, 101.
57 Bowman (1994b, 112).
58 van Driel-Murray (2002, 207).
59 Bowman (1994a; 1994b) and Bowman and Thomas (1996). Although it should be noted that the evidence at Vindolanda is in the form of wooden writing-tablets rather than seal boxes.
60 Bowman (1994a, 88–96; 1994b, 116). For a similar observation relating to literacy in Egypt and Pompeii, see Woolf (2000a, 881).
61 Roymans (1995, 48). Some stylus tablets have also been found in this area (Derks and Roymans 2002, 97–9), although it should be noted that Vindolanda-style writing-tablets have not. See Bowman (1994a, 97) and Woolf (1994, 88) for the scale of literacy in pre-Roman Gaul.
62 Bowman (1994a, 97).
63 *Ibid.*, 97.
64 *Ibid.*
65 van Driel-Murray (2002, 213) suggests that his 'inflammatory name' symbolizes deep tensions at all levels of the Batavian community.
66 Roymans (1995, 60).
67 Derks and Roymans (2002, 102) and Roymans (1995, 55).

68 Cooley (2002, 9). See Creighton (2000, 173) for Latin as an elite language in early Roman Britain.
69 Derks and Roymans (2002, 101).
70 Note Bowman's (1994b, 123) comments on the attempts by a number of the authors of the Vindolanda letters to 'manipulate institutional power'. See also Derks and Roymans (2002, 101).
71 Derks and Roymans (2002, 100).
72 Derks and Roymans (2002, 102–3). The point about savings is taken from van Driel-Murray (2002, 211).
73 Bowman (1994b, 112).
74 Bowman (1994a, 15–16).
75 Bowman (1994b, 112).
76 Haynes (2001, 71).
77 van Driel-Murray (2002, 215).
78 J. Adams (2003b, 693, 687) and Woolf (2000a, 881–4).
79 Woolf (2000a, 884–5) reviews evidence from surviving archives and stamps and painted labels on pots and amphorae.
80 Marichal (1988). See also, J. Adams (2003b, 687–719).
81 Marichal (1988).
82 *Ibid.*, 56.
83 Parca (2001, 69–70) and Woolf (1998, 96) suggest that the languages are intermixed on the dockets, possibly indicating that there was no clear understanding of Latin among the Gallic potters. J. Adams (2003b, 693–719), however, defines these texts as the result of 'code-switching' rather than fusion. The importance of this issue is that the individuals using the dockets on which mixed language occurs, if involved in code-switching, were able to distinguish both languages as distinct (*ibid.*, 694) and this may suggest a rather greater knowledge of Latin on the part of the potters than previously suggested. For a general discussion of code-switching as a social strategy, see Myres-Scotton (1993); for other applications of code-switching to the evidence from the Roman empire, see J. Adams *et al.* (eds) (2002) and Wallace-Hadrill (1998, 83–6).
84 See Giardina (1993b) and Parker (1987, 635). Giardina (1993b, 257) draws a distinction between small-scale and large-scale commerce; the latter, in contrast to the former, was not characterized as a 'sordid' profession (see also, Purcell 1995, 157). Giardina also acknowledges the elite status of most of the written sources that address trade (1993b, 254). For the negative influence of classical literature on our understanding of the status of those involved in industry and trade, see Joshel (1992, 130).
85 J. Adams (2003b, 698).
86 *Ibid.*, 689. For a discussion of Roman commercial law, which provides some understanding of the potential need for record-keeping, see Paterson (1998, 153–4).
87 Greene (1986, 166–7) discusses the process by which high-quality pottery is likely to have been traded.
88 J. Adams (2003a, 189–90; 2003b, 705).
89 Perkins (2000, 203). For the relative unity of these Roman-period redwares across much of the empire, see Vickers (1994, 245). Woolf (2001a) has discussed provincial appropriations of the central style of these vessels.
90 Greene (1986, 159–62) and Hayes (1997, 41).
91 Hayes (1997, 41) and Woolf (1992b, 288).
92 Hayes (1997, 42).
93 Perkins (2000, 203).

94 Hayes (1997, 14).
95 Walker (1991, 62).
96 Hayes (1997, 42) and Walker (1991). For gold vessels, see Vickers (1994, 246).
97 Woolf (2001a, 179).
98 Woolf (1998, 187; 2001a, 179).
99 Woolf (2001a, 179).
100 *Ibid.* For a critical review of this perspective, see Beltrán Lloris (1999, 133).
101 J. Adams (2003a, 190; 2003b, 705). The stamps were often prominently displayed in the centre of the bowl or plate (Perkins 2000, 205).
102 As suggested by J. Adams (2003a, 189).
103 For example, see Hanson and Conolly's study (2002) of styli and their occurrence on apparently fairly low-status rural settlements within Britain.
104 Parca (2001, 63–70). See Bowman and Woolf (1994, 2–3) for the complexities of the character of language and literacy across the Roman empire.
105 Woolf (2000a, 875). Directly contrasting approaches to this topic exist in Britain. Hanson and Conolly (2002) have evaluated the evidence for writing on sites in Britain that leads them to argue that the reading and writing of Latin was widespread in society, including among people who lived on non-villa and native settlements. Evans's (2001, 33–4) study of graffiti as an indication of literacy in Roman Britain, suggests that writing was restricted mainly to the occupants of military and urban sites.
106 Woolf (2000a, 887).
107 Woolf (2002, 185). For the character of this education, see Corbeill (2001) and T. Morgan (1998, 34–9).
108 Corbeill (2001, 282–4) and Woolf (2000a, 887).
109 Farrell (2001, 37–9).
110 Parca (2001, 72).
111 Bowman and Woolf (1994, 14). A recent volume on the rhetoric of classical learning (Too and Livingstone (eds) 1998) seeks to show that the character of authority and power that is associated with classical learning is far more complex than had previously been realized, as a result of its broad dissemination (Too 1998b, 8).
112 Bowman and Woolf (1994, 14) also note the significant emphasis upon Greek and Roman within classics and the downplaying of the Carthaginians, Semites, Egyptians and others.
113 See Woolf (2002, 185), who defines various forms of Latin literacy, including 'military', 'monumental', 'commercial', 'élite' and even 'un-Roman'. Even such a nuanced approach simplifies the complex and varying contexts in which literacy was adopted.
114 Spitulnik (2002, 212) provides an ethnographic parallel that stresses the complexity of the situation.
115 Woolf (2002, 185).
116 For the idea of the 'standard' trajectory, see pages 89–90.
117 Mattingly (1997a, 15). For additional individual studies of particular 'aberrant' areas and classes of sites that are not explored in detail here, see, for example, Terrenato (1998b) on the Romanization of Volaterrae in Italy; Dyson (2000) and van Dommelen (2001) on Sardinia; Hingley (2004) on northern areas of Roman Britain; Hingley (1989, 128, 159–60) and Fincham (2002) on the fenlands of Britain; and Hingley (1989; 1997; 2000, 151–2) and Taylor (2001) on 'non-villa' settlements in Britain.
118 Millett (2001b).
119 For studies, see, for example, Carrocera (1995), Da Silva (1995), Fernández

Ochoa and Morillo Cerdán (1999), Peralta Labrador (2003), Queiroga (2003), Ríos González and García de Castro Valdés (1998), Sayas (1996) and Vilas and Fuentes (1996).

120 Da Silva (1995, 275) and Orejas and Sánchez-Palencia (2002, 591).

121 Millett (2001b, 167) quotes a number of sources.

122 *Ibid.*, 167–8. See Pérez Losada (1998; 2002) and Orejas and Sánchez-Palencia (2002, 590), who argue that a *civitas* system may actually have extended right across the north-west of Iberia. Some urban centres are emerging across this area that may have served the purpose of *civitas* capitals (Pérez Losada 1998; 2002). This suggestion does not, necessarily, undermine the centralized recruitment model that Millett (2001b) champions, since military recruitment and mining may still have been organized through the *conventus* capitals of the region (Orejas and Sánchez-Palencia 2002, 590), but there is an on-going debate over this issue.

123 Orejas and Sánchez-Palencia (2002, 591), Sánchez-Palencia (1995) and Sánchez-Palencia (ed.) (2000).

124 Orejas and Sánchez-Palencia (2002, 582) draw explicitly upon Mattingly's (1997a) use of 'discrepant experiences'.

125 Fernández Ochoa and Morillo Cerdán (1999, 58–61) and Orejas and Sánchez-Palencia (2002, 591).

126 Fernández-Posse (2000a; 2000b) and Fernández-Posse and Fernández Manzano (2000).

127 Ruiz *et al.* (2000).

128 Orejas and Sánchez-Palencia (2002, 590–1).

129 Fernández Ochoa and Morillo Cerdán (1999, 53–5, 76–8) and Sevillano Fuertes and Vidal Encinas (2000).

130 Orejas and Sánchez-Palencia (2002, 592) and Sastre and Orejas (2000).

131 Orejas and Sánchez-Palencia (2002, 594) and Sastre and Orejas (2000).

132 Millett (2001b, 168) suggests that the nature of taxation (in men rather than cash) formed one reason for the gradual change to settlement patterns in north-western Iberia and the lower Rhine.

133 See Dyson (1995, 39). A. Gardner (2003, 1–2) has shown the complexity of the relationship between material remains and various postmodern approaches to textual analysis.

134 Myres (2001, 3) and M. P. Stone *et al.* (2000).

135 Howes (1996a, 2).

136 See Cooper (1996), Freeman (1993), Hawthorne (1997; 1998), Martins (2003) and Woolf (1998, 169–205; 2001a).

137 Wallace-Hadrill (2000, 309–12) and Woolf (1998, 169–205; 2001a).

138 For writings about the nature of the Roman economy, see Andreau (2002 [1995]), de Blois and Rich (eds) (2002), Duncan-Jones (1994), Garnsey and Saller (1987, 43–63), Greene (1986), Harris (1991), Howgego (1994), Meikle (2002), Purcell (1995, 162–3), Saller (2002), Temin (2001), Whittaker (1985) and Woolf (1992b). For the Roman economy in the context of the ancient economy as a whole, see Parkins (1998) and Scheidel and von Reden (eds) (2002).

139 Whittaker (1985) discusses the idea of elite-directed agriculture, industry and trade. The elite benefited from trade and industry, but the actual work was carried out by the 'lower orders'.

140 See Woolf (1992b, 283). For the minimalist view, see Finley (1985); for the integrated economy model, see works by Carandini referenced by Woolf (1992b) and also Temin (2001). For comparable divisions in the discussion of coinage and taxation, see Ducan-Jones (1994), Hopkins (1980; 2002) and Howgego (1994, 20).

141 Andreau (2002 [1995], 35), Gerrard (2002) and Saller (2002, 257).
142 Horden and Purcell (2000, 374).
143 Temin (2001). Haley (2003,12) notes Temin's failure to deal with non-market forces in the supply of the city of Rome and the army, while de Blois *et al.* (2002, xiv) argue that he places too much emphasis upon integration.
144 Greene (1986, 170), Howgego (1994, 5), Paterson (1998) and Woolf (1992b). For the importation of olive oil and wine from the provinces to Rome, see Panella and Tchernia (2002 [1994]).
145 Greene (1986, 179–80). Laurence (1998c) has argued that the costs of transport by sea and land were more comparable than earlier accounts have suggested. The Roman army also had a major part in encouraging trade (Fulford 1992).
146 Greene (1986, 178) and Hopkins (1980; 2002). Paterson (1998, 158–9) focuses upon the literary evidence for the elite, but we shall see that the quantity of manufactured items on many rural settlements across various areas indicates the production of surplus and access to consumer goods by various non-elite groups.
147 Hopkins (2002, 219), Mattingly and Salmon (2001, 8), Saller (2002) and Woolf (2001d, 57).
148 For this consumer boom, see Woolf (1992b; 1998, 169–74). Woolf suggests that in the absence of detailed information for prices, archaeological evidence forms the best means for choosing between the alternative models that have been offered for the economy of the empire (1992b, 283).
149 For trade and traders, see Fulford (1992), Greene (1986), Haley (2003), Horden and Purcell (2000, 371–2), Parker (1987), Paterson (1998), Perkins (2000, 197–201), Temin (2001), Wallace-Hadrill (2000, 309–12) and Woolf (1992b; 1998, 171); for the movement of people, see Laurence (1999; 2001a; 2001b).
150 See O'Gorman's (1993, 141) comments on Tacitus' writings about the Germans and the amber trade. Giardina (1993b, 248–9) discusses the ways that some classical writers justified undertaking commerce at the ends of the earth.
151 Paterson (1998, 150–1). The relationship between supply and demand was, perhaps, one of the forces that held the Roman empire together (Perkins 2000, 198).
152 For consumer goods and the Roman elite, see Wallace-Hadrill (2000, 309–12) and Whittaker (1995). For the context of elite consumption in Roman Gaul, see Woolf (1998, 169–70). For a theoretical discussion of consumption in the Roman world drawn from a contemporary marketing perspective, see Martins (2003).
153 Horden and Purcell (2000, 108) and Woolf (1998, 170–2).
154 See Wallace-Hadrill's (2000, 309) comments on the occurrence of imported household goods in relatively modest houses in Pompeii and Woolf's (1998, 171–2) observations on the nature of consumption in Gaul. See pages 113–14 for the limits of this approach. In Britain, however, certain people who did not readily adopt Roman architectural forms and practices for their dwellings may have been relatively powerful and wealthy (Hingley 1989, 159–61).
155 See Woolf's comment (1998, 173–4) on the situation in Roman Gaul.
156 Paterson (1998, 155) discusses traders. See Haley (2003, 172–80) for a discussion of the potential for agriculture to create surplus.
157 See Laurence (2001a; 2001b) who draws upon Horden and Purcell (2000).
158 Laurence (2001a, 91). This work derives from Laurence's earlier studies of Pompeii (1994b) and the Roman roads of Italy (1999).
159 Laurence (2001a, 91). See Horden and Purcell (2000, 126, 128) for Roman roads.
160 Laurence (2001a, 91).

161 Häussler (2002, 69) and James (2001a). Giardina (1993b, 264–9) considers some of the evidence for ways in which merchants in the Roman world represented themselves and the complex relationship of these ideas to images of elite identity. Trade associations are widely attested in Mediterranean urban centres and such groups may have formed one of the ways in which fashions and ideas spread (MacMullen 1974, 73–8). Some of those who made money from trade and industry had their occupation stated upon burial monuments and other inscriptions (Giardina 1993b, 264–6; Joshel 1992; MacMullen 1974, 70–1 and Perkins 2000, 205–8), indicating, once again, the complexity of identity in the Roman world.
162 James (2001a, 203).
163 *Ibid.* Terrenato (in press) explores this issue in terms of a 'loss of identity', resulting from the development of empire, cities and trade.
164 Laurence (2001a; 2001b).
165 Wallace-Hadrill (2000, 309) and Woolf (1998, 171).
166 *Ibid.*
167 Dyson (2003, 105).
168 Laurence (2001a).
169 Some studies have gone even further to suggest that Roman cities shared with contemporary examples a character as providers of an 'infinite tissue of signifiers' whose meaning changed with the viewer's class, ethnicity and gender (see Fredrick 2003, 204 for problems). The value of such a postmodern perspective lies in the way that it helps to break down the concrete understandings provided by some traditional approaches.
170 Morley (1997, 44). The emphasis that has been placed above upon the creation of urban space is justified, however, by the scale of the construction of public buildings that show a strong commitment on the part of the ruling elite and the emperor (Jongman 2002, 45). The idea of connectivity should not cause us to ignore the monumentality of urban space.
171 Morley (1997, 44–5).
172 For the potential contribution of pottery to an understanding of the Roman economy and society, see Greene (1986, 156), Vickers (1994, 235) and Woolf (1992b). Wallace-Hadrill (2000, 311–12) has noted that the focus of archaeological study upon production (to which we might add distribution), and the lack of consideration of consumption, limit the value of the information. Some recent studies of pottery in consumption are starting to change our understanding (Hawthorne 1997; 1998 and Meadows 1994; 1999).
173 Hayes (1997, 44).
174 Hawthorne (1998, 165).
175 *Ibid.*, 166, Perkins (2000, 203) and MacMullen (2000, 128).
176 See Meadows (1994; 1999) for some of the connotations.
177 Willis (1998).
178 J. Williams (2002, 144).
179 *Ibid.*, 145.
180 *Ibid.*, 146.
181 Willis (1998, Table 1).
182 *Ibid.*, 86. A contrast is likely to exist between military sites, at which the soldiers would have been familiar with samian vessels, and rural settlements at which the pots would have appeared dramatically different.
183 Willis (1998, Table 3). Although, for certain rural sites with high proportions of samian, see *ibid.*, 109.
184 Steve Willis, pers. com.

185 Greene (2002).
186 Howes (1996a, 5) and Tomlinson (1999, 84).
187 Bauman (1999, xxi). Even Coca-Cola, the ubiquitous product of the twentieth-century global economy, has been adapted and reinterpreted in differing ways in various societies (Howes 1996a, 6).
188 Bauman (1999, xxi).
189 Holton (1998, 16).
190 Bauman (1999, xxi).
191 J. Evans (2001, 35) and Willis (1998, 115–16).
192 Willis (1998, 116).
193 *Ibid.*, Tables 1 and 3.
194 Hingley (2004, 337) and Main (1998, 409).
195 Willis (in Main 1998, 327). See Erdrich *et al.* (2000) for the trimming down of sherds at the site of Traprain Law (East Lothian, Scotland).
196 *Ibid.*, 331.
197 It can be noted, in addition, that if used as lamps at Fairy Knowe, these fragments of *terra sigillata* could have drawn upon new ideas about lighting as a means of structuring domestic space and time (Eckardt 2002, 27).
198 Greene (1986, 164–5). Gerrard (2002) discusses problems with the economic marketing model.
199 Hawthorne (1997; 1998) and Meadows (1994; 1999).
200 For example, J. Evans and Dickinson (2000) and J. Evans (2001).
201 Meadows (1999).
202 J. Evans and Dickinson (2000); see also, J. Evans (2001).
203 J. Evans (2001, 28).
204 *Ibid.*, 27.
205 *Ibid.*, 33.
206 Meadows (1999).
207 Cooper (1996, 89).
208 Laurence (2001a; 2001b).
209 Hingley (1989) discusses the gradual changes to architecture on non-villa and native settlements in Britain.
210 Hingley (1989, 3–4; 1997, 84) considers the situation in Britain. It is likely that a comparable state of affairs pertains elsewhere.
211 Hingley (1989).
212 Haley (2003, 171, 186), in a 'theoretical' discussion of the evidence, argues that all non-slaves in the province will have seen a general growth in their income from *c.* 25 BC to AD 170.
213 Haley (2003, 8), who notes some criticism of an earlier version of this suggestion.
214 Particularly the number of urban centres that were elevated to colonial status early in the history of Roman rule (Haley 2003, 69). For other significant forms of production, see *ibid.*, 91–108. See Caballos Rufino (2001) and Étienne and Mayet (2001) for recent reviews of elites and merchants in Iberia.
215 Haley (2003, 4), although it should be noted that Baetica was one of the most Roman and highly urbanized of the provinces (de Blois *et al.* 2002, xv). Woolf (2001d, 58) proposes that an 'intermediate section' of society in Gaul had access to *terra sigillata* and wine. For suggestions about the influence of large-scale olive oil production in North Africa upon native society, see Hitchner (2002 [1993]) and Mattingly (1997b, 134).
216 For example, Garnsey and Saller (1987, 43), Jongman (2002, 29–31), MacMullen's study (1974, 12–22) of the evidence from Egypt, and Whittaker (1993,

276). See also additional works cited by Haley (2003, 4). MacMullen (1974, 89) attacked approaches that attempted to define a 'Roman middle class' and to locate it in the industrial and commercial elements of the Roman population. He did allow for a numerical middle class defined by the aristocracies of small cities, but argued that these groups formed the upper strata in their own local settings (*ibid.*, 89–90). On the other hand, Andreau (2002 [1995], 46–7) has criticized attempts to characterize the status of traders on legal grounds alone, arguing that this detracts from an understanding of particular situations and also from the evolution of Roman society.

217 Downs (2000, 209).

218 *Ibid.*, 208–9; see also Fear (1996) for the native input into the urban centres that developed in Roman Baetica. Downs does note the existence of items of portable culture on these sites, especially *terra sigillata* and amphorae, but the pottery is locally produced and adopts local traits (2000, 209).

219 *Ibid.,* 209. Fear (1996, 227–69) provides a discussion of the continuation of native practices in town and country, stressing, in particular, the contrast between the upland areas to the north and west and the Guadalquivir Valley. In the former area, towns were few and did not conform to the criteria normally accepted to define classical cities. The urban centres of Mediterranean coastal areas of the province and the Guadalquivir valley, by contrast, demonstrated many features of Roman life, although they still retained elements of 'otherness' (*ibid.*, 267–8).

220 Downs (2000) acknowledges that in the valleys of the Guadalquivir river and its tributaries a Roman and urban landscape did develop.

221 As Downs's approach recognizes. Mattingly (1997b, 117) discusses the problems with the concept of North Africa as a 'landscape of opportunity'.

222 Hingley (1997).

223 See Hingley (1997; 1999) for some initial thoughts on such an approach.

224 This suggestion that a high proportion of the population of Roman Britain was poor is based upon opinion rather than any quantitative assessment of the available information. In fact such a quantitative assessment would have limited validity since the excavation agenda remains dominated by the urban centres, military sites and villas, despite the changing balance of attention since the 1960s (Hingley 2000, 151–2). For statements about the relatively un-Roman populations in Britain, see Esmonde Cleary (2001, 96), Hingley (1989) and Hingley and Miles (2001, 161–2).

225 For a discussion of the focus that has occurred upon 'Roman' identity, and on urban and military sites, and the relative lack of impact of Roman culture upon rural settlements, see Cherry (1998, 159) and Mattingly and Hitchner (1995) for North Africa, and Okun (1991) for Germania Superior. For the villa-based research strategies that characterized earlier work in Italy and the reaction that has occurred away from these approaches as a result of regional survey work, see van Dommelen (1993), drawing upon the work of Vallat (1987; 1991).

6 'BACK TO THE FUTURE'? EMPIRE AND ROME

1 *Back to the Future* is the title of a film, but has also been used by Seth (2003) in a review of Hardt and Negri's book *Empire* (2000).

2 Hardt and Negri (2000, 163, 314–16).

3 *Ibid.*, 197–8.

4 See page 47.

5 Woolf (1997; 2001a).

6 Woolf (1997, 341).
7 Wilk (1995; 1996) provides a useful recent account derived from consideration of a beauty pageant in Belize.
8 For discussion of this concept, see Wilk (1995; 1996).
9 Toner (2002, 14).
10 Balakrishnan (2003, xiii) and Terrenato (in press).
11 See Chapter 1, note 115.
12 Curti (2001, 24).
13 See, for example, Legrain (2002).
14 Brennan (2003, 98). This reflects the argument discussed above that 'nativist' perspectives in Roman archaeology elide feelings of imperial guilt (pages 45–6).
15 As Brennan's (2003) observations on Hardt and Negri's *Empire* indicate.
16 These observations are derived from Balakrishnan's (2003, x) comments about Hardt and Negri's approach to contemporary empire, but also appear to reflect the current situation in Roman studies.
17 van Driel-Murray (2002) and Webster (in press).
18 Said (2003, xx–xxi) shows how the extreme views that appear increasingly powerful on both sites of the East–West divide derive from earlier views of the relationship between the two.
19 Mattingly (1997b, 135).
20 See Terrenato (2001a, 2).
21 Heath (2002, 11) and Sewell (1999, 57).

REFERENCES

ANCIENT WORKS

Dio (Cassius Dio) *Dio's Roman History, IV*, with an English translation by E. Cary (1914), London: Loeb.
— *Dio's Roman History, VII*, with an English translation by E. Cary (1924), London: Loeb.
Martial (Marcus Valerius Martialis) *Martial Book XI: A Commentary*, edited by N. M. Kay (1985), Oxford: Duckworth.
Polybius *The Rise of the Roman Empire*, translated by I. Scott-Kilvert (1979), London: Penguin.
Tacitus (Publius Cornelius Tacitus) *Agricola and Germany*, translated with an introduction by A. R. Birley (1999), Oxford: Oxford University Press.
Virgil (Publius Vergilius Maro) *The Aeneid: A New Prose Translation*, translated with an introduction by D. West (1991), London: Penguin.

MODERN WORKS

Adam, B. and Allan, S. (eds) (1995) *Theorizing Culture: An Interdisciplinary Critique after Postmodernism*, London: UCL Press.
Adams, J. N. (2003a) '"*Romanitas*" and the Latin language', *Classics Quarterly* 53: 184–205.
— (2003b) *Bilingualism and the Latin Language*, Cambridge: Cambridge University Press.
Adams, J. N., Janse, M. and Swain, S. C. R. (eds) (2002) *Bilingualism in Ancient Society: Language, Contact and the Written Text*, Oxford: Oxford University Press.
Alcock, S. (1993) *Graecia Capta: The Landscapes of Roman Greece*, Cambridge: Cambridge University Press.
— (1997a) 'The problem of Romanization, the power of Athens', in M. C. Hoff and S. I. Rotroff (eds) *The Romanization of Athens*, Oxford: Oxbow.
— (1997b) 'Preface: east is east', in S. Alcock (ed.) *The Early Roman Empire in the East*, Oxford: Oxbow.
— (2000) 'Heroic myths, but not for our times', in E. Fentress (ed.) *Romanization and the City: Creation, Transformations, and Failures, Journal of Roman Archaeology*, Supplementary Series no. 38.
— (2001) 'Vulgar Romanization and the domination of the elites', in S. Keay and N. Terrenato (eds) *Italy and the West: Comparative Issues in Romanization*, Oxford: Oxbow.

— (ed.) (1997) *The Early Roman Empire in the East*, Oxford: Oxbow.

Alcock, S., Dey, H. and Parker, G. (2001) 'Sitting down with the *Barrington Atlas*', *Journal of Roman Archaeology* 14: 454–61.

Alföldy, G. (1985) *The Social History of Rome*, originally published in German, London: Croom Helm.

— (1993) 'Two principles: Augustus and Sir Ronald Syme', *Athenaeum* 81: 101–22.

Alston, R. (1996) 'Conquest by text: Juvenal and Plutarch on Egypt', in J. Webster and N. Cooper (eds) *Roman Imperialism: Post-colonial Perspectives*, Leicester Archaeological Monographs no. 3, Leicester: School of Archaeological Studies, University of Leicester.

Amin, S. (1989) *Eurocentricism*, New York: Monthly Review Press.

Anderson, P. (1998) *The Origins of Postmodernity*, London: Verso.

Ando, C. (2000) *Imperial Ideology and Provincial Loyalty in the Roman Empire*, London: University of California Press.

Andreau, J. (2002 [1995]) 'Twenty years after Moses I. Finley's *The Ancient Economy*', in W. Scheidel and S. von Reden (eds) *The Ancient Economy*, Edinburgh: Edinburgh University Press.

Appadurai, A. (1985) 'Introduction: commodities and the politics of value', in A. Appadurai (ed.) *The Social Life of Things: Commodities in Cultural Perspective*, Cambridge: Cambridge University Press.

— (2002 [1996]) 'Disjuncture and difference in the global cultural economy', in J. X. Inda and R. Rosaldo (eds) *The Anthropology of Globalization: A Reader*, Oxford: Blackwell.

Aquilué, X., Dupré, X., Massó, J. and Ruiz de Arbulo, J. (1999) *Tàrraco: Guies del Museu d'Arqueologia de Catalunya*, Tarragona: Museu d'Arqueologia de Catalunya.

Arethusa (2003) *Centre and Periphery in the Roman World*, *Arethusa*, 36. 3.

Ashcroft, B., Griffiths, G. and Tiffin, H. (1989) *The Empire Writes Back: Theory and Practice in Post-colonial Literatures*, London: Routledge.

Atherton, C. (1998) 'Children, animals, slaves and grammar', in Y. L. Too and N. Livingstone (eds) *Pedagogy and Power: Rhetorics of Classical Learning*, Cambridge: Cambridge University Press.

Atkinson, J. A., Banks, I. and O'Sullivan, J. (eds) (1996) *Nationalism and Archaeology*, Glasgow: Scottish Archaeological Forum.

Babic, S. (2001) 'Janus on the bridge: a Balkan attitude towards ancient Rome', in R. Hingley (ed.) *Images of Rome: Perceptions of Ancient Rome in Europe and the United States of America in the Modern Age*, *Journal of Roman Archaeology*, Supplementary Series no. 44.

Bahrani, Z. (1999) 'Conjuring Mesopotamia: imaginative geography and a world past', in L. Meskell (ed.) *Archaeology Under Fire: Nationalism, Politics and Heritage in the Eastern Mediterranean and Middle East*, London, Routledge.

Balakrishnan, G. (2003) 'Introduction', in G. Balakrishnan (ed.) *Debating Empire*, London: Verso.

— (ed.) (2003) *Debating Empire*, London: Verso.

Ball, W. (2000) *Rome in the East: The Transformation of an Empire*, London: Routledge.

Balsdon, D. J. (1979) *Romans and Aliens*, London: Duckworth.

Barbanera, M. (1998) *L'archeologia degli italiani: storia, metodi e orientamenti dell'archeologia classica in Italia*, Rome: Editori Riuniti.

Barford, P. M. (2002) 'East is east and west is west? Power and paradigm in European archaeology', in P. F. Biehl, A. Gramsch and A. Marciniak (eds) *Archäologien Europas/Archaeologies of Europe*, Berlin: Waxmann: 77–97.

Barkan, L. (1999) *Unearthing the Past: Archaeology and Aesthetics in the Making of Renaissance Culture*, London: Yale University Press.

Barker, G. (1991) 'Approaches to archaeological survey', in G. Barker and J. Lloyd (eds) *Roman Landscapes: Archaeological Survey in the Mediterranean Region*, London: The British School at Rome, Archaeological Monographs.

Barker, G. and Lloyd, J. (eds) (1991) *Roman Landscapes: Archaeological Survey in the Mediterranean Region*, London: The British School at Rome, Archaeological Monographs.

Barrett, J. (1997a) 'Theorising Roman archaeology', in K. Meadows, C. Lemke and J. Heron (eds) *TRAC 1996: Proceedings of the Sixth Annual Theoretical Archaeology Conference Sheffield 1996*, Oxford: Oxbow.

— (1997b) 'Romanization: a critical comment', in D. J. Mattingly (ed.) *Dialogues in Roman Imperialism: Power, Discourse, and Discrepant Experiences in the Roman Empire*, *Journal of Roman Archaeology*, Supplementary Series, no. 23.

Barringer, T. and Flynn, T. (eds) (1998) *Colonialism and the Object: Empire, Material Culture and the Museum*, London: Routledge.

Bauman, Z. (1999) *Culture as Praxis*, London: Sage.

Beard, M. and Henderson, J. (1995) *Classics: A Very Short Introduction*, Oxford: Oxford University Press.

Becker, A. (2002) 'Die Ausgrabungen in Lahnau-Waldgirmes', in P. Freeman, J. Bennett, Z. T. Fiema and B. Hoffmann (eds) *Limes XVIII: Proceedings of the XVIIIth International Congress of Roman Frontier Studies held in Amman, Jordan (September 2000): vol. 1*, BAR International Series no. 1084, Oxford: British Archaeological Reports.

Becker, A. and Rasbach, G. (1998) 'Der spätaugusteische Stützpunkt Lahnau-Waldgirmes: Vorbericht über die Ausgrabungen 1996–1997', *Germania* 76: 673–92.

Beltrán Lloris, F. (1999) 'Writing, language and society: Iberians, Celts and Romans in Northeastern Spain in the 2nd and 1st centuries BC', *Bulletin of the Institute of Classical Studies* 43: 131–51.

Beltrán Lloris, F., Martín-Bueno, M. and Pina Polo, F. (2000) *Roma en la Cuenca Media del Ebro: La Romanización en Aragón*, Zaragoza: Colección 'Mariano de Pano y Ruata'.

Bénabou, M. (1976) *La résistance africaine à la romanisation*, Paris: François Maspero.

— (1978) 'Les Romains ont-ils conquis l'Afrique?', *Annales: Économies, Sociétés, Civilisations* 33: 83–8.

Benton, C. and Fear, T. (2003) 'Introduction: from Rome to Buffalo', *Arethusa* 36: 267–70.

Bergemann, J. (1998) *Die römische Kolonie von Butrint und die Romanisierung Griechenlands*, Munich: Pfeil.

Bernal, M. (1987) *Black Athena: The Afroasiatic Roots of Classical Civilisation, vol. 1*, London: Free Association Press.

— (1994) 'The image of Ancient Greece as a tool for colonialism and European hegemony', in G. Bond and A. Gilliam (eds) *Social Construction of the Past: Representations as Power*, London: Routledge.

Berrendonner, C. (2003) 'La romanisation de Volterra: "a case of mostly negotiated incorporation, that leaves the basic social and cultural structure intact"', *Digressus: The Internet Journal for the Classical World* 3: 46–59 <http://www.nottingham.ac.uk/classics/digressus/romaniz.html>.

Betts, R. F. (1971) 'The allusion to Rome in British imperial thought of the late nineteenth and early twentieth centuries', *Victorian Studies* 15: 149–59.
Bispham, E. (2000) 'Mimic? A case study in early Roman colonisation', in E. Herring and K. Lomas (eds) *The Emergence of State Identities in Italy in the First Millennium BC*, Accordia Specialist Studies in Italy, no. 8, London: Accordia Research Institute.
Blagg, T. and Millett, M. (eds) (1990) *The Early Roman Empire in the West*, Oxford: Oxbow.
Blázquez, J. M. (1989) *Nuevos Estudios sobre la Romanización*, Madrid: Ediciones Istmo.
Blázquez, J. M. and Alvar, J. (eds) (1996) *La Romanización en Occidente*, Madrid: Actas Editorial.
Bloemers, J. H. F., Louwe Kooijmans, L. P. and Sarfatij, H. (1981) *Verleden Land: archeologische opgravingen in Nederland*, Amsterdam: Meulenhoff Informatief.
Bodel, J. (2001) 'Epigraphy and the ancient historian', in J. Bodel (ed.) *Epigraphic Evidence: Ancient History from Inscriptions*, London: Routledge.
Bonfante, L. (2001) 'Introduction', in J. L. Sebesta and L. Bonfante (eds) *The World of Roman Costume*, London: University of Wisconsin Press.
Bowersock, G. W. (1990) *Hellenism in Late Antiquity*, Ann Arbor: University of Michigan Press.
Bowler, P. J. (1989) *The Invention of Progress: The Victorians and the Past*, Oxford: Blackwell.
Bowman, A. (1994a) *Life and Letters on the Roman Frontier*, London: British Museum Press.
— (1994b) 'The Roman imperial army: letters and literacy on the northern frontier', in A. Bowman and G. Woolf (eds) *Literacy and Power in the Ancient World*, Cambridge: Cambridge University Press.
Bowman, A. and Thomas, J. D. (1996) 'New writing-tablets from Vindolanda', *Britannia* 27: 299–328.
Bowman, A. and Woolf, G. (1994) 'Literacy and power in the ancient world', in A. Bowman and G. Woolf (eds) *Literacy and Power in the Ancient World*, Cambridge: Cambridge University Press.
Bowman, A. and Woolf, G. (eds) (1994) *Literacy and Power in the Ancient World*, Cambridge: Cambridge University Press.
Boyle, A. (2003) 'Introduction: reading Flavian Rome', in A. J. Boyle and W. J. Dominik (eds) *Flavian Rome: Culture, Image, Text*, Leiden: Brill.
Boyle, A. J. and Dominik, W. J. (eds) (2003) *Flavian Rome: Culture, Image, Text*, Leiden: Brill.
Brandt, R. and Slofstra, J. (eds) (1983) *Roman and Native in the Low Countries: Spheres of Interaction*, BAR, International Series no. 184, Oxford: British Archaeological Reports.
Braund, D. (1984) *Rome and the Friendly King: The Character of Client Kingship*, London: Croom Helm.
Brennan, T. (2003) 'The Italian ideology', in G. Balakrishnan (ed.) *Debating Empire*, London: Verso.
Brunt, P. A. (1987) 'Labour', in J. Wacher (ed.) *The Roman World*, vol. 2, London: Routledge.
— (1990 [1976]) 'The Romanization of the local ruling classes in the Roman Empire', in P. A. Brunt (ed.) *Roman Imperial Themes*, Oxford: Clarendon Press.

Bruun, P. (1999) 'Coins and the Roman imperial government', in G. M. Paul and M. Ierardi (eds) *Roman Coins and Public Life under the Empire*, E. Togo Salmon Papers II, Ann Arbor: University of Michigan Press.

Burnham, B. and Johnson, H. (eds) (1979) *Invasion and Response: The Case of Roman Britain*, BAR British Series no. 73, Oxford: British Archaeological Reports.

Burnham, B., Collis, J., Dobinson, C., Haselgrove, C. and Jones, M. (2001) 'Themes for urban research: *c.* 100 BC to AD 200', in S. James and M. Millett (eds) *Britons and Romans: Advancing an Archaeological Agenda*, York: Council for British Archaeology.

Butcher, K. (2003) *Roman Syria and the Near East*, London: British Museum.

Caballos Rufino, A. (2001) 'Los recursos económicos de los notables de la Bética', in M. Navarro Caballero and S. Demougin (eds) *Élites Hispaniques*, Bordeaux: Ausonius Publications no. 6.

Campbell, B. (2002) *War and Society in Imperial Rome, 31 BC–AD 284*, London: Routledge.

Carrié, J.-M. (1993) 'The soldier', in A. Giardina (ed.) *The Romans*, originally published in Italian, London: University of Chicago Press.

Carrocera, E. (1995) 'El territorio de los Astures: los castros', in *Astures: Pueblos y Culturas en la frontera del imperio Romano*, Gijón: Gran Enciclopedia Asturiana: 53–66.

Carroll, M. (2001) *Romans, Celts and Germans: The German Provinces of Rome*, Stroud: Tempus.

— (2003) 'The genesis of Roman towns on the lower Rhine', in P. Wilson (ed.) *The Archaeology of Roman Towns*, Oxford: Oxbow.

Cartledge, P. (1998) 'Classics: from discipline in crisis to (multi-)cultural capital', in Y. L. Too and N. Livingstone (eds) *Pedagogy and Power: Rhetorics of Classical Learning*, Cambridge: Cambridge University Press.

Chakrabarty, D. (2000) *Provincializing Europe: Postcolonial Thought and Historical Difference*, Oxford: Princeton University Press.

Champion, C. B. (ed.) (2004) *Roman Imperialism: Readings and Sources*, London: Blackwell.

Cherry, D. (1998) *Frontiers and Society in Roman North Africa*, Oxford: Clarendon Press.

Clarke, K. (1999) *Between Geography and History: Hellenistic Constructions of the Roman World*, Oxford: Clarendon Press.

— (2001) 'An island nation: re-reading Tacitus' *Agricola*', *Journal of Roman Studies* 91: 94–112.

— (2004) 'Ever-increasing circles: constructing the Roman Empire', in T. Minamikawa (ed.) *Material Culture, Mentality and Historical Identity in the Ancient World: Understanding the Celts, Greeks, Romans and Modern Europeans*, Kyoto: Kyoto University.

Collingwood, R. G. (1932) *Roman Britain*, Clarendon Press: Oxford.

Conte, G. B. (1994) 'The inventory of the world: form of nature and encyclopaedic project in the works of Pliny the Elder', in G. B. Conte (ed.) *Genres and Readers: Lucretius, Love Elegy, Pliny's Encyclopaedia*, London: Johns Hopkins University Press.

Cooley, A. (2002) 'Introduction', in A. Cooley (ed.) *Becoming Roman, Writing Latin? Literacy and Epigraphy in the Roman West*, *Journal of Roman Archaeology*, Supplementary Series no. 48.

— (ed.) (2002) *Becoming Roman, Writing Latin? Literacy and Epigraphy in the Roman West*, *Journal of Roman Archaeology*, Supplementary Series no. 48.

Cooper, N. (1996) 'Searching for the blank generation: consumer choice in Roman and post-Roman Britain', in J. Webster and N. Cooper (eds) *Roman Imperialism: Post-colonial Perspectives*, Leicester Archaeological Monographs no. 3, Leicester: School of Archaeological Studies, University of Leicester.

Corbeill, A. (2001) 'Education in the Roman Republic: creating traditions', in Y. L. Too (ed.) *Education in Greek and Roman Antiquity*, Leiden: Brill.

Cornell, T. J. (1993) 'The end of Roman imperial expansion', in J. Rich and G. Shipley (eds) *War and Society in the Roman World*, London: Routledge.

Coulston, J. and Dodge, H. (eds) (2000) *Ancient Rome: The Archaeology of the Eternal City*, Oxford: Oxbow.

Crawley Quinn, J. C. (2003) 'Roman Africa?', *Digressus: The Internet Journal for the Classical World* 3: 7–34 <http://www.nottingham.ac.uk/classics/digressus/romaniz.html>.

Creighton, J. (2000) *Coins and Power in Late Iron Age Britain*, Cambridge: Cambridge University Press.

Creighton, J. and Wilson, R. J. A. (eds) (1999) *Roman Germany: Studies in Cultural Interaction*, *Journal of Roman Archaeology*, Supplementary Series no. 32.

Croom, A. T. (2000) *Roman Clothing and Fashion*, Stroud: Tempus.

Culham, P. (1997) 'Did Roman women have an empire?' in M. Golden and P. Toohey (eds) *Inventing Ancient Culture: Historicism, Periodization, and the Ancient World*, London: Routledge.

Cunliffe, B. W. (1991) *Iron Age Communities in Britain*, third edition, London: Routledge.

Curchin, L. A. (2004) *The Romanization of Central Spain: Complexity, Diversity and Change in a Provincial Hinterland*, London: Routledge.

Curti, E. (2001) 'Toynbee's legacy: discussing aspects of the Romanization of Italy', in S. Keay and N. Terrenato (eds) *Italy and the West: Comparative Issues in Romanization*, Oxford: Oxbow.

Curti, E., Dench, E. and Patterson, J. R. (1996) 'The archaeology of central and southern Roman Italy: recent trends and approaches', *Journal of Roman Studies* 86: 170–89.

Da Silva, A. C. F. (1995) 'Portuguese castros: the evolution of the habitat and the proto-urbanization process', in B. W. Cunliffe and S. Keay (eds) *Social Complexity and the Development of Towns in Iberia: From the Copper Age to the Second Century AD*, Proceedings of the British Academy, no. 86, Oxford: Oxford University Press.

Dauge, Y. A. (1981) *Le Barbare: Recherches sur la conception romaine de la barbarie et de la civilisation*, Brussels: Collections Latomus.

David, J.-M. (1996) *The Roman Conquest of Italy*, originally published in French, Oxford: Blackwell.

de Blois, L. and Rich, J. (eds) (2002) *The Transformation of Economic Life under the Roman Empire*, Proceedings of the Second Workshop of the International Network, Impact of Empire (Roman Empire *c.* 200 BC–AD 476), Nottingham, 4–7 July 2001, Amsterdam: J. C. Gieben.

de Blois, L., Pleket, H. W. and Rich, J. (2002) 'Introduction', in L. de Blois and J. Rich (eds) *The Transformation of Economic Life under the Roman Empire*, Proceedings of the Second Workshop of the International Network, Impact of Empire (Roman Empire *c.* 200 BC–AD 476), Nottingham, 4–7 July 2001, Amsterdam: J. C. Gieben.

Delanty, G. (1995) *Inventing Europe: Ideas, Identity, Reality*, London: Macmillan.

Deletant, D. (1998) 'Rewriting the past: trends in contemporary Romanian historiography', in D. Deletant and M. Pearton (eds) *Romania Observed: Studies in Contemporary Romanian History*, Bucharest: Encyclopaedic Publishing House.

Delplace, C. (1993) *La romanisation du Picenum: l'exemple d'Urbs Salvia*, Rome: Ecole Française de Rome.

Demandt, A. (1990) 'Theodor Mommsen', in W. W. Briggs and W. M. Calder (eds) *Classical Scholarship: A Bibliographical Encyclopedia*, London: Garland.

Dench, E. (2003) 'Review of S. Keay and N. Terrenato (eds), *Italy and the West . . .*', *Journal of Roman Studies* 93: 327–9.

Derks, T. (1998) *Gods, Temples and Ritual Practices: The Transformation of Religious Ideas and Values in Roman Gaul*, Amsterdam: Amsterdam University Press.

Derks, T. and Roymans, N. (2002) 'Seal-boxes and the spread of Latin literacy in the Rhine delta', in A. Cooley (ed.) *Becoming Roman, Writing Latin? Literacy and Epigraphy in the Roman West*, *Journal of Roman Archaeology*, Supplementary Series no. 48.

Desideri, P. (1991) 'La Romanizzazione dell'impero', *Storia di Roma* 2, 2: 577–626.

de Souza, P. (1996) '"They are enemies of all mankind": justifying Roman imperialism in the Late Republic', in J. Webster and N. Cooper (eds) *Roman Imperialism: Post-colonial Perspectives*, Leicester Archaeological Monographs no. 3, Leicester: School of Archaeological Studies, University of Leicester.

Díaz-Andreu, M. (1998) 'Ethnicity and Iberians. The archaeological crossroads between perception and material culture', *European Journal of Archaeology* 2: 199–218.

— (2001) 'Ethnic identity/ethnicity and archaeology', in N. J. Smelser and P. B. Baltes (eds) *International Encyclopaedia of the Social and Behavioral Sciences*, Oxford: Elsevier Services.

Díaz-Andreu, M. and Champion, T. (eds) (1996) *Nationalism and Archaeology in Europe*, London: UCL Press.

Digressus (2003) *Romanization? Digressus: The Internet Journal for the Classical World*, 3 <http://www.nottingham.ac.uk/classics/digressus/romaniz.html>.

Dilke, O. A. W. (1985) *Greek and Roman Maps*, London: Thames and Hudson.

Dondin-Payre, M. (1991) '*L'exercitus Africae* inspiratrice de l'armée française d'Afrique: *Ense et aratro*', *Antiquités Africaines* 27, 141–9.

— (1996) 'Réussites et déboires d'une oeuvre archéologique unique: le colonel Carbuccia au nord de l'Aurès (1848–1850)', *Antiquités Africaines* 32, 145–465.

Dondin-Payre, M. and Raepsaet-Charlier, M.-T. (eds) (2001) *Noms, identités culturelles et Romanisation sous le Haut-Empire*, Séminaire d'histoire romaine et d'épigraphie latine, Brussels: Timperman.

Dougherty, C. (1993) *The Poetics of Colonization: From City to Text in Archaic Greece*, Oxford: Oxford University Press.

Dougherty, C. and Kurke, L. (2003) 'Introduction: the cultures within Greek culture', in C. Dougherty and L. Kurke (eds) *The Cultures within Greek Culture: Contact, Conflict, Collaboration*, Cambridge: Cambridge University Press.

Douglas, M. and Isherwood, B. (1996 [1979]) *The World of Goods: Towards an Anthropology of Consumption*, revised edition, London: Routledge.

Downs, M. (2000) 'Refiguring colonial categories on the Roman frontier in southern Spain', in E. Fentress (ed.) *Romanization and the City: Creation, Transformations, and Failures*, *Journal of Roman Archaeology*, Supplementary Series no. 38.

Drinkwater, J. F. (1987) 'Urbanization in Italy and the Western Empire', in J. Wacher (ed.) *The Roman World*, vol. 1, London: Routledge.
Dueck, D. (2000) *Strabo of Amasia: A Greek Man of Letters in Augustan Rome*, London: Routledge.
Duncan-Jones, R. (1994) *Money and Government in the Roman Empire*, Cambridge: Cambridge University Press.
Dyson, S. (1975) 'Native revolt patterns in the Western Empire', *Aufstieg und Niedergang der Römischen Welt*, 2, 3: 138–75.
— (1991) 'Introduction', in G. Barker and J. Lloyd (eds) *Roman Landscapes: Archaeological Survey in the Mediterranean Region*, London: The British School at Rome, Archaeological Monographs.
— (1993) 'From new to new age archaeology: archaeological theory and classical archaeology – a 1990s perspective', *American Journal of Archaeology* 97: 195–206.
— (1995) 'Is there a text in this site?', in D. B. Small (ed.) *Methods in the Mediterranean: Historical and Archaeological Views on Texts and Archaeology*, New York: E. J. Brill.
— (1998) *Ancient Marbles to American Shores*, Philadelphia: University of Pennsylvania Press.
— (2000) 'The limited nature of Roman urbanism in Sardinia', in E. Fentress (ed.) *Romanization and the City: Creation, Transformations, and Failures*, *Journal of Roman Archaeology*, Supplementary Series no. 38.
— (2001) 'Rome in America', in R. Hingley (ed.) *Images of Rome: Perceptions of Ancient Rome in Europe and the United States of America in the Modern Age*, *Journal of Roman Archaeology*, Supplementary Series no. 44.
— (2003) *The Roman Countryside*, London: Duckworth.
Eckardt, H. (2002) *Illuminating Roman Britain*, Montagnac: Éditions Monique Mergoil.
Eckstein, A. (1995) *Moral Vision in the Histories of Polybius*, London: University of California Press.
Eder, W. (1990) 'Augustus and the power of tradition: the Augustan Principate as binding link between Republic and Empire', in K. A. Raaflaub and M. Toher (eds) *Between Republic and Empire: Interpretations of Augustus and his Principate*, London: University of California Press.
Edwards, C. (1996) *Writing Rome: Textual Approaches to the City*, Cambridge: Cambridge University Press.
— (1999) 'Introduction: shadows and fragments', in C. Edwards (ed.) *Roman Presences: Receptions of Rome in European Culture, 1789–1945*, Cambridge: Cambridge University Press.
— (ed.) (1999) *Roman Presences: Receptions of Rome in European Culture, 1789–1945*, Cambridge: Cambridge University Press.
Edwards, C. and Woolf, G. (2003) 'Cosmopolis: Rome as world city', in C. Edwards and G. Woolf (eds) *Rome the Cosmopolis*, Cambridge: Cambridge University Press.
Edwards, C. and Woolf, G. (eds) (2003) *Rome the Cosmopolis*, Cambridge: Cambridge University Press.
Ellis, S. P. (2000) *Roman Housing*, London: Duckworth.
Elsner, J. (1996) 'Inventing imperium: texts and the propaganda of monuments in Augustan Rome', in J. Elsner (ed.) *Art and Text in Roman Culture*, Cambridge: Cambridge Univerity Press.
Erdrich, M., Gionnotta, K. and Hanson, W. (2000) 'Traprain Law: native and Roman on the northern frontier', *Proceedings of the Society of Antiquaries of Scotland*, 130: 441–56.

Esmonde Cleary, S. (2001) 'The Roman to medieval transition', in S. James and M. Millett (eds) *Britons and Romans: Advancing an Archaeological Agenda*, York: Council for British Archaeology.

Étienne, R. and Mayet, F. (2001) 'Les élites marchandes de la péninsule Ibérique', in M. Navarro Caballero and S. Demougin (eds) *Élites Hispaniques*, Bordeaux: Ausonius Publications no. 6.

Evans, J. (2001) 'Material approaches to the identification of different Romano-British site-types', in S. James and M. Millett (eds) *Britons and Romans: Advancing an Archaeological Agenda*, York: Council for British Archaeology.

Evans, J. and Dickinson, B. (2000) 'Roman pottery', in S. C. Palmer (ed.) 'Archaeological excavations in the Arrow Valley, Warwickshire', *Transactions of the Bristol and Gloucestershire Archaeological Society*, 103: 101–25.

Evans, R. (2003) 'Containment and corruption: the discourse of Flavian Empire', in A. J. Boyle and W. J. Dominik (eds) *Flavian Rome: Culture, Image, Text*, Leiden: Brill.

Evans, R. J. (1997) *In Defence of History*, London: Granta.

Fagan, G. G. (1999) *Bathing in Public in the Roman World*, Ann Arbor: University of Michigan Press.

Fantham, E. (1996) *Roman Literary Culture: From Cicero to Apuleius*, London: Johns Hopkins University Press.

Farrell, J. (2001) *Latin Language and Latin Culture: From Ancient to Modern Times*, Cambridge: Cambridge University Press.

Favro, D. (1996) *The Urban Image of Imperial Rome*, Cambridge: Cambridge University Press.

Fear, A. T. (1996) *Rome and Baetica: Urbanization in Southern Spain c. 50 BC–AD 150*, Oxford: Clarendon Press.

Featherstone, M. (1995) *Undoing Culture: Globalization, Postmodernism and Identity*, London: Sage.

Feeney, D. C. (1992) '*Si licet et fas est*: Ovid's *Fasti* and the problem of free speech under the principate', in A. Powell (ed.) *Roman Poetry and Propaganda in the Age of Augustus*, Bristol: Bristol Classical Press.

Fentress, E. (ed.) (2000) *Romanization and the City: Creation, Transformations, and Failures*, *Journal of Roman Archaeology*, Supplementary Series no. 38.

Ferguson, J. (1987) 'Ruler-worship', in J. Wacher (ed.) *The Roman World*, vol. 2, London: Routledge.

Fernández Ochoa, C. and Morillo Cerdán, Á. (1999) *La tierra de los Astures: Nuevas perspectivas sobre la implantación romana en la antigua Asturia*, Gijón: Ediciones Trea.

Fernández-Posse, M. D. (2000a) 'La organización interna de los castros preromanos', in F.-J. Sánchez-Palencia (ed.) *Las Médulas (León): Un Paisaje Cultural en la 'Asturia Augustana'*, León: Instituto Leonés de Cultura.

— (2000b) 'La organización territorial de los castros preromanos', in F.-J. Sánchez-Palencia (ed.) *Las Médulas (León): Un Paisaje Cultural en la 'Asturia Augustana'*, León: Instituto Leonés de Cultura.

Fernández-Posse, M. D. and Fernández Manzano, J. (2000) 'Los recintos de los castros. La función social de la muralla', in F.-J. Sánchez-Palencia (ed.) *Las Médulas (León): Un Paisaje Cultural en la 'Asturia Augustana'*, León: Instituto Leonés de Cultura.

Ferrary, J.-L. (1994) 'L'Empire romain, l'*oikoumène* et l'Europe', in M. Perrin (ed.) *L'idée de l'Europe au fil de deux millénaires*, Le Centre d'Histoire des Idées Université de Picardie Jules-Verne, Paris: Beauchesne.

Ferris, I. M. (2000) *Enemies of Rome: Barbarians through Roman Eyes*, Stroud: Sutton.

Février, P.-A. (1990) *Approches du Maghreb Romain: pouvoirs différences et conflicts*, Aix-en-Provence: Édisud.

Février, P.-A., Fixot, M. Goudineau, C. and Kruta, V. (1980) *Histoire de la France urbaine: vol. 1, La ville antique*, Paris: Seuil.

Fincham, G. (2002) *Landscapes of Imperialism: Roman and Native Interaction in the East Anglian Fenland*, BAR British Series no. 338, Oxford: British Archaeological Reports.

Finley, M. I. (1985) *The Ancient Economy*, second edition, Hogarth Press: London.

Fishwick, D. (1983) 'The altar of Augustus and the municipal cult of Tarraco', *Madrider Mitteilungen* 23: 222–33.

— (1999) 'Coinage and cult: the provincial monuments at Lugdunum, Taracco, and Emerita', in G. M. Paul and M. Ierardi (eds) *Roman Coins and Public Life under the Empire*, E. Togo Salmon Papers II, Ann Arbor: University of Michigan Press.

Forcey, C. (1997) 'Beyond "Romanization": technologies of power in Roman Britain', in K. Meadows, C. Lemke and J. Heron (eds) *TRAC 1996: Proceedings of the Sixth Annual Theoretical Archaeology Conference, Sheffield 1996*, Oxford: Oxbow.

Fowler, D. (2000) *Roman Constructions: Readings in Postmodern Latin*, Oxford: Oxford University Press.

Fredrick, D. (2003) 'Architecture and surveillance in Flavian Rome', in A. J. Boyle and W. J. Dominik (eds) *Flavian Rome: Culture, Image, Text*, Leiden: Brill.

Freeman, P. (1993) '"Romanisation" and Roman material culture', *Journal of Roman Archaeology* 6: 438–45.

— (1996) 'British imperialism and the Roman Empire', in J. Webster and N. Cooper (eds) *Roman Imperialism: Post-colonial Perspectives*, Leicester Archaeological Monographs no. 3, Leicester: School of Archaeological Studies, University of Leicester.

— (1997a) '"Romanization" – "Imperialism": What are we talking about?', in K. Meadows, C. Lemke and J. Heron (eds) *TRAC 1996: Proceedings of the Sixth Annual Theoretical Archaeology Conference, Sheffield 1996*, Oxford: Oxbow.

— (1997b) 'Mommsen through to Haverfield: the origins of Romanization studies in later 19th-c. Britain', in D. J. Mattingly (ed.) *Dialogues in Roman Imperialism: Power, Discourse, and Discrepant Experiences in the Roman Empire*, *Journal of Roman Archaeology*, Supplementary Series, no. 23.

Friedman, J. (1994) *Cultural Identity and Global Process*, London: Sage.

Frow, J. (1997) *Time and Commodity Culture: Essays in Cultural Theory and Postmodernity*, Oxford: Clarendon Press.

Fulford, M. (1992) 'Territorial expansion and the Roman empire', *World Archaeology* 23: 294–305.

Funari, P. P., Jones, S. and Hall, M. (1999) 'Introduction: archaeology in history', in P. P. Funari, M. Hall and S. Jones (eds) *Historical Archaeology: Back from the Edge*, London: Routledge.

Funari, P. P., Hall, M. and Jones, S. (eds) (1999) *Historical Archaeology: Back from the Edge*, London: Routledge.

Galinsky, K. (1992) *Classical and Modern Interactions: Postmodern Architecture, Multiculturalism, Decline and Other Issues*, Austin: University of Texas Press.

— (1996) *Augustan Culture: An Interpretative Introduction*, Princeton, NJ: Princeton University Press.

Gardner, A. (2003) 'Seeking a material turn: the artefactuality of the Roman Empire', in G. Carr, E. Swift and J. Weekes (eds) *TRAC 2002: Proceedings of the Twelfth Annual Theoretical Roman Archaeology Conference, Canterbury 2002*, Oxford: Oxbow.

Gardner, J. F. (1993) *Being a Roman Citizen*, London: Routledge.

Gardner, K. and Lewis, D. (1996) *Anthropology, Development and the Post-modern Challenge*, London: Pluto Press.

Gargola, D. J. (1995) *Lands, Laws and Gods: Magistrates and Ceremonies in the Regulation of Public Lands in Republican Rome*, London: University of North Carolina Press.

Garnsey, P. and Saller, R. (1987) *The Roman Empire: Economy, Society and Culture*, London: Duckworth.

Geertz, C. (1973) *The Interpretation of Cultures*, New York: Basic Books.

Gellner, E. (1983) *Nations and Nationalism*, Oxford: Blackwell.

— (1988) *Plough, Sword and Book: The Structure of Human History*, London: University of Chicago Press.

Gergel, R. A. (2001) 'Costume as geographical indicator: barbarians and prisoners on cuirassed statue breastplates', in J. L. Sebesta and L. Bonfante (eds) *The World of Roman Costume*, London: University of Wisconsin Press.

Gerrard, J. (2002) 'Pots for cash? A critique of the role of the "free market" in the late Roman economy', in M. Carruthers, C. van Driel-Murray, A. Gardner, J. Lucas, L. Revell and E. Swift (eds) *TRAC 2001 Proceedings of the Eleventh Annual Theoretical Roman Archaeology Conference, Glasgow 2001*, Oxford, Oxbow.

Giardina, A. (1993a) 'Introduction: Roman man', in A. Giardina (ed.) *The Romans*, originally published in Italian, London: University of Chicago Press.

— (1993b) 'The merchant', in A. Giardina (ed.) *The Romans*, originally published in Italian, London: University of Chicago Press.

— (1994) 'L'identità incompiuta dell'Italia Romana', in *L'Italie d'Auguste à Dioclétien*, Collection de l'École Française de Rome, Rome: École Française de Rome.

Giddens, A. (1984) *The Constitution of Society: Outline of a Theory of Structuration*, Cambridge: Polity Press.

Gilkes, O. and Miraj, L. (2000) 'The myth of Aeneas: The Italian archaeological mission in Albania, 1924–43', *Public Archaeology* 1: 109–24.

Golden, M. and Toohey, P. (1997a) 'General introduction', in M. Golden and P. Toohey (eds) *Inventing Ancient Culture: Historicism, Periodization, and the Ancient World*, London: Routledge.

— (1997b) 'Part one: introduction', in M. Golden and P. Toohey (eds) *Inventing Ancient Culture: Historicism, Periodization, and the Ancient World*, London: Routledge.

Gorges, J.-G. and Nogales Basarrate, T. (eds) (2000) *Sociedad y cultura en Lusitania romana*, Merida: Mesa Redonda Internacional IV.

Gosden, C. and Lock, G. (2003) 'Becoming Roman on the Berkshire Downs: the evidence from Alfred's Castle', *Britannia* 34: 64–80.

Gosden, C. and Marshall, Y. (1999) 'The cultural biography of objects', *World Archaeology*, 31: 169–78.

Goudineau, C. (1980) 'Sources et problèmes', in P.-A. Février, M. Fixot, C. Goudineau and V. Kruta (eds) *Histoire de la France urbaine: vol. 1, La Ville antique*, Paris: Seuil.

— (1998) *Regard sur la Gaule*, Paris: Editions Errance.

Goudineau, C., Février, P.-A. and Fixot, M. (1980) 'Le réseau urbain', in P.-A. Février, M. Fixot, C. Goudineau and V. Kruta (eds) *Histoire de la France urbaine: vol. 1, La Ville antique*, Paris: Seuil.

Grafton, A. (1992) *New Worlds, Ancient Texts: The Power of Tradition and the Shock of Discovery*, London: Harvard University Press.
Graves-Brown, P. M. (2000) 'Introduction', in P. M. Graves-Brown (ed.) *Matter, Materiality and Modern Culture*, London: Routledge.
Greene, K. (1986) *The Archaeology of the Roman Economy*, London: Batsford.
— (1995) *Archaeology: An Introduction*, London: Batsford.
— (2002) 'Pots and plots in Roman Britain', in M. Aldhouse-Green and P. Webster (eds) *Artefacts and Archaeology: Aspects of the Celtic and Roman World*, Cardiff: University of Wales Press.
Gregory, D. (2004) *The Colonial Present*, Oxford: Blackwell.
Griffin, M. (1991) '*Urbs Roma*, *plebs* and *princeps*', in L. Alexander (ed.) *Images of Empire*, Sheffield: JSOT Press.
Groenman-van Waateringe, W. (1980) 'Urbanization and the north-west frontier of the Roman empire', in W. S. Hanson and L. J. F. Keppie (eds) *Roman Frontier Studies 1979*, Oxford, BAR International Series no. 71, Oxford: British Archaeological Reports.
Gross, J., McMurray, D. and Swedenburg, T. (2002 [1996]) 'Arab noise and Ramadan nights: *Rai*, Rap, and Franco-Maghrebi identities', in J. X. Inda and R. Rosaldo (eds) *The Anthropology of Globalization: A Reader*, Oxford: Blackwell.
Gruen, E. S. (1990) 'The imperial policy of Augustus', in K. A. Raaflaub and M. Toher (eds) *Between Republic and Empire: Interpretations of Augustus and his Principate*, London: University of California Press.
— (1996) 'The expansion of the empire under Augustus', in A. K. Bowman, E. Champlin and A. Lintott (eds) *The Cambridge Ancient History, vol. X, The Augustan Empire, 43 BC to AD 69*, Cambridge: Cambridge University Press.
Gupta, A. and Ferguson, J. (2002 [1997]) 'Beyond "culture": space, identity, and politics of difference', in J. X. Inda and R. Rosaldo (eds) *The Anthropology of Globalization: A Reader*, Oxford: Blackwell.
Habinek, T. N. (1997) 'The invention of sexuality in the world-city of Rome', in T. N. Habinek and S. Schiesaro (eds) *The Roman Cultural Revolution*, Cambridge: Cambridge University Press.
— (1998) *The Politics of Latin Literature: Writing, Identity and Empire in Ancient Rome*, Princeton, NJ: Princeton University Press.
Habinek, T. N. and Schiesaro, S. (1997) 'Introduction', in T. N. Habinek and S. Schiesaro (eds) *The Roman Cultural Revolution*, Cambridge: Cambridge University Press.
Habinek, T. N. and Schiesaro, S. (eds) (1997) *The Roman Cultural Revolution*, Cambridge: Cambridge University Press.
Haffner, A. and von Schnurbein, S. (eds) (2000) *Kelten, Germanen, Römer im Mittelgebirgsraum zwischen Luxemburg und Thüringen, Akten des Internationalen Kolloquiums zum DFG-Schwerpunktprogamm 'Romanisierung' in Trier vom 28 bis 30, September 1998*, Bonn: Römisch-Germanische Kommission des Deutschen Archäologischen Instituts.
Hales, S. (2003) *The Roman House and Social Identity*, Cambridge: Cambridge University Press.
Haley, E. W. (2003) *Baetica Felix: People and Prosperity in Southern Spain from Caesar to Septimius Severus*, Austin: University of Texas Press.
Hall, E. (1989) *Inventing the Barbarian: Greek Self-definition through Tragedy*, Oxford: Clarendon Press.

— (2004) 'Introduction: why Greek tragedy in the late twentieth century?', in E. Hall, F. Macintosh and A. Wrigley (eds) *Dionysus since '69: Greek Tragedy at the Dawn of the Third Millennium*, Oxford: Oxford University Press.

Hanson, W. S. (1994) 'Dealing with barbarians: the Romanization of Britain', in B. Vyner (ed.) *Building on the Past: Papers Celebrating 150 Years of the Royal Archaeological Institute*, London: Royal Archaeological Institute.

— (1997) 'Forces of change and methods of control', in D. J. Mattingly (ed.) *Dialogues in Roman Imperialism: Power, Discourse, and Discrepant Experiences in the Roman Empire, Journal of Roman Archaeology*, Supplementary Series, no. 23.

— (2002) 'Why did the Roman empire cease to expand?', in P. Freeman, J. Bennett, Z. T. Fiema and B. Hoffmann (eds) *Limes XVIII: Proceedings of the XVIIIth International Congress of Roman Frontier Studies held in Amman, Jordan (September 2000): vol. 1*, BAR International Series no. 1084, Oxford: British Archaeological Reports.

Hanson, W. S. and Conolly, R. (2002) 'Language and literacy in Roman Britain: some archaeological considerations', in A. Cooley (ed.) *Becoming Roman, Writing Latin? Literacy and Epigraphy in the Roman West, Journal of Roman Archaeology*, Supplementary Series no. 48.

Hardie, P. (1992) 'Augustan poets and the mutability of Rome', in A. Powell (ed.) *Roman Poetry and Propaganda in the Age of Augustus*, Bristol: Bristol Classical Press.

— (2000) 'Coming to terms with the Empire: poetry of the late Augustan and Tiberian period', in O. Taplin (ed.) *Literature in the Roman World*, Oxford: Oxford University Press.

Hardt, M. and Negri, A. (2000) *Empire*, London: Harvard University Press.

Hardwick, L. (2000) *Translating Words, Translating Cultures*, London: Duckworth.

— (2003) *Reception*, Greece and Rome, New Surveys of the Classics, no. 33, Oxford: Oxford University Press.

Härke, H. (2000) 'The German experience', in H. Härke (ed.) *Archaeology, Ideology and Society: The German Experince*, Frankfurt-am-Main: Peter Lang.

Harris, W. V. (1991) 'Between archaic and modern: some current problems in the history of the Roman economy', in W. V. Harris (ed.) *The Inscribed Economy: Production and Distribution in the Roman Empire in the Light of* instrumentum domesticum, *Journal of Roman Archaeology*, Supplementary Series no. 6.

Harrison, S. J. (2001) 'General introduction: working together', in S. J. Harrison (ed.) *Texts, Ideas and the Classics: Scholarship, Theory and Classical Literature*, Oxford: Oxford University Press.

Hartog, F. (2001) *Memories of Odysseus: Frontier Tales from Ancient Greece*, Edinburgh: Edinburgh University Press.

Hassall, M. (1987) 'Romans and non-Romans', in J. Wacher (ed.) *The Roman World*, vol. 2, London: Routledge.

Haugerud, A., Stone, M. P. and Little, P. D. (eds) (2000) *Commodities and Globalization: Anthropological Perspectives*, Oxford: Rowman and Littlefield.

Häussler, R. (1999) 'Architecture, performance and ritual: the role of state architecture in the Roman Empire', in P. Baker, C. Forcey, S. Jundi and R. Witcher (eds) *TRAC 1998: Proceedings of the Eighth Annual Theoretical Roman Archaeology Conference, Leicester 1998*, Oxford: Oxbow.

— (2002) 'Writing Latin – from resistance to assimilation: language, culture and society in N. Italy and S. Gaul', in A. Cooley (ed.) *Becoming Roman, Writing Latin?*

Literacy and Epigraphy in the Roman West, Journal of Roman Archaeology, Supplementary Series no. 48.
Haverfield, F. (1905) 'The Romanization of Roman Britain', *Proceedings of the British Academy* 2: 185–217.
— (1909) 'Prefatory note', in T. Mommsen *The Provinces of the Roman Empire: From Caesar to Diocletian*, Parts 1 and 2, revised edition, London: Macmillan and Co.
— (1911) 'An inaugural address delivered before the first Annual General Meeting of the Society', *Journal of Roman Studies* 1: xi–xx.
— (1912) *The Romanization of Roman Britain*, second edition, Oxford: Clarendon Press.
— (1915) *The Romanization of Roman Britain*, third edition, Oxford: Clarendon Press.
Hawthorne, J. W. J. (1997) 'Post-processual economics: the role of African red slip ware vessel volumes in Mediterranean demography', in K. Meadows, C. Lemke and J. Heron (eds) *TRAC 1996: Proceedings of the Sixth Annual Theoretical Archaeology Conference Sheffield 1996*, Oxford: Oxbow.
— (1998) 'Pottery and paradigms in the early Western Empire', in C. Forcey, J. Hawthorne and R. Witcher (eds) *TRAC 1997: Proceedings of the Seventh Annual Theoretical Roman Archaeology Conference, Nottingham 1997*, Oxford: Oxbow.
Hayes, J. W. (1997) *Handbook of Mediterranean Roman Pottery*, London: British Museum.
Haynes, I. P. (2001) 'The impact of auxiliary recruitment on provincial societies from Augustus to Caracalla', in L. de Blois (ed.) *Administration, Prosopography and Appointment Policy in the Roman Empire*, Proceedings of the First Workshop of the International Network, Impact of Empire (Roman Empire, 27 BC–AD 406), Leiden, 28 June–1 July 2000, Amsterdam: J. C. Gieben.
Heath, M. (2002) *Interpreting Classical Texts*, London: Duckworth.
Helgerson, R. (1992) *Forms of Nationhood: The Elizabethan Writing of England*, London: University of Chicago Press.
Herrin, J. (1987) *The Formation of Christendom*, London: Princeton University Press.
Hessing, W. (2001) 'Foreign oppressors versus civilisers: the Batavian myth as the source for contrasting associations of Rome in Dutch historiography and archaeology', in R. Hingley (ed.) *Images of Rome: Perceptions of Ancient Rome in Europe and the United States of America in the Modern Age, Journal of Roman Archaeology*, Supplementary Series no. 44.
Hill, J. D. (2001) 'Romanisation, gender and class: recent approaches to identity in Britain and their possible consequences', in S. James and M. Millett (eds) *Britons and Romans: Advancing an Archaeological Agenda*, York: Council for British Archaeology.
Hingley, R. (1989) *Rural Settlement in Roman Britain*, London: Seaby.
— (1995) 'Britannia, origin myths and the British Empire', in S. Cottam, D. Dungworth, S. Scott and J. Taylor (eds) *TRAC 1994: Proceedings of the Fourth Theoretical Roman Archaeology Conference, Durham 1994*, Oxford: Oxbow.
— (1996) 'The "legacy" of Rome: the rise, decline and fall of the theory of Romanization', in J. Webster and N. Cooper (eds) *Roman Imperialism: Post-colonial Perspectives*, Leicester Archaeological Monographs no. 3, Leicester: School of Archaeological Studies, University of Leicester.
— (1997) 'Resistance and domination: social change in Roman Britain', in D. J. Mattingly (ed.) *Dialogues in Roman Imperialism: Power, Discourse, and Discrepant Experiences in the Roman Empire, Journal of Roman Archaeology*, Supplementary Series, no. 23.

— (1999) 'The imperial context of Romano-British studies and proposals for a new understanding of social change', in P. P. Funari, M. Hall and S. Jones (eds) *Historical Archaeology: Back from the Edge*, London: Routledge.
— (2000) *Roman Officers and English Gentlemen*, London: Routledge.
— (2001a) 'A comment on Ray Laurence's Roman narratives', *Archaeological Dialogues* 8: 111–13.
— (2001b) 'An imperial legacy: the contribution of classical Rome to the character of the English', in R. Hingley (ed.) *Images of Rome: Perceptions of Ancient Rome in Europe and the United States of America in the Modern Age*, *Journal of Roman Archaeology*, Supplementary Series no. 44.
— (2001c) 'Images of Rome', in R. Hingley (ed.) *Images of Rome: Perceptions of Ancient Rome in Europe and the United States of America in the Modern Age*, *Journal of Roman Archaeology*, Supplementary Series no. 44.
— (2003) 'Recreating coherence without reinventing Romanization', *Digressus: The Internet Journal for the Classical World* 3: 112–19 <http://www.nottingham.ac.uk/classics/digressus/romaniz.html>.
— (2004) 'Rural settlement in northern Britain', in M. Todd (ed.) *A Companion to Roman Britain*, Oxford, Blackwell.
Hingley, R. (ed.) (2001) *Images of Rome: Perceptions of Ancient Rome in Europe and the United States of America in the Modern Age*, *Journal of Roman Archaeology*, Supplementary Series no. 44.
Hingley, R. and Miles, D. (2001) 'The human impact on the landscape: agriculture, settlement, industry and infrastructure', in P. Salway (ed.) *The Roman Era: The Short Oxford History of the Roman Empire*, Oxford: Oxford University Press.
Hingley, R. and Unwin, C. (in press) *Boudica: From the Iron Age to the Internet*, London: Hambledon and London.
Hitchner, R. B. (2002 [1993]) 'Olive production and the Roman economy: the case for intensive growth in the Roman Empire', in W. Scheidel and S. von Reden (eds) *The Ancient Economy*, Edinburgh: Edinburgh University Press.
Hoff, M. C. and Rotroff, S. I. (eds) (1997) *The Romanization of Athens*, Oxford: Oxbow.
Holton, R. J. (1998) *Globalization and the Nation-State*, London: Macmillan Press.
Hope, V. (2000) 'Status and identity in the Roman world', in J. Huskinson (ed.) *Experiencing Rome: Culture, Identity and Power in the Roman Empire*, London: Routledge.
Hopkins, K. (1978) *Conquerors and Slaves*, Cambridge: Cambridge University Press.
— (1980) 'Taxes and trade in the Roman Empire (200 BC–AD 400)', *Journal of Roman Studies* 70: 101–25.
— (1983) *Death and Renewal*, Cambridge: Cambridge University Press.
— (2002 [1995/6]) 'Rome, taxes, rents and trade', in W. Scheidel and S. von Reden (eds) *The Ancient Economy*, Edinburgh: Edinburgh University Press.
Horden, P. and Purcell, N. (2000) *The Corrupting Sea: A Study of Mediterranean History*, Oxford: Blackwell.
Horsfall, N. (2001) 'The unity of Roman Italy: anomalies in context', *Scripta Classica Israelica* 20: 39–50.
Howes, D. (1996a) 'Introduction: commodities and cultural borders', in D. Howes (ed.) *Cross-cultural Consumption: Global Markets, Local Realities*, London: Routledge.
— (1996b) 'Cultural appropriation and resistance in the American southwest: decommodifying "Indianness"', in D. Howes (ed.) *Cross-cultural Consumption: Global Markets, Local Realities*, London: Routledge.

— (ed.) (1996) *Cross-cultural Consumption: Global Markets, Local Realities*, London: Routledge.

Howgego, C. (1994) 'Coin circulation and the integration of the Roman economy', *Journal of Roman Archaeology* 7: 5–21.

Huskinson, J. (2000a) 'Looking for culture, identity and power', in J. Huskinson (ed.) *Experiencing Rome: Culture, Identity and Power in the Roman Empire*, London: Routledge.

— (2000b) 'Élite culture and the identity of empire', in J. Huskinson (ed.) *Experiencing Rome: Culture, Identity and Power in the Roman Empire*, London: Routledge.

Iggers, G. G. (1997) *Historiography in the Twentieth Century: From Scientific Objectivity to the Postmodern Challenge*, London: Wesleyan University Press.

Inda, J. X. and Rosaldo, R. (2002) 'Introduction: a world in motion', in J. X. Inda and R. Rosaldo (eds) *The Anthropology of Globalization: A Reader*, Oxford: Blackwell.

Inda, J. X. and Rosaldo, R. (eds) (2002) *The Anthropology of Globalization: A Reader*, Oxford: Blackwell.

Isaac, B. (1990) *The Limits of Empire: The Roman Army in the East*, Oxford: Clarendon Press.

James, S. (1999) 'The community of the soldiers: a major identity and centre of power in the Roman empire', in P. Baker, C. Forcey, S. Jundi and R. Witcher (eds) *TRAC 1998: Proceedings of the Eighth Annual Theoretical Roman Archaeology Conference, Leicester 1998*, Oxford: Oxbow.

— (2001a) 'Romanization and the peoples of Britain', in S. Keay and N. Terrenato (eds) *Italy and the West: Comparative Issues in Romanization*, Oxford: Oxbow.

— (2001b) 'Soldiers and civilians: identity and interaction in Roman Britain', in S. James and M. Millett (eds) *Britons and Romans: Advancing an Archaeological Agenda*, York: Council for British Archaeology.

James, S. and Millett, M. (eds) (2001) *Britons and Romans: Advancing an Archaeological Agenda*, York: Council for British Archaeology.

Janik, L. and Zawadzka, H. (1996) 'One Europe – one past?', in P. M. Graves-Brown, S. Jones and C. Gamble (eds) *Cultural Identity and Archaeology: The Construction of European Communities*, London: Routledge.

Jenkins, K. (1995) *On 'What is History?'* London: Routledge.

Jenkyns, R. (1998) *Virgil's Experience. Nature and History: Time, Names and Places*, Oxford: Clarendon Press.

Johnson, C. (2004) *The Sorrows of Empire: Militarism, Secrecy, and the End of the Republic*, London: Verso.

Johnson, M. (1999a) *Archaeological Theory: An Introduction*, Oxford: Blackwell.

— (1999b) 'Rethinking historical archaeology', in P. P. Funari, M. Hall and S. Jones (eds) *Historical Archaeology: Back from the Edge*, London: Routledge.

Jones, M. and Miles, D. (1979) 'Celts and Romans in the Thames Valley: approaches to culture change', in B. Burnham and H. Johnson (eds) *Invasion and Response: The Case of Roman Britain*, BAR British Series no. 73, Oxford: British Archaeological Reports.

Jones, S. (1997) *The Archaeology of Ethnicity: Constructing Identities in the Past and Present*, London: Routledge.

Jones, S. and Graves-Brown, P. M. (1996) 'Introduction: archaeology and cultural identity in Europe', in P. M. Graves-Brown, S. Jones and C. Gamble (eds) *Cultural Identity and Archaeology: The Construction of European Communities*, London: Routledge.

Jones, W. R. (1971) 'The image of the barbarian in medieval Europe', *Comparative Studies in Society and History* 13: 376–407.

Jongman, W. M. (2002) 'The Roman economy: from cities to Empire', in L. de Blois and J. Rich (eds) *The Transformation of Economic Life under the Roman Empire*, Proceedings of the Second Workshop of the International Network, Impact of Empire (Roman Empire *c.* 200 BC–AD 476), Nottingham, 4–7 July 2001, Amsterdam: J. C. Gieben.

Joshel, S. R. (1992) *Work, Identity and Legal Status at Rome: A Study of the Occupational Inscriptions*, London: University of Oklahoma Press.

Jullian, C. (1929) *Histoire de la Gaule, vol. VI: La Civilisation gallo-romaine: état moral*, Paris: Librairie Hachette.

Keaveney, A. (1987) *Rome and the Unification of Italy*, London: Croom Helm.

Keay, S. (1988) *Roman Spain*, London: British Museum.

— (1995) 'Innovation and adaptation: the contribution of Rome to urbanism in Iberia', in B. W. Cunliffe and S. Keay (eds) *Social Complexity and the Development of Towns in Iberia: From the Copper Age to the Second Century AD*. Proceedings of the British Academy, no. 86, Oxford: Oxford University Press.

— (1997) 'Urban transformations and cultural change', in M. Díaz-Andreu and S. Keay (eds) *The Archaeology of Iberia: The Dynamics of Change*, London: Routledge.

— (2001) 'Romanization and the Hispaniae', in S. Keay and N. Terrenato (eds) *Italy and the West: Comparative Issues in Romanization*, Oxford: Oxbow.

— (2002) 'Closely observed élites in the Spanish provinces', *Journal of Roman Archaeology* 15: 581–6.

— (2003) 'Recent archaeological work in Roman Iberia (1990–2002)', *Journal of Roman Studies* 93: 146–211.

— (ed.) (1998) *The Archaeology of Early Roman Baetica*, *Journal of Roman Archaeology*, Supplementary Series no. 29.

Keay, S. and Terrenato, N. (2001) 'Preface', in S. Keay and N. Terrenato (eds) *Italy and the West: Comparative Issues in Romanization*, Oxford: Oxbow.

Keay, S. and Terrenato, N. (eds) (2001) *Italy and the West: Comparative Issues in Romanization*, Oxford: Oxbow.

Kellum, B. A. (1990) 'The city adorned: programmatic display at the *Aedes Concordiae Augustae*', in . K. A. Raaflaub and M. Toher (eds) *Between Republic and Empire: Interpretations of Augustus and his Principate*, London: University of California Press.

Kennedy, D. F. (1992) '"Augustan" and "Anti-Augustan": reflections on terms of reference', in A. Powell (ed.) *Roman Poetry and Propaganda in the Age of Augustus*, Bristol: Bristol Classical Press.

Kilmer, M. (1997) 'Painters and pederasts: Ancient art, sexuality, and social history', in M. Golden and P. Toohey (eds) *Inventing Ancient Culture: Historicism, Periodization, and the Ancient World*, London: Routledge.

King, A. (2001) 'Vercingetorix, Asterix and the Gauls: Gallic symbols in French politics and culture', in R. Hingley (ed.) *Images of Rome: Perceptions of Ancient Rome in Europe and the United States of America in the Modern Age*, *Journal of Roman Archaeology*, Supplementary Series no. 44.

King, C. E. (1999) 'Roman portraiture: images of power?', in G. M. Paul and M. Ierardi (eds) *Roman Coins and Public Life under the Empire*, E. Togo Salmon Papers II, Ann Arbor: University of Michigan Press.

Knauft, B. M. (2002) 'Critically modern: an introduction', in B. M. Knauft (ed.) *Criti-*

cally Modern: Alternatives, Alterities, Anthropologies, Bloomington: Indiana University Press.
— (ed.) (2002) *Critically Modern: Alternatives, Alterities, Anthropologies*, Bloomington: Indiana University Press.
Konstan, D. (1997) 'Philosophy, friendship, and cultural history', in M. Golden and P. Toohey (eds) *Inventing Ancient Culture: Historicism, Periodization, and the Ancient World*, London: Routledge.
Kraus, C. S. (2000) 'Forging a national identity: prose literature down to the time of Augustus', in O. Taplin (ed.) *Literature in the Roman World*, Oxford: Oxford University Press.
Krausse, D. (2000) 'Zentrale Fragestellung', in A. Haffner and S. von Schnurbein (eds) *Kelten, Germanen, Römer im Mittelgebirgsraum zwischen Luxemburg und Thüringen, Akten des Internationalen Kolloquiums zum DFG-Schwerpunktprogramm 'Romanisierung' in Trier vom 28 bis 30 September 1998*, Bonn: Römisch-Germanische Kommission des Deutschen Archäologischen Instituts.
— (2001) 'Farewell to Romanisation?', *Archaeological Dialogues* 8: 108–10.
Kristiansen, K. (1996) 'European origins – "civilisation" and "barbarism"', in P. M. Graves-Brown, S. Jones and C. Gamble (eds) *Cultural Identity and Archaeology: the Construction of European Communities*, London: Routledge.
Kühlborn, J.-S. (2000) 'Die Feldzüge unter Augustus und Tiberius in Nordwestdeutschland', in L. Wamser (ed.) *Die Römer zwischen Alpen und Nordmeer: zivilisatorisches Erbe einer europäischen Militärmacht*, Mainz: Philipp von Zabern.
Lanham, C. D. (ed.) (2002) *Latin Grammar and Rhetoric: From Classical Theory to Medieval Practice*, London: Continuum.
Laroui, A. (1970) *L'histoire du Maghreb, un essai de synthèse*, Paris: François Maspero.
— (1977) *The History of the Maghrib: An Interpretative Essay*, Princeton, NJ: Princeton University Press.
Latouche, S. (1996) *The Westernization of the World: The Significance, Scope and Limits of the Drive toward Global Uniformity*,Cambridge: Polity Press.
Laurence, R. (1994a) 'Modern ideology and the creation of ancient town planning', *European Review of History* 1: 9–18.
— (1994b) *Roman Pompeii: Space and Society*, London: Routledge.
— (1998a) 'Introduction', in R. Laurence and J. Berry (eds) *Cultural Identity in the Roman World*, London: Routledge.
— (1998b) 'Territory, ethnonyms and geography: the construction of identity in Roman Italy', in R. Laurence and J. Berry (eds) *Cultural Identity in the Roman World*, London: Routledge.
— (1998c) 'Land transport in ancient Italy: cost, practice and the economy', in H. Parkins and C. Smith (eds) *Trade, Traders and the Ancient City*, London: Routledge.
— (1999) *The Roads of Roman Italy: Mobility and Cultural Change*, London: Routledge.
— (2001a) 'Roman narratives: the writing of archaeological discourse – a view from Britain?' *Archaeological Dialogues* 8: 90–101.
— (2001b) 'The creation of geography: an interpretation of Roman Britain', in C. Adams and R. Laurence (eds) *Travel and Geography in the Roman Empire*, London: Routledge.
Le Bohec, Y. (1989) *Les Unites auxiliaires de l'armée romaine en Afrique Proconsulaire et Numidie sous le Haut Empire*, Études d'Antiquités Africaines, Paris: CNRS.

Lee, R. Y. T. (2003) *Romanization in Palestine: A Study of Urban Development from Herod the Great to AD 70*, BAR International Series no. 1180, Oxford: British Archaeological Reports.

Legrain, P. (2002) *One World: The Truth about Globalisation*, London: Abacus.

Lendon, J. E. (1997) *Empire of Honour*, Oxford: Oxford University Press.

Leveau, P. (1978) 'La Situation coloniale de l'Afrique romaine', *Annales: Économies, Sociétés, Civilisations* 33: 89–92.

Levick, B. (1999) 'Messages on the Roman coinages: types and inscriptions', in G. M. Paul and M. Ierardi (eds) *Roman Coins and Public Life under the Empire*, E. Togo Salmon Papers II, Ann Arbor: University of Michigan Press.

Linderski, J. (1984) '*Si vis pacem, para bellum*: concepts of defensive imperialism', in W. V. Harris (ed.) *The Imperialism of Mid-Republican Rome*, Rome: American Academy in Rome, Papers and Monographs no. 29.

Lintott, A. (1981) 'What was the "Imperium Romanum"?' *Greece and Rome* 28: 53–67.

Lloyd, J. (1991) 'Forms of rural settlement in the early Roman empire', in G. Barker and J. Lloyd (eds) *Roman Landscapes: Archaeological Survey in the Mediterranean Region*, London: The British School at Rome, Archaeological Monographs.

Lomas, K. (1995) 'Urban elites and cultural definition: Romanization in southern Italy', in T. J. Cornell and K. Lomas (eds) *Urban Society in Roman Italy*, London: UCL Press.

López Castro, J. L. (1992) 'El concepto de romanización y los fenicos en la Hispania republicana: problemas historiográficos', in *La colonización Fenicia en el Sur de la Península Iberica: 100 Años de Investigación*, Actas del Seminario, Almería, 5–7 de Junio de 1990, Maracena: Instituto de Estudios Almerienses: 151–70.

Lowenthal, D. (1988) 'Classical antiquities as national and global heritage', *Antiquity* 62, 726–35.

MacCormack, S. (2001) 'Cuzco, another Rome?', in S. Alcock, T. N. D'Altroy, K. D. Morrison and C. M. Sinopoli (eds) *Empires: Perspectives from Archaeology and History*, Cambridge: Cambridge University Press.

McCracken, G. D. (1988) *Culture and Consumption: New Approaches to the Symbolic Character of Consumer Goods and Activities*, Bloomington: Indiana University Press.

MacDonald, W. L. (1986) 'Empire imagery in Augustan architecture', in R. Winkes (ed.) *The Age of Augustus*, Louvain: Publications d'Histoire de l'Art et d'Archéologie de l'Université Catholique de Louvain no. 94.

MacMullen, R. (1974) *Roman Social Relations: 50 BC to AD 284*, London: Yale University Press.

— (1982) 'The epigraphic habit in the Roman empire.' *American Journal of Philology* 103: 233–46.

— (2000) *Romanization in the Time of Augustus*, London, Yale University Press.

Main, L. (1998) 'Excavations of a timber round-house and broch at the Fairy Knowe, Buchlyvie, Stirlingshire, 1975–8', *Proceedings of the Society of Antiquaries of Scotland* 128: 293–418.

Majeed, J. (1999) 'Comparativism and references to Rome in British imperial attitudes to India', in C. Edwards (ed.) *Writing Rome: Textual Approaches to the City*, Cambridge: Cambridge University Press.

Malkin, I. (1998) *The Return of Odysseus: Colonization and Ethnicity*, London: University of California Press.

Manacorda, D, and Tamassia, R. (1985) *Il piccone del regime*, Rome: Biblioteca di Archeologia, Armando Curcio.

Marichal, R. (1988) *Les Graffites de la Graufesenque*, *Gallia*, Supplement no. XLVII, Paris: Centre National de la Recherche Scientifique.

Martindale, C. (1993) *Redeeming the Text: Latin Poetry and the Hermenutics of Reception*, Cambridge: Cambridge University Press.

Martins, C. (2003) 'Becoming consumers: looking beyond wealth as an explanation for villa variability', in G. Carr, E. Swift and J. Weekes (eds) *TRAC 2002: Proceedings of the Twelfth Annual Theoretical Roman Archaeology Conference, Canterbury 2002*, Oxford: Oxbow.

Mattern, S. P. (1999) *Roman and the Enemy: Imperial Strategy in the Principate*, London: University of California Press.

Mattingly, D. J. (1996) 'From one colonialism to another: imperialism and the Maghreb', in J. Webster and N. Cooper (eds) *Roman Imperialism: Post-colonial Perspectives*, Leicester Archaeological Monographs no. 3, Leicester: School of Archaeological Studies, University of Leicester.

— (1997a) 'Dialogues of power and experience in the Roman Empire', in D. J. Mattingly (ed.) *Dialogues in Roman Imperialism: Power, Discourse, and Discrepant Experiences in the Roman Empire*, *Journal of Roman Archaeology*, Supplementary Series no. 23.

— (1997b) 'Africa: a landscape of opportunity', in D. J. Mattingly (ed.) *Dialogues in Roman Imperialism: Power, Discourse, and Discrepant Experiences in the Roman Empire, Journal of Roman Archaeology*, Supplementary Series no. 23.

— (2002) 'Vulgar and weak "Romanization", or time for a paradigm shift?' *Journal of Roman Archaeology* 15: 536–40.

— (ed.) (1997) *Dialogues in Roman Imperialism: Power, Discourse, and Discrepant Experiences in the Roman Empire*, *Journal of Roman Archaeology*, Supplementary Series no. 23.

Mattingly, D. J. and Hitchner, R. B. (1995) 'Roman Africa: an archaeological review', *Journal of Roman Studies* 85: 165–213.

Mattingly, D. J. and Salmon, J. (2001) 'The productive past: economies beyond agriculture', in D. J. Mattingly and J. Salmon (ed.) *Economies Beyond Agriculture in the Classical World*, London: Routledge.

Meadows, K. (1994) 'You are what you eat: diet, identity and Romanisation', in S. Cottam, D. Dungworth, S. Scott and J. Taylor (eds) *TRAC 1994: Proceedings of the Fourth Theoretical Roman Archaeology Conference*, Durham 1994, Oxford: Oxbow.

— (1999) 'The appetites of households in early Roman Britain', in P. M. Allison (ed.) *The Archaeology of Household Activities*, London: Routledge.

Meikle, S. (2002) 'Modernism, economics and the ancient economy', in W. Scheidel and S. von Reden (eds) *The Ancient Economy*, Edinburgh: Edinburgh University Press.

Merryweather, A. D. and Prag, J. R. W. (2003) 'Preface', *Romanization: Digressus. The Internet Journal for the Classical World* 3: 5–6 <http://www.nottingham.ac.uk/classics/digressus/romaniz.html>.

Meskell, L. (1999) 'Introduction: archaeology matters', in L. Meskell (ed.) *Archaeology under Fire: Nationalism, Politics and Heritage in the Eastern Mediterranean and Middle East*, London, Routledge.

— (ed.) (1999) *Archaeology Under Fire: Nationalism, Politics and Heritage in the Eastern Mediterranean and Middle East*, London: Routledge.

Metzler, J., Millett, M., Roymans, N. and Slofstra, J. (eds) (1995) *Integration in the Early Roman West: The Role of Culture and Ideology*, Dossiers d'Archéologie du Musée National d'Histoire et d'Art, no. 4, Luxembourg: Musée National d'Histoire et d'Art.

Mierse, W. E. (1990) 'Augustan building programs in the western provinces', in K. A. Raaflaub and M. Toher (eds) *Between Republic and Empire: Interpretations of Augustus and his Principate*, London: University of California Press.
— (1999) *Temples and Towns in Roman Iberia: The Social and Architectural Dynamics of Sanctuary Design from the Third Century BC to the Third Century AD*, London: University of California Press.
Mikalachki, J. (1998) *The Legacy of Boadicea: Gender and Nation in Early Modern England*, London: Routledge.
Miles, R. (2000) 'Communicating culture, identity and power', in J. Huskinson (ed.) *Experiencing Rome: Culture, Identity and Power in the Roman Empire*, London: Routledge.
Miller, D. (1985) *Artefacts as Categories: A Study of Ceramic Variability in Central India*, Cambridge: Cambridge University Press.
— (1987) *Material Culture and Mass Consumption*, Oxford: Blackwell.
— (1995) 'Introduction: anthropology, modernity and consumption', in D. Miller (ed.) *Worlds Apart: Modernity through the Prism of the Local*, London: Routledge.
— (ed.) (1995) *Worlds Apart: Modernity through the Prism of the Local*, London: Routledge.
Millett, M. (1990a) *The Romanization of Britain: An Essay in Archaeological Interpretation*, Cambridge: Cambridge University Press.
— (1990b) 'Romanization: historical issues and archaeological interpretations', in T. Blagg and M. Millett (eds) *The Early Roman Empire in the West*, Oxford: Oxbow.
— (2001a) 'Approaches to urban societies', in S. James and M. Millett (eds) *Britons and Romans: Advancing an Archaeological Agenda*, York: Council for British Archaeology.
— (2001b) 'Roman interaction in north-western Iberia', *Oxford Journal of Archaeology* 20: 157–70.
Miró, M. T. (1998) 'El nucli ibèric de Tàrraco: dels inicis a la integració dins la ciutat romana', in M. Mayer, J. M. Nolla and J. Pardo (eds) *De les Estructures Indígenes a l'Organització Provincial Romana de la Hispània Citerior*, Barcelona: Ítaca, Annexos 1.
Moatti, C. (1993) *The Search for Ancient Rome*, London: Thames and Hudson.
— (1997) *La Raison de Rome: Naissance de l'esprit critique à la fin de la République (IIe–Ier siècle avant Jésus-Christ)*, Paris: Éditions du Seuil.
Mommsen, T. (1886) *The Provinces of the Roman Empire: From Caesar to Diocletian, Parts 1 and 2*, translated by W. P. Dickson, London: Macmillan and Co.
Mora, G. (2001) 'The image of Rome in Spain: scholars, artists and architects in Italy during the 16th to 18th c.', in R. Hingley (ed.) *Images of Rome: Perceptions of Ancient Rome in Europe and the United States of America in the Modern Age*, *Journal of Roman Archaeology*, Supplementary Series no. 44.
Moreland, J. (2001a) *Archaeology and Text*, London: Duckworth.
— (2001b) 'The Carolingian empire: Rome reborn?', in S. Alcock, N. T. D'Altroy, K. D. Morrison and C. M. Sinopoli (eds) *Empires: Perspectives from Archaeology and History*, Cambridge: Cambridge University Press.
Morgan, L. (2000) 'Creativity out of chaos: poetry between the death of Caesar and the death of Virgil', in O. Taplin (ed.) *Literature in the Roman World*, Oxford: Oxford University Press.
Morgan, T. (1998) *Literate Education in the Hellenistic and Roman Worlds*, Cambridge: Cambridge University Press.
Morley, N. (1997) 'Cities in context: urban systems in Roman Italy', in H. M. Parkins (ed.) *Roman Urbanism: Beyond the Consumer City*, London: Routledge.

— (1999) *Writing Ancient History*, London: Duckworth.
Morris, I. (1994a) 'Introduction', in I. Morris (ed.) *Classical Greece: Ancient Histories and Modern Archaeologies*, Cambridge: Cambridge University Press.
— (1994b) 'Archaeologies of Greece', in I. Morris (ed.) *Classical Greece: Ancient Histories and Modern Archaeologies*, Cambridge: Cambridge University Press.
— (2000) *Archaeology as Cultural History: Words and Things in Iron Age Greece*, London: Blackwell.
— (ed.) (1994) *Classical Greece: Ancient Histories and Modern Archaeologies*, Cambridge: Cambridge University Press.
Mouritsen, H. (1998) *Italian Unification: A Study in Ancient and Modern Historiography*, London: Institute of Classical Studies.
Musco Mendes, N. (2000) 'Cultura e sociedade: conceito e prática da romanização na Lusitânia', in J.-G. Gorges and T. Nogales Basarrate (eds) *Sociedad y Cultura en Lusitania Romana*, Merida: Mesa Redonda Internacional IV.
Myres, F. R. (2001) 'Introduction: the empire of things', in F. R. Myres (ed.) *The Empire of Things: Regimes of Value and Material Culture*, Oxford: School of American Research Press/James Curry.
Myres-Scotton, C. (1993) *Social Motivations for Codeswitching: Evidence from Africa*, Oxford: Clarendon Press.
Nevett, L. and Perkins, P. (2000) Urbanism and urbanization in the Roman world', in J. Huskinson (ed.) *Experiencing Rome: Culture, Identity and Power in the Roman Empire*, London: Routledge.
Niblett, R. (1999) *The Excavation of a Ceremonial Site at Folly Lane, Verulamium*, London: Society for the Promotion of Roman Studies.
— (2001) *Verulamium: The Roman City of St Albans*, Stroud: Tempus.
Nicolet, C. (1991) *Space, Geography, and Politics in the Early Roman Empire*, Ann Arbor: University of Michigan Press.
— (1993) 'The citizen', in A. Giardina (ed.) *The Romans*, originally published in Italian, London: University of Chicago Press.
Nippel, W. (2002 [1996]) 'The construction of the "other"', in T. Harrison (ed.) *Greeks and Barbarians*, Edinburgh, Edinburgh University Press.
Noelke, P. (ed.) (2003) *Romanisation und Resistenz in Plastik, Architektur und Inschriften der Provinzen des Imperium Romanum: Neue Funde und Forschungen. Akten des VII, Internationalen Colloquiums über Probleme des Provinzialrömischen Kunstschaffens, Köln 2. bis 6. Mai 2001*, Mainz-am-Rhein: Philip von Zabern.
Noy, D. (2000) *Foreigners at Rome: Citizens and Strangers*, London: Duckworth.
O'Gorman, E. (1993) 'No place like Rome: identity and difference in the *Germania* of Tacitus', *Ramus* 22: 135–54.
Okun, M. L. (1991) 'Pluralism in Germania Superior', in V. Maxfield and M. J. Dobson (eds) *Roman Frontier Studies 1989: Proceedings of the XVth International Congress of Roman Frontier Studies*, Exeter: University of Exeter Press.
Olivier, L. (1999) 'The origins of French archaeology', *Antiquity* 73: 176–83.
Orejas, A. and Sánchez-Palencia, F.-J. (2002) 'Mines, territorial organization, and social structure in Roman Iberia', *American Journal of Archaeology* 106: 581–99.
Orr, D. G. (1983) 'The Roman city: a philosophical and cultural Summa', in R. T. Marchese (ed.) *Aspects of Graeco-Roman Urbanism: Essays on the Classical City*, BAR International Series no. 188, Oxford: British Archaeological Reports.
Owens, E. J. (1991) *The City in the Greek and Roman World*, London: Routledge.

Pagden, A. (1995) *Lords of all the World: Ideologies of Empire in Spain, Britain and France c.1500–c.1800*, London: Yale University Press.
— (2002) 'Europe: conceptualizing a continent', in A. Pagden (ed.) *The Idea of Europe: From Antiquity to the European Union*, Cambridge: Cambridge University Press.
Pallottino, M. (1991) *A History of Earliest Italy*, originally published in Italian, Ann Arbor: University of Michigan Press.
Panella, C. and Tchernia, A. (2002 [1994]) 'Agricultural products transported in amphorae: olive and wine', in W. Scheidel and S. von Reden (eds) *The Ancient Economy*, Edinburgh: Edinburgh University Press.
Parca, M. (2001) 'Local languages and native cultures', in J. Bodel (ed.) *Epigraphic Evidence: Ancient History from Inscriptions*, London: Routledge.
Parker, A. J. (1987) 'Trade within the empire and beyond the frontiers', in J. Wacher (ed.) *The Roman World*, vol. 2, London: Routledge.
Parkins, H. (1998) 'Time for change? Shaping the future of the ancient economy', in H. Parkins and C. Smith (eds) *Trade, Traders and the Ancient City*, London: Routledge.
Parkins, H. and Smith, C. (eds) (1998) *Trade, Traders and the Ancient City*, London: Routledge.
Parrinder, P. (1999) 'Ancients and moderns: literature and the "Western Canon"', in M. Wyke and M. Biddiss (eds) *The Uses and Abuses of Antiquity*, Bern: Peter Lang.
Passavant, P. A. and Dean, J. (eds) (2004) *Empire's New Clothes: Reading Hardt and Negri*, London: Routledge.
Pastor Muñoz, M. (2000) 'La figura de Viriato y su importancia en la sociedad lusitana', in J.-G. Gorges and T. Nogales Basarrate (eds) *Sociedad y Cultura en Lusitania Romana*, Merida: Mesa Redonda Internacional IV.
— (2003) *Viriato: A Luta pela Liberdade*, originally published in Spanish, Lisbon: Ésquilo.
Paterson, J. (1998) 'Trade and traders in the Roman world: scale, structure, and organisation', in H. Parkins and C. Smith (eds) *Trade, Traders and the Ancient City*, London: Routledge.
Patterson, T. C. (1997) *Inventing Western Civilisation*, New York: Monthly Review Press.
Peralta Labrador, E. (2003) *Los Cántabros: Antes de Roma*, Madrid: Real Academia de la Historia.
Percival, J. (1976) *The Roman Villa: An Historical Introduction*, London: Batsford.
Pérez Losada, F. (1998) 'Cidades e aldeias na Galiza romana. Uma proposta de classificação hierárquica do habitat galaico-romano', *O Arqueólogo Portugues* 4: 157–74.
— (2002) *Entre a Cidade e a Aldea: Estudio Arqueohistórico dos 'Aglomerados Secundarios' Romanos en Galicia*, La Coruña: Museo Arquelóxico e Histórico da Coruña (*Brigantium* 13).
Perkins, P. (2000) 'Power, culture and identity in the Roman economy', in J. Huskinson (ed.) *Experiencing Rome: Culture, Identity and Power in the Roman Empire*, London: Routledge.
Perring, D. (2002) *The Roman House in Britain*, London: Routledge.
Petras, J. and Veltmeyer, H. (2001) *Globalization Unmasked: Imperialism in the 21st Century*, London: Zed.
Pflaum, H.-G. (1973) 'La romanisation de l'Afrique.' *Akten des VI. Internationalen Kongresses für Griechische und Lateinische Epigraphik, München 1972*: 55–68.
Piggott, S. (1968) *The Druids*, London: Thames and Hudson.

— (1989) *Ancient Britons and the Antiquarian Imagination*, London: Thames and Hudson.

Pollard, S. (1968) *The Idea of Progress: History and Society*, London: C. A. Watts.

Pollini, J. (2002) *Gallo-Roman Bronzes and the Process of Romanization: The Cobannus Hoard*, Leiden: Brill.

Pomeroy, A. J. (2003) 'Centre and periphery in Tacitus's *Histories*', *Arethusa* 36: 361–74.

Potter, D. S. (1999) *Literary Texts and the Roman Historian*, London: Routledge.

Powell, A. (1992) 'The *Aeneid* and the embarrassment of Augustus', in A. Powell (ed.) *Roman Poetry and Propaganda in the Age of Augustus*, Bristol: Bristol Classical Press.

Prag, J. R. (2002) 'Epigraphy by numbers: Latin and the epigraphic structure in Sicily', in A. Cooley (ed.) *Becoming Roman, Writing Latin? Literacy and Epigraphy in the Roman West, Journal of Roman Archaeology*, Supplementary Series no. 48.

Purcell, N. (1987) 'Town in country and country in town', in E. B. MacDougall (ed.) *Ancient Roman Villa Gardens*, Dumbarton Oaks Colloquium on the History of Landscape Architecture, Washington DC, Cambridge, MA: Harvard University Press.

— (1990) 'The creation of provincial landscape: the Roman impact on Cisalpine Gaul', in T. Blagg and M. Millett (eds) *The Early Roman Empire in the West*, Oxford: Oxbow.

— (1995) 'The Roman *villa* and the landscape of production', in T. J. Cornell and K. Lomas (eds) *Urban Society in Roman Italy*, London: UCL Press.

Purnell, R. (1978) 'Theoretical approaches to international relations: the contribution of the Graeco-Roman world', in T. Taylor (ed.) *Approaches and Theory in International Relations*, London: Longman.

Quartermaine, L. (1995) '"Slouching towards Rome": Mussolini's imperial vision', in T. J. Cornell and K. Lomas (eds) *Urban Society in Roman Italy*, London: UCL Press.

Queiroga, F. M. V. R. (2003) *War and the Castros: New Approaches to the Northwestern Portuguese Iron Age*, BAR International Series no. 1198, Oxford: British Archaeological Reports.

Raaflaub, K. A. and Samons, L. J. (1990) 'Opposition to Augustus', in K. A. Raaflaub and M. Toher (eds) *Between Republic and Empire: Interpretations of Augustus and his Principate*, London: University of California Press.

Ramage, E. S. (1973) *Urbanitas: Ancient Sophistication and Refinement*, Norman: University of Oklahoma Press.

Rasbach, G. and Becker, A. (2000) 'Neue Forschungsergebnisse der Grabungen in Lahnau-Waldgirmes in Hessen', in L. Wamser (ed.) *Die Römer zwischen Alpen und Nordmeer: Zivilisatorisches Erbe einer Europäischen Militärmacht*, Mainz: Philipp von Zabern.

Rawson, E. (1991 [1987]) '*Discrimina Ordinum*: the *Lex Julia Theatralis*', in E. Rawson, *Roman Culture and Society: Collected Papers*, Oxford: Clarendon Press.

Reece, R. (1980) 'Town and country: the end of Roman Britain', *World Archaeology* 12: 77–91.

— (1988) *My Roman Britain*, Oxford: Oxbow.

Remola, J. A. and Ruiz de Arbulo, J. (2002) 'L'Aigua a la Colònia Tarraco', *Empúries* 53: 29–65.

Renfrew, C. (1995) 'Foreword', in N. Spencer (ed.) *Time, Tradition and Society in Greek Archaeology: Bridging the 'Great Divide'*, London: Routledge.

Révolution Romaine, La (2000) *La Révolution Romaine après Ronald Syme: Bilans et perspectives*, Entretiens sur l'antiquité classique, Geneva: Vandœuvres.
Rich, J. (1993) 'Introduction', in J. Rich and G. Shipley (eds) *War and Society in the Roman World*, London: Routledge.
Rich, J. and Shipley, G. (eds) (1993) *War and Society in the Roman World*, London: Routledge.
Richardson, J. S. (1991) '*Imperium Romanum*: empire and the language of power', *Journal of Roman Studies* 81: 1–9.
Richardson, L. (1992) *A New Topographical Dictionary of Ancient Rome*, London: Johns Hopkins University Press.
Richardson, P. (2002) *City and Sanctuary: Religion and Architecture in the Roman Near East*, London: SCM Press.
Richlin, A. (1997) 'Toward a history of body history', in M. Golden and P. Toohey (eds) *Inventing Ancient Culture: Historicism, Periodization, and the Ancient World*, London: Routledge.
Ridley, R. T. (1992) *The Eagle and the Spade: The Archaeology of Rome during the Napoleonic Era*, Cambridge: Cambridge University Press.
Ríos González, S. and García de Castro Valdés, C. (1998) *Asturias Castreña*, Gijón: Ediciones Trea.
Rist, G. (1997) *The History of Development: From Western Origins to Global Faith*, London: Zed.
Ritzer, G. (1993) *The McDonaldization of Society*, London: Sage.
— (1998) *The McDonaldization Thesis*, London: Sage.
Rives, J. (2001) 'Civic and religious life', in J. Bodel (ed.) *Epigraphic Evidence: Ancient History from Inscriptions*, London: Routledge.
Robertson, R. (1992) *Globalization: Social Theory and Global Culture*, London: Sage.
— (2003) *The Three Waves of Globalization: A History of the Developing Global Consciousness*, London: Zed.
Roerkohl, A. (1992) *Das Hermannsdenkmal*, Münster: Druckerei Blach.
Rofel, L. (2002) 'Modernity's masculine fantasies', in B. M. Knauft (ed.) *Critically Modern: Alternatives, Alterities, Anthropologies*, Bloomington: Indiana University Press.
Roller, M. B. (2001) *Constructing Autocracy: Aristocrats and Emperors in Julio-Claudian Rome*, Oxford: Princeton University Press.
Romanisation du Samnium, La (1991) *La Romanisation du Samnium aux IIe et Ier siècles av. J.-C.*, Naples: Bibliothèque de l'Institut Français de Naples.
Romm, J. S. (1992) *The Edges of the Earth in Ancient Thought: Geography, Exploration and Fiction*, Princeton, NJ: Princeton University Press.
Roth, R. (2003) 'Towards a ceramic approach to social identity in the Roman world: some theoretical considerations', *Digressus: The Internet Journal for the Classical World* 3: 35–45 <http://www.nottingham.ac.uk/classics/digressus/romaniz.html>.
Rowlands, M. (1987) 'The concept of Europe in prehistory', *Man* 22: 558–9.
Roymans, N. (1995) 'Romanization, cultural identity and the ethnic discussion: the integration of the lower Rhine populations in the Roman empire', in J. Metzler, M. Millett, N. Roymans and J. Slofstra (eds) *Integration in the Early Roman West: The Role of Culture and Ideology*, Dossiers d'Archéologie du Musée National d'Histoire et d'Art, no. 4, Luxembourg: Musée National d'Histoire et d'Art.
— (1996) 'The sword or the plough: regional dynamics in the Romanisation of

Belgic Gaul and the Rhineland area', in N. Roymans (ed.) *From the Sword to the Plough*, Amsterdam: Amsterdam Archaeological Studies no. 1.

Ruestes i Bitrià, C. (2001) *L'espai públic a les ciutats romanes del conuentus Tarraconensis: els fòrums*, Barcelona: Universitat Autònoma de Barcelona.

Ruiz, A. M., Sastre, I. and Plácido, D. (2000) 'El nuevo modelo de ocupación del territorio', in F.-J. Sánchez-Palencia (ed.) *Las Médulas (León): Un Paisaje Cultural en la 'Asturia Augustana'*, León: Instituto Leonés de Cultura.

Ruiz de Arbulo Bayona, J. (1998) 'Tarraco: escenografía del poder, administracíon y justicia en una capital provincial Romana (s. II aC–II dC)', *Empúries* 51: 31–61.

Ruiz Zapatero, G. (1996) 'Celts and Iberians: ideological manipulations in Spanish archaeology', in P. M. Graves-Brown, S. Jones and C. Gamble (eds) *Cultural Identity and Archaeology: The Construction of European Communities*, London: Routledge.

Rykwert, J. (1988) *The Idea of a Town: The Anthropology of Urban Form in Rome, Italy and the Ancient World*, revised edition, London: MIT Press.

Said, E. W. (1993) *Culture and Imperialism*, London: Chatto and Windus.

— (2003 [1978]) *Orientalism*, new edition, London: Penguin.

— (2003) 'Preface (2003)', in E. W. Said, *Orientalism*, new edition, London: Penguin.

Saller, R. (2002) 'Framing the debate over growth in the ancient economy', in W. Scheidel and S. von Reden (eds) *The Ancient Economy*, Edinburgh: Edinburgh University Press.

Sánchez-Palencia, F.-J. (1995) 'Minería y metalurgia de la región astur en la antigüedad', in *Astures: Pueblos y Culturas en la frontera del imperio Romano*, Gijón: Gran Enciclopedia Asturiana.

Sánchez-Palencia, F.-J. (ed.) (2000) *Las Médulas (León): Un Paisaje Cultural en la 'Asturia Augustana'*, León: Instituto Leonés de Cultura.

Santos Yanguas, N. (1991) *La Romanízación de Asturîas*, Madrid: Ediciones ISTMO.

Sastre, I. and Orejas, A. (2000) 'Las aristocracias locales y la administración de las minas', in F.-J. Sánchez-Palencia (ed.) *Las Médulas (León): Un Paisaje Cultural en la 'Asturia Augustana'*, León: Instituto Leonés de Cultura.

Savino, E. (1999) *Città di Frontiera nell'Impero Romano: Forme della Romanizzazione da Augusto ai Severi*, Bari: Edipuglia.

Sayas, J. J. (1996) 'Galaicos, astures, cántabros y vascones bajo el dominio romano', in J. M. Blázquez and J. Alvar (eds) *La Romanización en Occidente*, Madrid: Actas Editorial.

Scheidel, W. and von Reden, S. (eds) (2002) *The Ancient Economy*, Edinburgh: Edinburgh University Press.

Schiffer, M. (1999) *The Material Life of Human Beings: Artefacts, Behavior and Communication*, London: Routledge.

Schnapp, A. (1996) *The Discovery of the Past*, London: British Museum Press.

Scott, E. (1991) 'Animal and infant burials in Romano-British villas', in P. Garwood, D. Jennings, R. Skeates and J. Toms (eds) *Sacred and Profane*, Oxford University Committee for Archaeology Monograph no. 32, Oxford: Oxford University Committee for Archaeology.

— (1993) 'Writing the Roman empire', in E. Scott (ed.) *Theoretical Roman Archaeology: First Conference Proceedings*, Aldershot: Avebury.

— (1998) 'Tales from a Romanist: a personal view of archaeology and "equal opportunities"', in C. Forcey, J. Hawthorn and R. Witcher (eds) *TRAC 1997: Proceedings of the Seventh Annual Theoretical Roman Archaeology Conference, Nottingham 1997*, Oxford: Oxbow.

Segrè, C. G. (1974) *Fourth Shore: the Italian Colonization of Libya*, Chicago: University of Chicago Press.

Seth, S. (2003) 'Back to the future?', in G. Balakrishnan (ed.) *Debating Empire*, London: Verso.

Sevillano Fuertes, Á. and Vidal Encinas, J. M. (2000) *Urbs Magnífica. Una Aproximación a la Arqueología de Astúrica Augusta (Astorga, Léon), Museo Romano (Guía-Catálogo)*, Léon: Ayuntamiento de Astorga.

Sewell, W. H. (1999) 'The concept(s) of culture', in V. E. Bonnell and L. Hunt (eds) *Beyond the Cultural Turn*, London: University of California Press.

Shahîd, I. (1984) *Rome and the Arabs: A Prolegomenon to the Study of Byzantium and the Arabs*, Washington, DC: Dumbarton Oaks.

Shanin, T. (1997) 'The idea of progress', in M. Rahnema and V. Bawtree (eds) *The Post-Development Reader*, London: Zed.

Shaw, B. D. (1983) 'Eaters of flesh, drinkers of milk: the ancient Mediterranean ideology of the pastoral nomad', *Ancient Society* 13/14: 5–31.

Sheldon, R. (1982) 'Romanizzazione, acculturazione e resistenza: problemi concettuali nella storia del Nordafrica', *Dialoghi di Archeologia* 4: 102–6.

Sherwin-White, A. N. (1973) *The Roman Citizenship*, Oxford: Clarendon Press.

Shohat, E. and Stam, R. (1994) *Unthinking Eurocentricism: Multiculturalism and the Media*, London: Routledge.

Shore, C. (2002) 'Introduction: towards an anthropology of elites', in C. Shore and S. Nugent (eds) *Elite Cultures: Anthropological Perspectives*, ASA Monograph no. 38, London: Routledge.

Slofstra, J. (2002) 'Batavians and Romans on the Lower Rhine', *Archaeological Dialogues* 9: 16–38.

Small, D. B. (1995) 'Introduction', in D. B. Small (ed.) *Methods in the Mediterranean: Historical and Archaeological Views on Texts and Archaeology*, New York: E. J. Brill.

— (1999) 'The tyranny of the text: lost social strategies in current historical period archaeology in the classical Mediterranean', in P. P. Funari, M. Hall and S. Jones (eds) *Historical Archaeology: Back from the Edge*, London: Routledge.

— (ed.) (1995) *Methods in the Mediterranean: Historical and Archaeological Views on Texts and Archaeology*, New York: E. J. Brill.

Smiles, S. (1994) *The Image of Antiquity: Ancient Britain and the Romantic Imagination*, London: Yale University Press.

Smith, A. D. (1986) *The Ethnic Origins of Nations*, Oxford: Blackwell.

Smith, J. T. (1978) 'Villas as a key to social structure', in M. Todd (ed.) *Studies in the Romano-British Villa*, Leicester: Leicester University Press.

— (1997) *Roman Villas: A Study in Social Structure*, London: Routledge.

Snodgrass, A. (1983) 'Archaeology', in M. Crawford (ed.) *Sources for Ancient History*, Cambridge: Cambridge University Press.

Spencer, N. (1995) 'Introduction', in N. Spencer (ed.) *Time, Tradition and Society in Greek Archaeology: Bridging the 'Great Divide'*, London: Routledge.

Spitulnik, D. A. (2002) 'Accessing "local" modernities: reflections on the place of linguistic evidence in ethnography', in B. M. Knauft (ed.) *Critically Modern: Alternatives, Alterities, Anthropologies*, Bloomington: Indiana University Press.

Stahl, H.-P. (1998) 'Editor's introduction: changing views of the political *Aeneid*', in H.-P. Stahl (ed.) *Vergil's* Aeneid*: Augustan Epic and Political Context*, London: Duckworth.

Stone, M. (1999) 'A flexible Rome: fascism and the cult of *romanità*', in C. Edwards (ed.) *Writing Rome: Textual Approaches to the City*, Cambridge: Cambridge University Press.

Stone, M. P., Haugerud, A. and Little, P. D. (2000) 'Commodities and globalisation: anthropological perspectives', in A. Haugerud, P. Stone and P. D. Little (eds) *Commodities and Globalization: Anthropological Perspectives*, Oxford: Rowman and Littlefield.

Stone, S. (2001) 'The toga: from national to ceremonial costume', in J. L. Sebesta and L. Bonfante (eds) *The World of Roman Costume*, London: University of Wisconsin Press.

Storey, G. R. (1999) 'Archaeology and Roman society: integrating textual and archaeological data', *Journal of Archaeological Research* 7: 203–45.

Stout, A. (2001) 'Jewelry as a symbol of status in the Roman Empire', in J. L. Sebesta and L. Bonfante (eds) *The World of Roman Costume*, London: University of Wisconsin Press.

Stray, C. (1998) *Classics Transformed: Schools, University and Society in England, 1830–1960*, Oxford: Oxford University Press.

Struck, M. (2001) 'The *Heilige Römische Reich Deutscher Nation* and Herman the German', in R. Hingley (ed.) *Images of Rome: Perceptions of Ancient Rome in Europe and the United States of America in the Modern Age*, *Journal of Roman Archaeology*, Supplementary Series no. 44.

Sturgeon, M. C. (2000) 'East meets west: toward a global perspective on the Roman empire', *Journal of Roman Archaeology* 13: 659–67.

Syme, R. (1939) *The Roman Revolution*, Oxford: Clarendon Press.

— (1988 [1983]) 'Rome and the nations', in R. Syme, *Roman Papers IV*, edited by E. Birley, Oxford: Clarendon Press: 62–93.

Taplin, O. (2000) 'Introduction', in O. Taplin (ed.) *Literature in the Roman World*, Oxford: Oxford University Press.

Taylor, J. (2001) 'Rural society in Roman Britain', in S. James and M. Millett (eds) *Britons and Romans: Advancing an Archaeological Agenda*, York: Council for British Archaeology.

Temin, P. (2001) 'A market economy in the early Roman Empire', *Journal of Roman Studies* 91: 169–81.

Terrenato, N. (1998a) 'The Romanization of Italy: global acculturation or cultural *bricolage*?' in C. Forcey, J. Hawthorne and R. Witcher (eds) *TRAC 1997: Proceedings of the Seventh Annual Theoretical Roman Archaeology Conference, Nottingham 1997*, Oxford: Oxbow.

— (1998b) '*Tam firmum municipium*. The Romanization of Volaterrae and its cultural implications', *Journal of Roman Studies* 88: 94–114.

— (2001a) 'Introduction', in S. Keay and N. Terrenato (eds) *Italy and the West: Comparative Issues in Romanization*, Oxford: Oxbow.

— (2001b) 'Ancestor cults: the perception of ancient Rome in modern Italian culture', in R. Hingley (ed.) *Images of Rome: Perceptions of Ancient Rome in Europe and the United States of America in the Modern Age*, *Journal of Roman Archaeology*, Supplementary Series no. 44.

— (2001c) 'A tale of three cities: the Romanization of northern coastal Etruria', in S. Keay and N. Terrenato (eds) *Italy and the West: Comparative Issues in Romanization*, Oxford: Oxbow.

— (2001d) 'The Auditorium site in Rome and the origins of the villa', *Journal of Roman Archaeology* 14: 5–32.
— (in press) 'The deceptive archetype: Roman colonialism in Italy and postcolonial thought', in H. Hurst and S. Owen (eds) *Ancient Colonizations: Analogy, Similarity and Difference*, London: Duckworth.
Thébert, Y. (1978) 'Romanisation et déromanisation en Afrique: histoire décolonisée ou histoire inversée?' *Annales: Économies, Sociétés, Civilisations* 33: 64–82.
Thollard, P. (1987) *Barbarie et civilisation chez Strabon*, Paris: Centre de Recherches d'Histoire Ancienne.
Thomas, C. (ed.) (1966) *Rural Settlement in Roman Britain*, London: Council for British Archaeology.
Thomas, R. F. (2001) *Virgil and the Augustan Reception*, Cambridge: Cambridge University Press.
Thompson, D. (1971) *The Idea of Rome: From Antiquity to the Renaissance*, Albuquerque: University of New Mexico Press.
Tomlinson, J. (1991) *Cultural Imperialism*, London: Continuum.
— (1999) *Globalisation and Culture*, Oxford: Polity Press.
Toner, J. (2002) *Rethinking Roman History*, Cambridge: Oleander Press.
Too, Y. L. (1998a) *The Idea of Ancient Literary Criticism*, Oxford: Clarendon Press.
— (1998b) 'Introduction', in Y. L. Too and N. Livingstone (eds) *Pedagogy and Power: Rhetorics of Classical Learning*, Cambridge: Cambridge University Press.
Too, Y. L. and Livingstone, N. (eds) (1998) *Pedagogy and Power: Rhetorics of Classical Learning*, Cambridge: Cambridge University Press.
Torelli, M. (1995) *Studies in the Romanization of Italy*, originally published in Italian, Edmonton, Alberta: University of Alberta Press.
Trigger, B. G. (1984) 'Alternative archaeologies: nationalist, colonialist, imperialist', *Man* 19: 355–70.
Trimble, J. (2001) 'Rethinking "Romanization" in early imperial Greece', *Journal of Roman Archaeology* 14: 625–8.
Tsing, A. (2002 [2000]) 'Conclusion: the global situation', in J. X. Inda and R. Rosaldo (eds) *The Anthropology of Globalization: A Reader*, Oxford: Blackwell.
Turner, F. M. (1981) *The Greek Heritage in Victorian Britain*, London: Yale University Press.
— (1989) 'Why the Greeks and not the Romans in Victorian Britain?', in G. W. Clarke (ed.) *Rediscovering Hellenism: The Hellenistic Inheritance and the English Imagination*, Cambridge: Cambridge University Press.
Vallat, J.-P. (1987) 'Les structures agraires de l'Italie républicaine', *Annales: Économies, Sociétés, Civilisations* 42: 181–218.
— (1991) 'Survey archaeology and rural history – a difficult but productive relationship', in G. Barker and J. Lloyd (eds) *Roman Landscapes: Archaeological Survey in the Mediterranean Region*, London: The British School at Rome, Archaeological Monographs.
— (2001) 'The Romanization of Italy: conclusions', in S. Keay and N. Terrenato (eds) *Italy and the West: Comparative Issues in Romanization*, Oxford: Oxbow.
van Dommelen, P. (1993) 'Roman peasants and rural organization in central Italy: an archaeological perspective', in E. Scott (ed.) *Theoretical Roman Archaeology: First Conference Proceedings*, Aldershot: Avebury.
— (1997) 'Colonial constructs: colonialism and archaeology in the Mediterranean', *World Archaeology* 28: 305–23.

— (2001) 'Cultural imaginings: Punic tradition and local identity in Roman Republican Sardinia', in S. Keay and N. Terrenato (eds) *Italy and the West: Comparative Issues in Romanization*, Oxford: Oxbow.

van Driel-Murray, C. (2002) 'Ethnic soldiers: the experience of the lower Rhine tribes', in T. Grünewald and S. Seibel (eds) *Kontinuität und Diskontinuität: Germania inferior am Beginn und am Ende der römischen Herrschaft. Beiträge des Deutsch-niederländischen Kolloquiums in der Katholieke Universiteit Nijmegen (27. bis 30.06.2001)*, Berlin: Walter de Gruyter.

van Enckevort, H. and Thijssen, J. (2003) 'Nijmegen – a Roman town in the frontier zone of *Germania Inferior*', in P. Wilson (ed.) *The Archaeology of Roman Towns*, Oxford: Oxbow.

van Es, W. A. (1983) 'Introduction', in R. Brandt and J. Slofstra (eds) *Roman and Native in the Low Countries: Spheres of Interaction*, BAR International Series no. 184, Oxford: British Archaeological Reports.

Vance, N. (1997) *The Victorians and Ancient Rome*, Oxford: Blackwell.

Vance, W. L. (1989) *America's Rome*, New Haven, CT: Yale University Press.

Vasunia, P. (2001) *The Gift of the Nile: Hellenizing Egypt from Aeschylus to Alexander*, London: University of California Press.

— (2003) 'Hellenism and empire: reading Edward Said', *Parallax* 9: 88–97.

Vercingétorix et Alésia (1994) *Vercingétorix et Alésia*, St-Germain-en-Laye: Musée des Antiquités Nationales.

Veyne, P. (1993) '*Humanitas*: Romans and non-Romans', in A. Giardina (ed.) *The Romans*, originally published in Italian, London: University of Chicago Press.

Vickers, M. (1994) 'Nabataea, India, Gaul and Carthage: reflections on Hellenistic and Roman gold vessels and red-gloss pottery', *American Journal of Archaeology* 98: 231–48.

Vilas, F. A. and Fuentes, C. D. (1996) *Museo do Castro de Viladonga*, Lugo: Xunta de Galicia.

von Schnurbein, S. (2003) 'Augustus in *Germania* and his new "town" at Waldgirmes east of the Rhine', *Journal of Roman Archaeology* 16: 93–108.

Wacher, J. (1987) *The Roman Empire*, London: Dent.

— (1995) *The Towns of Roman Britain*, second edition, London: Routledge.

Walbank, F. W. (1979) 'Introduction', in Polybius, *The Rise of the Roman Empire*, London: Penguin.

Walker, S. (1991) *Roman Art*, London: British Museum.

Wallace-Hadrill, A. (1989) 'Rome's cultural revolution', *Journal of Roman Studies* 79: 157–64.

— (1994) *Houses and Society in Pompeii and Herculaneum*, Princeton, NJ: Princeton University Press.

— (1997) '*Mutatio morum*: the idea of a cultural revolution', in N. T. Habinek and S. Schiesaro (eds) *The Roman Cultural Revolution*, Cambridge: Cambridge University Press.

— (1998) 'To be Greek, go Greek: thoughts on Hellenization at Rome', in M. Austin, J. Harries and C. Smith (eds) *Modus Operandi: Essays in Honour of Geoffrey Rickman*, London: Institute of Classical Studies.

— (2000) 'The Roman revolution and material culture', in *La Révolution Romaine après Ronald Syme: Bilans et perspectives*, Entretiens sur l'antiquité classique, Geneva: Vandœuvres.

— (2001) *The British School at Rome. One Hundred Years*, London: British School at Rome.

Waquet, F. (2001) *Latin or the Empire of a Sign, from the Sixteenth to the Twentieth Centuries*, originally published in French, London: Verso.

Ward-Perkins, J. B. (1970) 'From Republic to Empire: reflections on the early provincial architecture of the Roman West', *Journal of Roman Studies* 60: 1–19.

Webster, J. (1995) 'The just war: Graeco-Roman text as colonial discourse', in S. Cottam, D. Dungworth, S. Scott and J. Taylor (eds) *TRAC 1994: Proceedings of the Fourth Theoretical Roman Archaeology Conference, Durham 1994*, Oxford: Oxbow.

— (1996) 'Roman imperialism and the "post-imperial age"', in J. Webster and N. Cooper (eds) *Roman Imperialism: Post-colonial Perspectives*, Leicester Archaeological Monographs no. 3, Leicester: School of Archaeological Studies, University of Leicester.

— (1999) 'A new Roman Britain? Recent developments in Romano-British archaeology', *American Journal of Archaeology* 103: 122–5.

— (2001) 'Creolizing the Roman provinces', *American Journal of Archaeology* 105: 209–25.

— (in press) 'Archaeologies of slavery and servitude: bringing "New World" perspectives to Roman Britain', in H. Hurst and S. Owen (eds) *Ancient Colonizations: Analogy, Similarity and Difference*, London: Duckworth.

Wells, C. M. (1972) *The German Policy of Augustus: An Examination of the Archaeological Evidence*, Oxford: Clarendon Press.

Wells, P. S. (2003) *The Battle that Stopped Rome: Emperor Augustus, Arminius, and the Slaughter of the Legions in the Teutoburg Forest*, London: W. W. Norton.

Whitley, J. (2001) *The Archaeology of Ancient Greece*, Cambridge: Cambridge University Press.

Whittaker, C. R. (1985) 'Trade and the aristocracy in the Roman Empire', *Opus* 4: 49–76.

— (1993) 'The poor', in A. Giardina (ed.) *The Romans*, originally published in Italian, London: University of Chicago Press.

— (1994) *Frontiers of the Roman Empire*, London: Johns Hopkins University Press.

— (1995) 'Integration of the early Roman West: the example of Africa', in J. Metzler, M. Millett, N. Roymans and J. Slofstra (eds) *Integration in the Early Roman West: The Role of Culture and Ideology*, Dossiers d'Archéologie du Musée National d'Histoire et d'Art, no. 4, Luxembourg: Musée National d'Histoire et d'Art.

— (1997) 'Imperialism and culture: the Roman initiative', in D. J. Mattingly (ed.) *Dialogues in Roman Imperialism: Power, Discourse, and Discrepant Experiences in the Roman Empire*, *Journal of Roman Archaeology*, Supplementary Series no. 23.

Wightman, E. M. (1975) 'The pattern of rural settlement in Roman Gaul', *Aufstieg und Niedergang der Römischen Welt* II, 4: 584–657.

Wilk, R. (1995) 'Learning to be local in Belize: global systems of common difference', in D. Miller (ed.) *Worlds Apart: Modernity through the Prism of the Local*, London: Routledge.

— (1996) 'Connections and contradictions: from the Crooked Tree Cashew Queen to Miss World Belize', in C. B. Cohen, R. Wilk and B. Stoeltje (eds) *Beauty Queens on the Global Stage: Gender, Contests and Power*, London: Routledge.

Willems, W. J. H. (1984) 'Romans and Batavians: a regional study in the Dutch East Rivers area II', *Berichten van de Rijksdienst voor het Oudheidkundig Bodemonderzoek* 34: 39–332.

Williams, J. H. C. (2001) 'Roman intentions and Romanization: Republican northern Italy', in S. Keay and N. Terrenato (eds) *Italy and the West: Comparative Issues in Romanization*, Oxford: Oxbow.

— (2002) 'Pottery stamps, coin designs, and writing in late Iron Age Britain', in A. Cooley (ed.) *Becoming Roman, Writing Latin? Literacy and Epigraphy in the Roman West, Journal of Roman Archaeology*, Supplementary Series no. 48.

Williams, P. and Chrisman, L. (eds) (1993) *Colonial Discourse and Post-colonial Theory: A Reader*, London: Harvester.

Williams, R. (1981) *Keywords: A Vocabulary of Culture and Society*, London: Flamingo.

Willis, S. (1995) 'Roman imports into late Iron Age British societies: towards a critique of existing models', in S. Cottam, D. Dungworth, S. Scott and J. Taylor (eds) *TRAC 1994: Proceedings of the Fourth Theoretical Roman Archaeology Conference, Durham 1994*, Oxford: Oxbow.

— (1998) 'Samian pottery in Britain: exploring its distribution and archaeological potential', *Archaeological Journal* 155: 82–133.

Witcher, R. (1998) 'Roman roads: phenomenological perspectives on roads in the landscape', in C. Forcey, J. Hawthorne and J. Witcher (eds) *TRAC 1997: Proceedings of the Seventh Annual Theoretical Roman Archaeology Conference, Nottingham 1997*, Oxford: Oxbow.

— (2000) 'Globalisation and Roman imperialism: perspectives on identities in Roman Italy', in E. Herring and K. Lomas (eds) *The Emergence of State Identities in Italy in the First Millennium BC*, Accordia Specialist Studies in Italy no. 8, London: Accordia Research Institute.

Wood, M. and Queiroga, F. (eds) (1992) *Current Research on the Romanization of the Western Provinces*, BAR International Series no. 575, Oxford: British Archaeological Reports.

Woolf, G. (1992a) 'The unity and diversity of Romanisation,' *Journal of Roman Archaeology* 5: 349–52.

— (1992b) 'Imperialism, empire and the integration of the Roman economy', *World Archaeology* 23: 283–93.

— (1993) 'Roman peace', in J. Rich and G. Shipley (eds) *War and Society in the Roman World*, London: Routledge.

— (1994) 'Power and the spread of writing in the West', in A. Bowman and G. Woolf (eds) *Literacy and Power in the Ancient World*, Cambridge: Cambridge University Press.

— (1995) 'The formation of Roman provincial cultures', in J. Metzler, M. Millett, N. Roymans and J. Slofstra (eds) *Integration in the Early Roman West: The Role of Culture and Ideology*, Dossiers d'Archéologie du Musée National d'Histoire et d'Art, no. 4, Luxembourg: Musée National d'Histoire et d'Art.

— (1996) 'Monumental writing and the expansion of Roman society in the early Empire', *Journal of Roman Studies* 86: 22–39.

— (1997) 'Beyond Roman and natives', *World Archaeology* 28: 339–50.

— (1998) *Becoming Roman: The Origins of Provincial Civilization in Gaul*, Cambridge: Cambridge University Press.

— (2000a) 'Literacy', in A. Bowman, P. Garnsey and D. Rathbone (eds) *Cambridge Ancient History, vol. XI: The High Empire, AD 70–192*, Cambridge: Cambridge University Press.

— (2000b) 'Urbanization and its discontents in early Roman Gaul', in E. Fentress

(ed.) *Romanization and the City: Creation, Transformations, and Failures*, *Journal of Roman Archaeology*, Supplementary Series no. 38.
— (2001a) 'The Roman cultural revolution in Gaul', in S. Keay and N. Terrenato (eds) *Italy and the West: Comparative Issues in Romanization*, Oxford: Oxbow.
— (2001b) 'Inventing empire in ancient Rome', in S. Alcock, T. N. D'Altroy, K. D. Morrison and C. M. Sinopoli (eds) *Empires: Perspectives from Archaeology and History*, Cambridge: Cambridge University Press.
— (2001c) 'MacMullen's Romanization', *Journal of Roman Archaeology* 14: 575–9.
— (2001d) 'Regional productions in early Roman Gaul', in D. J. Mattingly and J. Salmon (eds) *Economies beyond Agriculture in the Classical World*, London: Routledge.
— (2002) 'Afterword: how the Latin West was won', in A. Cooley (ed.) *Becoming Roman, Writing Latin? Literacy and Epigraphy in the Roman West*, *Journal of Roman Archaeology*, Supplementary Series no. 48.
Wyke, M. (1999) 'Sawdust Caesar: Mussolini, Julius Caesar, and the drama of dictatorship', in M. Wyke and M. Biddiss (eds) *The Uses and Abuses of Antiquity*, Bern: Peter Lang.
Wyke, M. and Biddiss, M. (1999) 'Introduction: using and abusing antiquity', in M. Wyke and M. Biddiss (eds) *The Uses and Abuses of Antiquity*, Bern: Peter Lang.
Wyke, M. and Biddiss, M. (eds) (1999) *The Uses and Abuses of Antiquity*, Bern: Peter Lang.
Zanker, P. (1987) *Augustus und die Macht der Bilder*, Munich: Beck.
— (1988) *The Power of Images in the Age of Augustus*, originally published in German, Ann Arbor: University of Michigan Press.
— (2000) 'The city as symbol: Rome and the creation of an urban image', in E. Fentress (ed.) *Romanization and the City: Creation, Transformations, and Failures*, *Journal of Roman Archaeology*, Supplementary Series no. 38.

INDEX

academics 92; British 8
administration 45, 47, 65, 67, 78, 82, 87, 95, 96, 99, 102, 104, 105, 112; in Germania 66; Iberian 104; in Lower Rhine Valley 95; models of 69; provincial 70
administrators: English 26; late Victorian 26; provincial 68; Roman 35, 54
aesthetics 58
Africa 28, 56; North 2, 17, 28, 39, 40
African Red Slip ware 109
age: definition of 76
agency 37, 42, 95
Agricola, Julius 25 (Figure 3), 35, 65, 66, 68
agriculture 88, 107, 115, 119; arable 95; products of 106
Agrippa 79
ahistoricism 6, 7
Albania 28
Alcester 113
Alcock, Susan 17
alder 99
Alföldy, Géza 115
Algeria: French colonial occupation of 8
allies of Rome 32, 56
altars: dedicated to Augustus 84; provincial 81
American commercial imperialism 108
amphitheatres: in Rome and Italy 81; provincial 81; at Tarraco 84
amphorae 106, 110, 114
anachronism 12, 13
analogy, ethnographic 28
ancestry 19, 23; Greek 62; national 27; Roman 79; tribal 87
Ando, Clifford 74
Anglo-Saxons 33
animals 10
anthropologists 73
anthropology 1, 36, 41, 48, 51, 73; social 52
antiquarianism 23
appearance, personal: provincial 75, 76; Roman 72, 74, 76
Appian 8, 32
Apulia: Daunia 10
aqueduct 81
arable agriculture 95
Arabs 28
arcades 35, 66, 75
archaeological approaches: inherited 92
archaeological research 65, 73, 88, 92, 105; strategy 91
archaeological signatures 47
archaeological survey 93, 113
archaeologists 2, 3, 4, 10, 11, 14, 15, 16, 17, 23, 36, 41, 44, 73, 75, 92, 105, 109, 110, 113, 114, 115, 116
archaeology 20, 30, 33, 44, 66, 73, 85, 98, 102, 103, 114; classical 3, 18, 22, 29; democratization of 10; French colonial 40; funding of 36; interpretative 4; post-processual 4; prehistoric 23; relationship with history 10, 11; research in 11, 23; role of 10; Roman period 10, 11, 39, 40, 92; 'text-aided' 4
arches, triumphal 62
architectural rules, Roman 89
architectural traditions, domestic 110
architecture 46; Augustan 80; classical models for 6; domestic 88; European 20; of forts 94; monumental 30, 69, 76, 77, 109; provincial 75, 79, 81, 88; of public buildings 80; Roman 72, 74, 75, 79, 81, 88, 95, 100; Roman concepts of 82; at Tarraco 85; urban 43, 69; of villas 88
Arezzo 100
aristocracy: conduct of Roman 60, 62;

Iberian 104; provincial native 70; Roman 49, 60, 61, 63; *see also* elite
Arminius 23, 66
army, Roman 22, 44, 54, 56, 68, 70, 94, 95, 96–9, 100, 102, 104; *see also* auxiliary army, legions, military
Arretine ware 100
Arretium 100
Arrow Valley113
art 34; ancient 10, 18; Augustan 57; classical models for 6; European 20; imperial monumental 62; objects 4; Roman 15, 30, 39, 74, 75; styles of 58
artefacts 11 (Table 1.1); circulation of 54, 107; origins of 23; prehistoric 24; Roman 74, 80; transport of 108
artists: European 23; Roman 61
Asia: pairing with Europe of 28
Asia Minor 100
assimilation 34, 43, 48, 50, 55, 64, 82, 111
Astúrica Augusta (Astorga) 104
Athens 17, 100
Augustan cultural revolution 101, 58, 118
Augustan culture 6, 7, 9, 51, 58, 70
Augustan ideology 51
Augustan period 6, 7, 9, 55, 80, 100
Augustodunum 68
Augustus 2, 5, 6, 7, 8, 9, 16, 32, 43, 55, 56, 57, 58, 60, 69, 76, 78, 79, 80, 81, 82, 84, 93, 101; altar dedicated to 84; cult of 85; Divine, temple of 84; invention of empire 57; mausoleum of 79; portrayals of 80; *Res Gestae* 92; visit to Tarraco 84, 85
Autun 68
auxiliary army, Roman 56, 98, 102, 104; Batavians in 96–8; commanders of 97

Baetica 91, 115
Ball, Warwick 29, 55
banquets 35, 65, 66, 75
barbarians 8, 15, 17, 22–4, 26–9, 30, 32, 38, 39, 43, 52, 61–2, 63–4, 69, 77; conquest of 63; German 66; Greek definition of 62; invasions of 27; non-Greek-speakers 61; origins of 62, 64; populations 20; privileged 66
barbarism 16, 17, 23, 27, 38, 64, 65; and civilization 22; inherited 29
Barnard, Edward: *The New, Comprehensive, Impartial and Complete History of England* 25 (Figure 3)
Barrett, John 13, 46, 48, 71
barrows 24
basilica 81, 104; at Tarraco 84; at Verulamium 85
Batavians 22, 95, 97–8, 99, 102, 114; military recruitment of 96; Ninth Cohort of 98; at Vindolanda 97;
bathhouses 24, 35, 43, 65, 66, 75, 76, 81, 88, 108
bathing 76, 81
Bauman, Zygmunt 49, 53
Beard, Mary 10, 19, 20
behaviour: aristocratic 60, 63, 72; barbarian 61; Greek 63
beliefs 20, 70; transport of 108
Benton, Cindy 4
Berbers 29
Bernal, Martin 27
binary opposites 38, 48, 64
birch 99
Black Sea 61
Boadicea *see* Boudica
boats 106
Bonfante, Larissa 72
books 17, 18; circulation of 68
Boudica 23
boundaries 118
bowls 109, 113
Brennan, Timothy 119
bric-à-brac 73, 107
bricolage, cultural 55
Britain 17, 18, 22, 23, 24, 26, 32, 33, 34, 35, 36, 37, 40, 41, 45, 46, 51, 57, 66, 68, 75, 77, 82, 85, 89, 94, 100, 107, 110–14, 115, 116
Britannia 35, 65, 68, 97
Britons, ancient 22, 33, 35, 41, 65–6
broch 112 (Figure 10)
Brunt, P. A. 45; 'The Romanization of the Local Ruling Classes of the Roman Empire', 41
building: materials 89; programmes in Gaul 80; traditions, Roman 89
buildings 58, 62, 69, 72–3, 74, 77, 80, 98; Augustan 82; cult 84; elite 109; monumental 74, 85; pre-Roman 89; provincial 75, 80–1, 90, 104; public 74, 84, 80, 82, 84, 87, 89, 102, 105, 108; stone-built 81, 89; at Tarraco 84–5; *see also* amphitheatres, basilica, bathhouses, broch, byre, castros, churches, henges, houses, hut of Romulus, temples
burials: early Roman 87; at Folly Lane, Verulamium 87; of Roman citizens 75

business: activities 99; language of 100
byre 95
Byzantine civilization 29

Caesar, Julius 1, 33, 56
campaigns, Roman 61
Camulodunum 87
capitalism 19
Capitolium 78
Caracalla 57
casa Romuli see hut of Romulus
castros 102, 103–4; pre-Roman origins of 102; 103 (Figure 9)
cattle: ownership of 98; rearing 95
cellar 95
'Celtic qualities' 35
censuses 57
'central enclosure' 85
centurions 68
Cerialis, Flavius 98
ceremonies 76
Charlemagne 20
chiefs 68
Christianity 19, 20, 21
churches 24
circulation of pottery 109
circus 84
cities 1, 30, 34, 36, 39, 44, 46, 49, 54, 66, 76–9, 81, 89, 92, 95, 101, 102, 104, 105, 107, 109; gates of 79; Graeco-Roman concept of 109; idealized 78; modern concept of 17; provincial form of 82; Roman concept of 78; Roman model for 81; standard Roman 80, 87
citizens, Roman 16, 56–7, 60, 64, 75, 76, 82; burials of 75
citizenship, Roman 34, 56–7, 64, 75, 76, 98
city planning 46
city-states: Greek 61; of Rome 54
civil policy, Roman 8
Civilis 23
civilization: classical 18, 22, 24, 26, 39, 62; concept of 64; displacement of 21; European 38; gift of 28; Graeco-Roman 35; Greek 63; inheritance from Rome of 21, 27, 29; Mediterranean 26, 27; modern 38; native 24; passage to 38, 62, 63; prehistoric 24; Roman 17, 20, 26, 33–6, 39, 40, 43, 45, 62, 64, 66, 108, 115; Roman accounts of 15; Roman concept of 69; self- 67; Western 18, 20, 22, 38, 58, 91
civilization and barbarism 22
civilization, Byzantine 29
civilizing missions 38, 64; European 27; modern imperial 65; Roman 8, 24, 28, 33, 65, 66, 70
civitas capital 82, 85
Clarke, Katherine 12
classicists 4, 10, 11
classics, classical studies 4, 8, 10, 11, 18, 19, 20, 23, 37
classification 23, 61, 64, 73
Claudia Rufina 66
cleanliness 81
clients 88
cloth 76
clothing 74; barbarian 61; at Vindolanda 98; *see also* garments
coins 73; Iron Age 111; Roman 43, 72, 74, 80–1, 84, 94, 105, 107
Colchester 87
Collingwood, R. G. 35
colonial administrators 18, 28
colonial adventurers 8
Colonial Office 67
colonial possessions 28
colonialism 8, 18, 22, 27, 40, 72; British 67; discourse of 41, 42, 92; European 28; French 28; Italian 28; *see also* neo-colonialism
colonies: Roman 77–8; Tarraco 84
colonization 36, 47; European 27; Greek 61
colonizers 28; Roman 36
colonnades 65, 88
commonwealth, Roman 10
Communism 19
conquest 17, 62, 68; modern justification of 65; Roman 17, 24, 26, 27, 30, 48, 54, 55, 64, 67, 68, 69, 70, 77, 82, 85, 90, 110, 111, 115; Roman justification of 63; Spanish 20; strategy for 70
consumer culture 106–7
consumer revolution 108, 115
consumers 101
consumption 73, 106, 113; of food and drink 76; of pottery 109; varying patterns of 113
council, local provincial 79
countryside 88, 89, 92
courtyard 88
craftsmen 108; Gallo-Roman 95
craftspeople 108
Cranborne Chase 34

crops 10
cults: imperial 87; local provincial 79; in Rome 84; at Tarraco 84, 85; of tribal ancestor 87
cultural anxiety 63
cultural 'mapping' 63
cultural power, Roman 50
cultural revolution 47, 58, 69
cultural studies 51–2, 54
culture-history 51
cultures: identification of 90
cups 110, 113
Curchin, Leonard 18

Dacia 23
Dacians 22
Danube 56
Decabalus 23
descent 56
decline and fall 26
decolonization 40
decoration: architectural 88; personal 34
democracy 21
denarius 2 (Figure 1)
denationalization 34
deportation 120
Derks, Ton 95, 97–8, 102
destiny, imperial 60
destructuring, archaeological 10
deterritorialization 53
development theory 37
dictators, twentieth-century 7
dining: creation of Roman ways of 110, 113; rooms 89
Dio, Cassius 1, 65, 66, 82
Diocletian 33
discrepant experiences 102
dishes 113
diversity 53; cultural 37, 102; of identities 108; local 60; of priesthood 85; regional 2, 10, 120; of responses to incorporation 36; of writing styles 98
documents 11 (Table 1.1), 92, 94, 97
domestic occupation 81
domestic space 87–8, 95
domination 4, 5, 6, 29, 93; Augustan 61, 79; discourse of 6, 8, 10, 21, 60, 92; facilitated by roads 78; imperial 8, 26; justification of 63; language of 88; Roman 26, 31, 67, 70, 79; Western 21
Dougherty, Carol 91
Douglas, Mary 73
Downs, Mary 48, 91, 115
drawings of prehistoric peoples 28
dress: adoption of new forms of 105; military 94; provincial 75–6, 105; Roman 35, 65, 72, 73, 75–6; standardization of 76; styles of 66; *see also* clothing, garments, toga
drinking 110, 111, 113
dynastic strategies, Julio-Claudian 87
dynasties, imperial 87
Dyson, Steve 108

East, the 3, 5, 15, 19
eating 76, 89, 110, 111, 114, 115
economic growth 106
education 64; classical 39, 44, 49, 60, 64, 67, 68, 69, 101; elite 11 (Table 1.1), 72; European 20; Greek 63; Greek principles of 60; modern Western 67; of native rulers 35; process of 66; provincial 68, 70; Roman 57, 58, 67, 68
elite 11 (Table 1.1), 14, 53, 59, 60; domestic space 88; modern European 20, 22
elite-focused perspectives 48
elite-focused strategy 92
elite, native 27, 42, 43, 45, 46, 47, 56, 65, 67, 68–70, 75, 76, 79, 81, 82, 91, 115, 118; families 97; officials 95
elite negotiation 48, 54
elite, provincial 34, 37, 45, 49, 50–1, 64, 67, 70–1, 79, 80, 82, 85, 87–9, 91, 92, 93, 95, 104–5, 107, 110, 115; at Autun 68; housing of 89; Iberian 104; identifier of 76; localized identity of 71; male 91; military 94; relationship with emperor and Rome 79; Romano-British 35, 75; in southern Spain 48; visits to other provinces of 69; visits to Rome of 69
elite, Roman 26, 57, 60, 61, 62–3, 64, 65–6, 70, 72, 77, 81, 88, 92, 93, 94, 98, 99, 106, 107, 109, 119; author 35; buildings 109; culture 49, 94, 98, 101; identity 50, 94; Italian 54, 55, 92; late Republican 88; male 8, 60, 76; of Rome 60, 101; settlement developments 88; values 75
Elsner, Jas 57
Empel 97
emperors 58, 79, 85; Augustus 2, 56, 57, 58, 60; authority of 78; Caracalla 57; cult of 87; image on coins 81; Julio-Claudian 84; name on milestones 81; physical

influence of 80; representations of 81; Tiberius 84; worship of 80, 82, 84, 87
empire, British 26, 40
empire, discourse of 70
empire, Germanic 20
empire imagery 80–1, 89
empire, Roman 3 (Figure 2); Augustan discourse of 70; creation of 49, 50; early 15; Eastern 17, 19, 29, 55; extent of 62; later 55; northern 34, 44; north-west 65; *Pax Romana* 21; periphery of 55, 61; political system of 70; Roman accounts of 15; southern 29; Western 3, 11, 15, 17, 19, 20, 22, 27, 29, 34–5, 39, 42–4, 55, 64, 78, 79, 80, 82, 84, 85, 87–8, 89, 91, 92, 98, 99, 101, 102, 104, 107, 109, 110, 114, 115, 118
empires, ancient 120
empires, modern: concepts of 16; European 27; *Pax Americana* 21; *Pax Britannica* 21; Western 22, 28, 34, 38, 40, 41, 65; of the world 27
enclosure, ditched 87
English 26; character of 33
engravings: of prehistoric peoples 28
Enlightenment, the 5
enslavement 65, 120; *see also* slavery
epic poetry 101
epigraphy 85; sources of 36
equestrians 60, 98
ethics 63, 64, 67
ethnic past 24
ethnicity 38, 51, 56, 61, 99; terms of 22, 23; *see also* identity, ethnic
ethnography 28, 61
Etruscans 15, 22, 79; settlement developments of 88
Eurocentrism 21, 22, 92; discourse of 29
Europe 2, 4, 5, 14, 18, 19, 20, 21, 22, 23, 24, 27, 28, 29, 33, 35, 36, 44, 51, 55, 56; Christian 20; eastern 19; northern 17, 22, 54, 55, 68, 78, 99, 107; pairing with Asia of 28; prehistoric 23; present-day 21; western 10, 20, 22, 23, 24, 26, 31, 35, 36, 38, 39, 43, 69, 89
Europeans 19, 21
Evans, Jerry 113
Evans, Rhiannon 65
evolutionary theory 5, 37, 38
excavations 10–11, 36, 92, 104; reports 107; strategies 92; at Vindolanda 98
exchange 73, 77, 100, 106, 107
exclusionism 24
factories, pottery 100
Fairy Knowe 111 (Figure 10)
families: native elite 85, 88, 97; of soldiers 99
farmers 10
farms 106, 115
Farrell, Joseph 61
Fascism 7
favour 65; divine 67
Fear, Trevor 5
Featherstone, Mike 53
Ferguson, James 117
fetishism 73
fiction 13
finance 108
finds *see* objects
Flavian period 65, 66, 84
Flavius Cerialis *see* Cerialis, Flavius
floors, mosaic 89
Folly Lane, Verulamium 87
food 10, 114; consumption of 74, 110, 113, 114; new types of 110; preparation of 74, 110, 114; serving 114; at Vindolanda 98
fortresses 94
forts 24, 30, 36, 39, 92, 94, 101
forum 81, 102, 104; at Rome 79; at Tarraco 84; at Verulamium 85, 87
fountains 81
France 22, 24, 35, 89; south-eastern 99
Fredrick, David 46
free men and women 56, 64
free women 56
freed slaves 56, 108
Freeman, Philip 44, 45
friendly kingdoms: sons of leaders of 69
Frisians 69
frontiers 36, 62, 107, 117; areas of 94, 95; military 110; modern issues of 26; policy 6, 7, 65; works on 24, 92
furniture 88, 89

Galinsky, Karl 6, 7, 8, 9, 58; *Augustan Culture* 6, 7
Gallic culture 35
Gallo-Roman pottery 101
Gallo-Romans: contribution to imperial culture 101; craftsmen 95; officials 95; soldiers 95; veterans 95
garments, Roman 76; colour of 76
Gaul 17, 18, 23, 32, 45, 69, 80, 95, 100, 104, 115; central 77; northern 95, 97; pottery factories in 100; southern 94

Gaulish writing 99
Gauls 22, 48
Gellner, Ernest 9
gender 56, 118
generals, Roman 22, 67
genocide 120
geography 9, 12, 45, 50, 53, 61; knowledge of 27; Roman imperial concepts of 79
geography of connectivity 108
Germania 66, 95
Germania Inferior 94
Germanic peoples, modern 24
Germans 22, 33
Germany 7, 8, 18, 23, 24, 31, 45, 51, 66, 77, 82, 94, 100
gestures 76
Getae 68
Giddens, Anthony 5, 6
globalization 1, 5, 6, 9, 48, 53, 118, 120; local 111
globalizing 49, 72, 109, 119
globe 1 (Figure 1)
glocalization 111
gold, mining 102
goods 43, 73, 75, 100, 106; acquisition of 107; adoption of 105; attributed as Roman 45; availability of 108; in building styles 89; circulation of 54, 108; consumption of 73; definition of 44; in interdependent relationships 73; movement of 106–7, 111; new 45, 107; range of 107; reasons for acquiring 73; reception of 106; Roman attitudes to 107; in social exchange 72; superior 47; transport of 99
government 50; elite discourse of 108; local 79, 81, 85, 115; Roman 57, 69, 75, 77; systems of 69
governors, provincial 67
Graeco-Roman: concept of the city 109; culture 102, 119; mythology 101; perspective 40
Grafton, Anthony 9
Grand Tour 18
Greece classical 17, 18, 19, 20, 21, 26, 29, 55, 63
Greek: cultural models 55; culture 26, 29, 63, 91; educational principles 60; language 60, 62, 68; literature 68; *see also* Hellenization, Latin–Greek civilizing process
Greeks 19, 26, 61, 79
grooming 76
guilt, post-colonial 46, 65
Gupta, Akhil 117

Habinek, Thomas 8, 10, 51, 61
Haley, Evan W. 115
Hanson, Bill 17, 42, 45
Hardt, Michael and Negri, Antonio: *Empire* 9, 117, 119
Haverfield, Francis 16, 18, 33–5, 37, 38, 39, 42, 43, 44, 45, 48; *The Romanization of Roman Britain* 33
Hayes, John 100
hearth 109
heating 89
hegemony: European 9; global Roman 118; Roman aristocratic, 63; social 4; universal Roman 1
Hellenism 20
Hellenistic: culture 88; Greek imagery 100
Hellenization 55
Henderson, John 10, 19, 20
henges 24
Herman *see* Arminius
Hertfordshire 85
hillforts 24
hilltop sites 103 (Figure 9), 104
historians 3, 4, 5, 7, 10, 14, 15, 16–17, 56, 61, 75, 92
historiography 39; analysis by 12
history: ancient 10, 20, 22; anti-Oriental interpretation of 29; assumed pattern of 9; British imperial 40, 46; family 56; link with historical archaeology 11; mythical 87; relationship with archaeology 10; rewriting of 117; Western 20, 29, 37; Western imperial 31, 65; world 28; writing of 12, 21
homogeneity 32, 39, 60
honestiores 57
households, provincial 89, 114
houses 73, 74; Batavian 95; Greek styles of 88; high-status 88–9; late Republican, in Italy 88; local concepts of 90; long 95; lower status 89, 92, 107, 116; prehistoric 24, 90; provincial 87, 88, 90
Howes, David 52
humanitas 26–7, 35, 43, 62–4, 67–70; origin of 63
humiliores 57
hut of Romulus 62
hybridization 111
hypocausts 88, 89, 90

Iberia 17, 23, 80, 82, 84–5, 89; north-western 102, 104, 114
Iberians 22
idealism 4, 7
identity 1, 2, 14, 15, 19, 53; adopted 118; alternative aspects of 45; barbarian 22, 23, 24, 30; Batavian 104; British 33; civilized 64; classical 61; of community 80; of consumers 101; contemporary attitudes to 117; cultural 26, 99, 118; elite 21, 51, 68, 71, 91, 94, 109; ethnic 24, 92; European 19, 21, 27; flexible 37; hybrid 30; ideas about 74, 114; imperial 9, 58; of incomers 108; joint 71; local 39, 40, 49, 51, 71, 72, 104, 111; localized ethnic 92; monolithic 41; national 22–4, 28, 38; native 17, 34, 35, 52; negotiated 48; pre-Roman 104; recasting of 87; recent approaches to 91; regional aspects of 45; Romano-British 35
identity, provincial 30, 94; communication of 82; complexities of 114
identity, Roman 6, 14, 26, 30, 33–4, 42–50, 54–7, 60, 62, 64, 66, 69, 70, 72, 75, 78, 84, 91–3, 100, 102, 105, 108, 114, 118; commemoration of 75; elite 49–50, 68, 72, 74, 91, 94, 107; expression of 109; fragmented 48, 118; fragmenting 91; individualized 81, 108; military 94; monolithic image of 37; new forms of 108–10, 119; of producers 101; range of 108; recasting 87; religious 67; self- 23; source of 41; spiritual 44; variable 71; Western 19, 21, 29, 31, 39, 53
ideology: Augustan 51; imperial 51
imitation 43, 58
immigrants, Gallo-Roman 95
imperial actions: justification for 38
imperial culture 17, 30, 36, 47–8, 51, 54–5, 58, 61, 89, 102, 109, 115, 117
imperial discourse 51, 69, 70, 76; Augustan 79; Roman 63, 70, 74, 81
imperial expansion: Roman 1, 22, 23, 26, 49, 58, 77, 104, 114, 118; modern Western 38
imperial mission, British 41
imperial system, Roman 70
imperialism 5, 29, 119; American commercial 108; Augustan 1; British 8, 22; and culture 49; discourse of 51; European 27; Flavian 65; French 8, 22; ideas of 27; modern 14, 21, 26, 28–9, 31; ideology behind 70; modernist discourses of 37; Roman 45, 65, 58, 60, 67, 72, 78, 102–3, 109, 115–18; unifying character of 35
imperialists: modern 65; Roman 27
imported objects 105
incomers 108; elite 85
incorporation 1, 2, 5, 15, 17, 24, 27, 33, 34, 38–9, 40, 46, 49–50, 54, 56, 64, 65–8, 70–1, 72, 77, 78, 82, 85, 87, 90, 104, 105, 106, 107, 108, 114, 118, 119; of barbarians 63; responses to 36
indigenization 111
indoctrination 35
industry 81, 88, 94, 100, 106, 107, 108, 109, 116, 119; products 106; workers 48, 118
inequality 88
ink 99
innovation 27, 29, 35, 39, 43–4, 46, 78, 88, 90, 95, 99, 101, 116
inscriptions 11, 102, 104; Augustan 81; funerary 104; on Iron Age coins 111; provincial 81; *Res Gestae* 79; Roman 74, 75, 80; at Tarraco 84, 85
integration 5, 11, 31, 41, 48, 52, 65; political 106
intellectuals 27
interest rates 106
interventionism, Roman 64; perspective of 46
invasion: barbarian 27; Roman 24, 43
Iron Age 113; coins 111; enclosure 85; imports 111; the Latin 54
Isherwood, Baron 73
Islam 20
'Italian question, the' 12, 32
Italians 28, 33, 40
Italy 3, 8, 10, 12, 15, 16–17, 18, 20, 22, 28, 30, 31, 32–3, 36, 39, 44, 48, 49, 54, 55, 56, 57, 58, 64, 69, 76, 77, 78, 80, 81, 88, 89, 92, 100, 102, 106, 107, 118; indigenous peoples of 118; modern unification of 12, 32; Roman unification of 92

James, Simon 93
jars 113
Johnson, Matthew 10, 11 (Table 1.1)
Judaeo-Christianity 38
Julio-Claudian period 98
Jullian, Camille 16, 35
Juno 61, 75
Jupiter 61

Keay, Simon 54, 85
Kiene, A. 31
kiln dockets 99, 100
kinship: between Romans and native peoples 62
Kurke, Leslie 91

La Graufesenque 99–101
labour 49, 106, 109
lamps, pottery 113
land 106
landowners 116
landscapes 23, 36; archaeological 13; cultural 47; provincial 58; non-villa 95; settlement 73, 89, 103; survey 36
language 20, 34, 35, 58; boundaries 99; correct form of 101; cultural 88; Greek 55, 61, 68; inheritance from Rome of 21; Latinized Gallic 100; studies of 110; of success 55; *see also* Latin
Las Médulas 103
Latin 20, 35, 51, 55, 60, 61, 63, 66, 68, 70, 75, 94–102, 105, 114; adoption of 98–9, 102; association with *terra sigillata* 110; identity 75; on Iron Age coins 111; on kiln dockets 99; knowledge of 101; language 60, 61, 63, 68–9, 75, 94, 98, 99, 101, 105, 114; literacy 94, 96; literature 63, 68, 69; myth of origin 61; names on pottery 99, 100, 101; non-elite forms of 101; pottery stamp 100; in provincial contexts 98; sources 88; writing 60, 99, 100, 101
Latin–Greek civilizing process 32
Latinization 102
Latouche, Serge 14, 19
Laurence, Ray 107
law 46, 58, 76
lead 89
leaders, native 23
legions 34, 56, 66
León 103, 104
lifestyles 93, 108; adopted 118, 105; barbarian 61; developing 110; military 94; new 10, 13, 34, 40, 43, 48, 52, 53, 57, 58, 60, 66, 69, 70, 74, 75–6, 77, 80, 81, 82, 85, 89, 104, 109, 114, 115, 116
literacy 73; in the army 94; association with *terra sigillata* 110; Latin 94, 96; provincial 98; among rural Batavians 96–8; at Vindolanda 98;
literature 4, 46, 75, 119; Augustan 6, 61; classical 26, 31, 58, 60, 61, 64, 77, 92, 101; classical models for 6; European 20; Graeco-Roman 11; Greek 68; Latin 63, 68, 69; styles of 58
loans 108
local centres 92
local discourses 71
localization 41
logic: alternative cultural 47, 117; colonial 28; of Haverfield 35, 39; of historical development 37; of Mommsen 39; of Western history 37
Lomas, Kathryn 18
long houses 95
Low Countries 17, 36

MacDonald, William L. 80
MacMullen, Ramsey: *Romanization in the Time of Augustus* 43
Maghreb 28–9, 41
maps 23, 28; archaeological 89; cognitive 85; monumental 79
marble 89
marketing 100, 101
markets 66, 76, 94; conglomeration of 106; economy of 106; international 100; local 106, 113; principles of 106; system of 106; transactions at 80; unified 106
Martial: *Epigrams* 66, 68
Martindale, Charles 4
mass-communication 67
material culture as text 11
mausoleum 79
media, the 1
Mediterranean region 10, 15, 16, 17, 22, 24, 36, 44, 54, 55, 56, 57, 69, 77, 78, 80, 89, 94, 100, 106, 107, 110, 111; central 55; eastern 61; peoples of 55
meeting place 78; at Tarraco 84; at Verulamium 85
meetings 76
metal, precious 100
metalwork, Roman 100
methodology, archaeological 23
Middle Ages 20, 21
Middle East 19
milestones 81
militarized zone 95
military, Roman 78, 97; administration of 78; commanders 97–8; communication 78; control 78; culture 94; organization 34; policy 8, 10; power 50; recruitment 96, 97, 98, 99, 102, 120; superiority 62; units,

at Vindolanda 98; zone 35; *see also* sites, soldiers
military service 95, 98, 104, 108, 116; benefits of 97
Millett, Martin 41–3, 44, 45, 46, 47, 102; *The Romanization of Britain* 41
minerals 103, 104
mines 104; *see also* mining
mining 102, 103, 104; at Las Médulas 103
missions civilisatrices 27
modernism 30, 31, 37, 38, 39, 41, 51, 52
modernity 5, 6, 15, 31, 38, 42
modernization 38
Mommsen, Theodor 16, 18, 31–2, 33, 35, 37, 38, 39, 42, 44, 45; *Römische Geschichte* 31; *The Provinces of the Roman Empire: From Caesar to Diocletian* 33
monarchy, Spanish 20
Mongols 28
monumentality, provincial 82
monuments 26; burial 76; classical 10, 31; origins of 23; prehistoric 23, 24; provincial 76, 81; Roman 28, 72, 79, 92; in Rome 79; visiting 18
morality 16, 33, 61, 63–4, 67, 68; decline of Roman 62
Morley, Neville 109
Morris, Ian 37
mortar 89
mortaria 110
mosaics 88, 89, 90, 108
Mouritsen, Henrik 12
municipium 82, 85, 87
Muslim, definition of the East as 19
Muslims 28
Mussolini, Benito 7
myth 13, 119
mythological scenes 100, 101
mythology, Graeco-Roman 101
myths of origin *see* origin, myths of

names: of ethnic groups 22; Latinized Gallic 100; Latinized, on pottery 101; of potters 99; of Roman citizens 75; Romanized Gallic 102
nation, British 33
nation state, rise of 51
nationalism, regional 24; justification for 38
nationhood 16, 26; German 33
native leaders: Batavian 96; sons of 69
native peoples 64, 67; corruption of 66; German 66; of the New World 28; of the northern Roman empire 34; of the Roman Western empire 39; Romanized 26; upwardly mobile 43; *see also* Britons, ancient
nativism 46; accounts 40–2
Near East 2, 21, 22, 28–9, 39, 40, 54; Roman 29
negotiation 46, 48, 58, 91, 119–20; elite 54
Negri, Antonio and Hardt, Michael: *Empire* 9, 117, 119
neo-colonialism 27
neo-evolutionary theory 37
Netherlands, the 23
New Archaeology 51
New World 27, 28
Nicolet, Claude 78
Nijmegen 95, 97 (Figure 8)
Ninth Cohort of Batavians 98
Nippel, Wilfried 28
non-elite 34, 43, 48, 90, 93; military culture 94; provincial 37, 43, 92–3, 101, 105, 108
non-militarized zone 95
non-villa landscapes 102
non-villa settlements 98, 111, 113, 114; Batavian 97
North Sea 23
North Wales 34
novelists, British 8; Roman 61
nucleated sites 77

oak 99
objects: adoption of 45; acquisition of 73, 106; 'art' 4; assimilation of 111; collection of 18, 54; distinct groups of 52; in everyday use 104; imported 44, 105; messages conveyed by 74; new 111; of personal decoration 34; pottery, names of 100; producers of 100; reinterpretation of 13; related to elite Roman identity 107; Roman 45; in Roman empire 16; use of 45
Octavian 2 (Figure 1)
officers: modern 92; provincial 68; Roman army 92, 98
officials: Gallo-Roman 95; modern British 67; modern imperial 92; native elite 95; Roman 35, 67
olive oil 115
oppida 85, 77
Oppidum Batavorum 95
orbis 1
order, imposition of 120

Orejas, Almudena 103
oriental revolution 55
origin, mixed racial 24
origin, myths of: barbarian 19, 23–4, 62; English 33; Latin 61; Roman 19, 22, 62
origins, native cultural 92
ornaments: domestic 89; personal 73
osmosis 43, 90
'otherness' 61, 117; of barbarians 22, 62; of classical culture 6; of the New World 27; Roman 62
Ottoman civilization 29

pagans 28
paideia 63
paintings 72; on wall plaster 89, 108
Palatine Hill 62
Palestine 18
papyrus, writing on 11
parades 74
Parca, Maryline 102
Parthenon 19
patronage 48, 68, 108
patrons 88
Pax Americana 21
Pax Britannica 21
Pax Hispanica 21
Pax Romana 21
'peasantry' 35
philosophers 38
philosophy 40
physique, barbarian 61
pigments 89
plaster 88, 90; painted 89, 95
plates 110
plumbing 89
poetry 60, 68
poets, Roman 61; *see also* Martial
policy: of *humanitas* 67; of intervention 65; Roman foreign 34, 120; Roman settlement 95; of urbanization 82
polishers, pottery 112–13
politicians: British 8; English 26; modern 27; Victorian 26
politics 1, 46, 55; classical models for 6; European 20; local power- 76; Mediterranean 69; modern 31; present-day 9, 17; Roman 74, 81
Polybius 9, 12
Pompey, Theatre of 69
poor, the 34, 115
populations: barbarian 20; Batavian 96, 97, 98; Berber 29; freeborn 57; indigenous 17, 41, 43, 115; literate 81; local 62; local control of 78; of Lower Rhine Valley 98; modern 67; poor 115, 116; prehistoric 17, 26; provincial 67, 114; of Roman empire 56, 57, 106, 107; un-Roman 101;
portable items 73, 105
portico 95
portraits, imperial 84
Posidonius 8, 12
post-colonialism 14, 17, 21, 29, 40, 41; guilt 46, 65
postmodernism 4, 6, 9, 12, 30, 37, 38, 42, 50, 52, 119; accounts 42
Potter, David 8, 10
potters 94, 101; Gallic 101, 114; local 100; names of 99; record-keeping by 100; training of 100
pottery 34, 43, 73, 74, 105, 107, 109; amphorae 106, 110, 114; character of 110; decoration on 100, 101; dimensions of 99; distribution of 113; fabric 100, 113; factories 100; forms 101, 113; high-quality 110; high-status 44, 45; imported 113; Italian 43; local 113; production 99, 101; reuse of 112–13; Roman-style 34; significance of broken 113; stamps 100, 101; styles 45, 113; symbolism of 100; techniques 45; types of 113; use of 113–14; use in new ways 110; use in sets 110; wheel-made 45; *see also terra sigillata*
pottery studies: Evans 113; Willis 110, 111
praefectus 98
pragmatism 58
prehistoric cultures 52
prehistoric society 23, 105
prehistory 5, 23, 24, 26, 28, 39
prejudice 29
prices 99; of land 106
priesthood 85
primitiveness 39
primitives 28; *see also* barbarians
Principate, the 59 (Figure 4)
prisoners, barbarian 61; parading of 61
'privileging' of ancient literature 4
processions, triumphal 61
proclamations 102
production 107, 114; agricultural 116; character of 106; expansion of 106, 115–16; industrial 106; of inscriptions 81; of literature 58; of olive oil 115; of pottery 45, 99, 100–1, 109–10; processes

100; surplus 107; of *terra sigillata* 113; of togas 76
professions, low-status 100
progress 2, 11, 27, 30, 31, 32, 34, 37–9, 41, 43–4, 46, 52, 63
progressive accounts 44
propaganda 7, 13, 58; Augustan 57; Roman 51, 60, 115
provinces: indigenous peoples of 118; north-western 16; of Gaul 45; peripheral 57
provincial capital, in Iberia 85
Prussia 31

race 24, 26, 27, 28, 33, 34, 38, 51; relations 26
racial difference 38
racial mixing 33
racism 24
rationality 38
rebels, native 23
reception 7; of Roman attributes and assumptions 18; of Virgil's *Aeneid* 8
record-keeping 100
recruitment, military: pre-Roman native 96; *see also* military recruitment
redistribution 106
Reece, Richard 40
reinterpretation 58
rejection 58
relativism, cultural 37, 42
religion 19, 34; Greek 61; inheritance from Rome of 21; Roman 57, 74, 75; provincial 80; state 69
religious observances, Roman 80
religious power, Roman 50
Renaissance 18, 20–1
renegotiation 58
Republican period, Roman 7, 15, 50, 56, 60, 61, 79, 82, 102
Republican Rome 21; traditions of 57
Republican system, Roman 9
Res Gestae 79, 92
res publica 7
resistance 11, 23, 40, 70, 116
resources, control of 71
rhetoric 15, 66
Rhine Valley, Lower 95, 98, 102, 104; population of 98
Rhône Valley 69
ritual landscape 87
rituals 74, 78, 79, 80, 85, 87; Roman-period 40
roads 24, 36, 44, 78, 87, 92, 107; as Roman identifiers 78; system of 78; at Verulamium 87
roadside settlements 111
Roller, Matthew 63
Romanisierung 17
Romanising 32, 33; *see also* Romanization
Romanitas 44
Romanization 2, 10, 14–27, 30–46, 48, 49, 50, 52, 65, 90, 92–3, 95, 105, 111, 114; accounts of 29; approaches to 18; interpretation of 30; modernist 31–7; use in book titles 18; *see also* Romanizing
Romanizing 45
Romano-centrism 23, 29, 30, 36, 39, 42, 48, 92, 105, 119
Rome, city of 1, 54, 57, 61–2, 64, 69, 70, 76, 77, 78–80, 85, 106
roofs 89, 95
Roymans, Nico 95, 97, 98, 102
rubbers, pottery 112–13
ruins, observation of 18
rulers, native 35, 82, 57, 94
rural production 88

St Albans *see* Verulamium
samian *see terra sigillata*
Sánchez-Palencia, Francisco Javier 103
Sanfins, Cîtania de 103 (Figure 9)
savagery 28
Schiesaro, Alessandro 51
scholarship 2, 12; classical 51; European 39; modern 10; Roman-period 35; in social sciences 73; twentieth-century 39; Western tradition of 4
schools: at Autun 68; in Britain 68
Scotland 111
sculpture 72; commissions of 80
seal boxes 96 (Figure 7), 97, 98
self-government 47, 82
semi-urban centres, Iberian 104
Senate, of Rome 1, 61
senators 60
sense of place 24
servants 88, 89
settlement 10, 34, 36, 40, 73, 104; Batavian 95, 97, 98; development of 102; evolution 105; landscapes 89; non-villa 92; open 104; pre-Roman 82, 85, 102; provincial domestic 90; provincial forms of 77, 89; Roman elite 92; Roman process of 78; rural 36; secondary agglomerations 92; *see also oppida*, urban centres

settlers, of Lower Rhine Valley 95
sexual conduct 58
Shanin, Theodor 38
ships 106
shipwrecks 6
shoes 76
silver: mining 102; plate 100
sites 4, 10, 11, 24; archaeological 13, 36, 75, 91, 103; military 94, 97, 107, 111, 114; native rural 111; native-type 92; urban 111
slavery 49; *see also* enslavement
slaves 88; freed 56; household 98
small towns 92, 111, 113
social change 2, 14, 15, 16, 30, 33, 38, 39, 41, 42, 44, 45, 46, 47, 56, 66, 72, 92, 109, 114, 120; contemporary attitudes to 117; non-elite 110
social relations, Roman 88
social sciences 1, 36, 37, 52 *see also* anthropology, archaeology, sociology
social scientists 38
society: Batavian 97, 98; classical 7, 10, 15, 19, 21, 31, 32, 38; creation of 74; elite-focused 115; European 72; evolution of 5, 92; exploitation of 120; grades of 81; Graeco-Roman 77; Greek 22, 61; hierarchically structured 8; indigenous 72; Italian 44; local 54, 91; lower-status 107, 116; material elements of 73; middle stratum 115; modern 5, 27, 31, 39, 40, 43; native 67, 95, 98, 100, 115; native British 42; native Dutch 36; non-elite 101; poor 118; prehistoric 95, 108, 105; pre-modern 5; present-day 19; provincial 37, 42, 43, 47, 60, 68, 69, 89, 90, 92, 93, 98, 101, 102, 105, 115; Roman 1, 4, 41, 44, 47, 48, 53, 54, 55, 56, 60, 61, 69, 72, 73, 76, 89, 91, 92; Roman military 94; rural 116; structure of 59 (Figure 4); substantiation of 74; Western 19, 20, 22, 29, 31, 38; *see also* elite, non-elite
sociology 1, 36, 41, 48, 51, 73
soldiers 48, 93, 108, 118; auxiliary 56, 98, 104, 56, 99; Batavian 97, 104; dress of 94; enculturation of 94; ethnic 99; Gallo-Roman 95; Iberian 102, 104; military duties of 94; as non-elite Roman 'sub-culture' 93; religious duties of 94; retired 56, 94, 95; Roman 66; savings of 99; training of 94; veterans 95; at Vindolanda 97
Spain 17, 18, 20, 36, 48, 56, 82, 84, 100
specialists 14, 15, 30, 91
stability 7, 47, 52, 54, 64, 72, 75; historical 50
Stahl, Hans-Peter 8
stamps, pottery 100, 101
states, European 8
statues: of Julius Caesar 1; Roman 72, 74; provincial 81, 84, 85
status 3, 8, 16, 26, 84; communication of 76, 82; conquered 62; definition of 68, 76; elite 55; improvement of 118; in Italy 88; in native community 98; projection of 76; provincial 60, 82; of Roman citizenship 57; of Roman identity 56; *see also* toga, appearance
status anxiety 75; Augustan 61
stone 81, 88, 89, 95; dressed 89
storage 76
Strabo 12
street system: orthogonal 82; at Tarraco 84; at Verulamium 85
streets 79
structures *see* buildings
students, Roman 60
stylus *see* wax stylus-tablets
sub-cultures 53, 91, 93
sub-groups, political: of Rome 60
superiority: European 27; of Greece 20, 55; Roman 26, 61, 63, 79; of Roman identity 37; Roman military 62; Western 21
super-powers 9
survey, archaeological 10, 23, 92, 93, 113; landscape 30, 36; regional 36; strategies of 92
Syme, Ronald 7, 15, 58: *Roman Revolution* 7
Syria 57

tableware 110–11, 113–14
Tacitus 62, 65–6, 68; *Agricola* 35, 65, 75; *Annals* 69, 84
Tarraco (Tarragona) 82, 83 (Figure 5), 84–5, 87; archaeology at 85; delegation to Tiberius 84; layout of 85; pre-Augustan 85
Tarraconensis 82
taxation 44, 80–1, 104, 106, 107
technology 6, 27, 38, 118; adoption of 102; of food 110; key 55; pottery 100; Roman innovations in 39; of writing 98–9
teleology 5, 22, 27, 31, 37–9, 44
temples 79; to Augustus 84; to Divine Augustus 84; at Empel 97; at Folly Lane 87; provincial 80; at Tarraco 84

terra sigillata 45, 99, 100–1, 102, 113; association with Latin 110; decorated 111; import of 110; mortaria 110; sets of 110; stamps on 111
Terrenato, Nicola 48, 54, 88
territorialization 53
texts 13, 75; ancient written 11, 13; Augustan 57; classical 3, 4, 7, 9, 10, 15, 20, 22, 23, 24, 27, 67, 68, 72; Greek 68; Latin 68; material culture as 11, 105; monumental forms as 72; pre-Roman 68
theatres 79, 81; at Folly Lane 87; provincial 81; in Rome and Italy 81; at Tarraco 84; Theatre of Pompey 69; at Verulamium 85
theory 15; archaeological 51; in classical studies 37; colonial discourse 41, 42, 92; development 37; diffusionist 38; postmodern 4, 38; schools of 16; *see also* Eurocentrism, evolutionary theory, globalization, neo-evolutionary theory, Romanization
Thrace, northern 68
Tiberius 84
Tiel-Passewaaij 96 (Figure 7)
tiles 89, 95
timber 89, 95 *see also* wood
toga 35, 65, 75–6; provincial 76
Tomlinson, John 5, 6
Toner, Jerry 1, 4
Torelli, Mario 10
town centres 108
towns 24, 34, 40, 45, 66, 84, 92, 95, 115; monumentalization of 107
towns, small 92, 111, 113
trade 45, 55, 73, 77, 81, 88, 94, 105–7, 108, 109, 113, 116, 119; cross-regional 6; Mediterranean 6; pre-Roman 107; small-scale 100; state 106
traders 48, 68, 99, 100, 108, 118; local 100; Roman 22
travel 69
treaties 96
tria nomina 75
tribal ancestor: burial of 87; cult of 87
tribal centre 95
tribal terms 23
tribes 97; Batavians 95, 98, 99; Germanic 69; Frisians 69
tribute 103
trophies 62
tugurium Romuli see hut of Romulus
Tungrians 97
Turks 28
Tuscany 45; north 100

unification, of Italy *see* Italy
unitary model 31
United States of America 4, 7, 8–9, 14, 17, 21, 31, 36
units: Batavian 96–7; cultural 31; Roman army 96–8, 100; territorial 24
upper classes *see* elite
urban centres 74, 69, 108; development of space in 85; elite of 85; form of 77, 78, 82, 85; Iberian 84, 104; local 95; of Lower Rhine Valley 95; of militarized zone 95; Oppidum Batavorum 95; pre-Roman 77, 82; pre-Roman origins of 85; provincial 77, 79, 80, 81, 82, 88, 89, 101, 109, 111; provincial idea of 82; Roman 85, 87; Roman Republican 84; Roman-style 102; at Tarraco 84, 85; at Verulamium 85; *see also* towns
urban living, Mediterranean 69
urban planning 76, 78, 82; Etruscan 79; Greek 79; orthogonal 79; provincial 77, 79
urban space 77; provincial 75; at Tarraco 85
urbanism 66, 69, 79, 82, 95, 109
urbanization 34, 77; native 96; provincial 82
urbs 1

valour, barbarian 24, 26
values of Roman imperial culture 89; Roman order of 102
van Driel-Murray, Carol 91
variability: classical cultural 44; of imperial relations 48, 55; of response to Roman control 17, 18, 54, 119
variation 30, 32, 52, 93; local 90, 91; regional 40
Varus, Quintilius 66, 82
Vercingetorix 23
Verulamium (St Albans) 82, 85, 86 (Figure 6), 87
veteran soldiers *see* soldiers, retired
villas 24, 30, 34, 36, 39, 40, 89, 92, 96, 102, 105, 107, 108, 111; architecture of 88; building of 98; enclosure system 113; redefinition of 88; terminology 88; zones 95
villa-type building 104
Vindolanda 97–8; writing-tablets from 99
Vinogradoff, Paul 40
Virgil 60–1, 75, 101; *Aeneid* 8, 19, 61, 67, 75

Viriatus 23
virtue 64
visitor attractions 4
visitors of urban centres 80; to Verulamium 87
vocabulary, Latin 63, 101
voyages, sixteenth-century 27

wages 106
wall plaster 88, 89, 90; painted 95
Wallace-Hadrill, Andrew 51, 55
wall-paintings 108
Warwickshire 113–14
water systems 79
wax stylus-tablets 99
Western perspective 9, 37
Whittaker, Dick 43, 46
Williams, Jonathan 45, 67
Willis, Steve 110, 111
wine 43, 110
wood: alder 99; birch 99; oak 99; writing on 11; in writing-tablets 99;
Woolf, Greg 47, 48, 58, 62, 69, 73, 101, 102, 117, 118
workshops 100
writing 6, 8, 10, 11, 114; adoption of 99; classical 60; Gaulish 99; in Latin 60, 94, 98, 99, 100, 101; practice of 98; pre-Roman 68; Roman 15, 74; spread of 99; studies of 110; styles of 98; technologies of 98, 99, 101; *see also* writing tablets, wax stylus-tablets
writing-tablets 11, 98, 99

Zanker, Paul 70, 77–8, 79–81